Jean Renoir

Leo Braudy is Associate Professor of English at Columbia University, author of *Narrative Form in History and Fiction: Hume, Fielding, and Gibbon*, and editor of anthologies about Norman Mailer and Truffaut's *Shoot the Piano Player*.

Jean Renoir

THE WORLD OF HIS FILMS

BY

LEO BRAUDY

ANCHOR BOOKS
DOUBLEDAY & COMPANY, INC.
GARDEN CITY, NEW YORK
1972

Jean Renoir: The World of His Films was originally published in a
hard cover edition by Doubleday & Company, Inc. in 1972.

ANCHOR BOOKS EDITION: 1972

For Mary Feldbauer, Peter Scarlet, and Bill Rothman,
in memory of the Seven Arts Luncheonette
in the fall of 1969.

Contents

Acknowledgments

Until there is greater co-ordination between film collections, and until some of the great repositories decide to let us know, or find out for themselves, what they own, the preliminaries of film research will remain an art form somewhere between mosaics and jigsaw puzzles. Luckily I met many people who helped me through the maze.

I would like to thank especially Dan Herrara, Darrell Flugg, Nick Stanos, and Marilyn Pettis of McGraw-Hill Contemporary Films, as well as Mary Meerson, Lotte Eisner, and Sybille de Luze of the Cinémathèque Française, who enabled me to see many of Renoir's films with the leisure that this study requires.

Other portions of information and support were given me by Tom Brandon; Pierre Sauvage; Bernard Rabb of Grove Press; Mme. G. Courtois-Doynel of the Compagnie Jean Renoir; Jacques Charrière of l'Avant-Scène; Violette de Mazia of the Barnes Foundation; Gene Stavis; Gerald Weales; Paul Wagner and Diane Frankel of National Telefilm Associates; David L. Loew; and George Pratt of Eastman House, who has always given me the greatest help and enthusiasm whenever I asked, for whatever project I was engaged in.

Steve Weisman, Mike Wood, Peter Biskind, and Martin

Meisel gave me great help with the text itself; Brian and Marlene Finney lent their kitchen table; Anne Alexander enormously eased the burden of research; Joanne Jaffe and David Lait supplied fine pictures when I was too nervous to get the aperture right. Pauline Kael gave encouragement, information, and advice all the way through, and Bill White-head, my editor, gave the preparations and the manuscript itself the kind of attention only someone deeply interested in the subject can supply.

But my final and deepest thanks must go to Mr. and Mrs. Jean Renoir, whose unfailing grace and courtesy, both by mail and in person, made the difficult time of writing a little softer.

A Note on Translation

I have translated into English all but the briefest statements by Renoir included in the text (as well as all quotations from French critics). While this practice makes it difficult to distinguish between the flavors of Renoir's English and his French formulations, I hope that it will carry the reader through the text with fewer lurches or dead stops. Those French film titles that do not have obvious English equivalents, or are not familiarly known by their French titles, I have translated on their first appearance and then returned to the French.

A Note on the Illustrations

Using stills to illustrate a book about films might be unfairly, but not too inaccurately, compared to the method of literary analysis that works up a list of a poet's ten favorite words and then proceeds to generalize about his poems on that basis. The illustrations that follow are not meant to give any direct idea of Renoir's visual style. Some are photographs taken on the set and therefore slightly different from what was seen by camera. But even if they were all reproductions from the frames, they would still be only single shots from works meant to be seen as sequences of shots. At best, they can illustrate some of Renoir's more static motifs, for example, his interest in various kinds of framing, or his use of objects, like the table. They can give some idea of the actors and how they look, and they can furnish some look behind the scenes into the world of production that surrounds each film.

The author wishes gratefully to acknowledge the following for the use of stills in this book: Grove Press, Inc., Contemporary Films/McGraw-Hill, David L. Loew, National Telefilm Associates, Inc., Janus Films, Twentieth-Century Fox, Kenneth McEldowney, RKO Pictures, the Cinémathèque Française, The British Film Institute, National Film Archive, and the New York Museum of Modern Art Film Department.

CHAPTER ONE

Introduction

Je suis fait de sable friable et ce qui m'environne m'influence beaucoup.

—JEAN RENOIR, 1962

The need to write a book about any creative artist begins in one's first feelings that the subject is separate from other artists with whom he may share superficial similarities, that he has passed through that unspecifiable boundary beyond which a writer, composer, sculptor, painter, or film director becomes a country unto himself. This need is perhaps most pressing and yet most difficult to realize when the artist is a film director, although an understanding of the playwright involves many of the same problems. The characteristic submergence in the play of the playwright's controlling vision, like the disappearance of the director in his motion picture, leaves the spectator with little of the palpable feeling of connection with a maker and shaper that we get from the strokes of the brush or the curves of the statue or the pages of the novel. In films especially the artistic integrity of the work is always in danger of fragmenting before our eyes because of our knowledge of the work behind the scenes, the elaborate detail of the credits, the technicians and administrators swarming in every corner of the film. The spectator may just

throw up his hands, muttering "entertainment," and re-
fuse to go beyond either the seeming fragmentation of control or the elaboration of physical fact that is in the nature of
every film. On the other hand, he may seek for coherences,
within an individual film, or within the career of a particular
director, that are especially moving and artistically worthy.

How, then, should one deal with Jean Renoir, with thirty-
six films to his credit, films made in four countries in the
space of forty-six years? In all these films there throbs a
strongly felt continuity that demands to be brought into the
world of critical discourse. How does one talk about the
continuities of thematic preoccupation, treatment, and technical method? If there is a world of Renoir's films, what are its
principles?

Renoir has of course been an important director for some
time. The two most usual approaches to his work have been
the blandly celebrating and the cultic (whose celebrations are
a little more idiosyncratic). Praise from the first group invokes Renoir's "humanism," his "love for little people," and
his "joy in nature." The cult appreciation of Renoir in its
turn tends to concentrate on details that run through the
films—the frequent appearance of laundresses, for example,
like some Dickens Society discussion of Bucket's finger in
Bleak House. Both approaches flatten out Renoir's films and
reduce their complexities to a series of simple philosophic
pieties or a continuity of visual quirks. One should instead, I
think, be more interested in the vital relation of such details, or preferably more important ones, to the large themes
and attitudes of Renoir's entire body of work. One should
balance between consideration of the preoccupations that
bind together a career and the artistic sensibility that exists
most perfectly only in an artist's best works.

An emphasis on the director automatically raises the specter of *auteur* theory. Renoir himself may be partially re-

sponsible for the framework of the *politique des auteurs* as promulgated by François Truffaut in a 1954 issue of *Cahiers du Cinéma*. The particular usage seems to derive from a remark made by Renoir on the set of *La Règle du Jeu* in 1939:

> It used to be the era of the actor: the film was equivalent to its star, and so we had the Mary Pickfords, the Douglas Fairbankses, the Greta Garbos. Then we had the age of the directors (*metteurs-en-scène*): and the films of King Vidor, Sternberg, Feyder, Clair. Now a new epoch is beginning: the epoch of the writers (*auteurs*); because from now on it is the scenarist who will create the film. . . .

Renoir's statement obviously deals with the role of the writer in making the film, and by extension the need of the director to be a writer. *Auteur*, as he uses it here (and, I might point out, as Truffaut uses it in his article), has none of the blandly congratulatory and complacent aura that now surrounds it, when it has become too frequently the mark of either a cult of personality, in which the director's name authenticates beyond the recall of critical judgment, or it is a search for invariable motifs—a desperate attempt to supply coherence and personality where on the surface there is none. *Auteur*, in English and American film criticism at least, is only a shuttlecock between opposing critical schools, each affirming or denying it, as their momentary polemical taste warrants. Why apologize for or even discuss an impulse as basic as the need to find a creator? In many films the search will be fruitless, because the imaginative and technical control is weak. The *auteur*, the strongest creative presence in the film, may be an actor or a technician, or perhaps the film must be appreciated more for its place in the history of art and society than for its individual power.

But instead of presenting great works alone, to ratify an artist by his "masterpieces," one should study the complexity

of thought and feeling within a particular work and across
many such works. Renoir makes his world energetic and
compelling through the complexity and irony with which he
treats even his most cherished themes. His films do not
come to a stop in the sense of the self-enclosed great work;
they have a richness that eludes total schematization, a constant edge of self-awareness that never yields to either formal
pomposities or fashionable fragmentation. Renoir has said that
every director struggles between interior reality, the reality
of the constructed world of the studio, and exterior reality,
the reality of the world of nature. But his point is not the
final commitment to one or the other, but the dynamics of
the struggle itself. Robert Venturi, the architect, has called
the basic principle of art "complexity and contradiction." In
Renoir's films, the energy for his ongoing art springs from
irony and self-awareness. In 1954 Renoir spoke about the
process of his film-making: ". . . I am incapable of impro-
vising completely. . . . I am obliged to know in advance what
I'm going to film; but even though I know what I'm going to
do, what I finally film turns out to be something quite different." Problems are never solved, but films are completed.
Within the frame of his chosen aesthetic form, Renoir can
revolve without conclusion those issues that can never be
resolved. The greatness of his films more often lies in their
inconclusiveness, their openness, and their rich tentativeness
than in any absolute formulation of the truths of nature or
the truths of theater, the claims of the individual or the
claims of society.

Jean Renoir is an appropriate subject for extensive study
because of both the continuity in his interests and the variety
of their expression. He has a sense of the possibilities of
film that allows him to work in a much larger variety of
forms than most other directors—farce and epic, social drama,
neo-realism and baroque theater, detective story, satire, and

parody. In his film career he has played all the major roles: producer, writer, technician, and actor. And as a director he has co-ordinated these forces and abilities into thirty-six films, remarkable for their variety, complexity, and artistic self-sufficiency. When at the beginning of my work on this book I saw thirty-two Renoir films in the space of two weeks, I was prepared for cloying. If I had seen so many films by many other directors I like (Ford, Hitchcock, or Hawks, for example) I am sure I would have been reduced to the cataloguing of motifs, as the films ran together before my eyes into one epic oeuvre for each director. But I was fascinated to find that each of the films of Jean Renoir stayed whole, establishing its continuity with the other films, at the same time that it refused to lose its individual artistic identity. As André Bazin, the great French film critic and one of Renoir's most fervent admirers, has said, "Other great directors have suffered from not knowing how to rise above their success: they remain the prisoners of the kind of cinema that first gave them glory when the secret of success was in a temporary relation between subject, style, and the particular expectations of a historical period. After this mysterious harmony between the artist's message and the expectations of his contemporaries had passed, his artistic inspiration became irrelevant. This misfortune has never happened to Jean Renoir, whose humane sensibility has adapted itself to both the restlessness of history and the changes in culture." (Bazin, André, *Jean Renoir*, edited and introduced by François Truffaut. Paris: Editions Champ Libre, 1971, p. 65.)

Renoir's variety has influenced directors as different as François Truffaut and Philippe de Broca, Roberto Rossellini and Luchino Visconti, Robert Aldrich and Arthur Penn, Fritz Lang and Luis Buñuel. His art is not a pure austere art that repeats the same motifs and methods from film to film, elaborating a simple sensibility. Like his critical statements, Renoir's films are not categorical and theoretical, but capacious and ironic. They present a rich critical problem, because nothing is ever single-valued in Renoir's world, no character can be easily made hero or villain, no set of ideas has automatic consent. Within the borders of his artistic vision and the continuity of his career, many of his basic interests remain the same: nature, the theater, society, the place of the hero. But the expression of these themes changes throughout the years, as the external pressure of new projects, new ideas, and new events works its way on him. His attitudes are never simple, but the nature of their complexity varies enormously. His method commits itself to a sense of the immediate and the improvised, projecting a willingness to learn from events: ". . . one discovers the contents of a film only in the process of making it." *Partie de Campagne,* for example, was originally written with a sunny setting. But it rained almost all through the shooting. And the film changed into something else, something discovered along the way. Improvisation mixes with and qualifies artistic order to achieve a new harmony of vitality and form.

At the tapering off of the industrial revolution, films appeared as the first mechanical art, in which the uniformity of the assembly line was harnessed in the interest of artistic uniqueness. To complement his love for the eighteenth century, Renoir's films exemplify the best possibilities of film, in their return to the early eighteenth-century belief that technical competence and mechanical method could help liberate both human feelings and artistic sensiblity. Despite the fears Walter Benjamin voices in his essay "The Work of Art in the Age of Mechanical Reproduction," movies are not by their technical nature doomed to the ultimate ends of fascistic facelessness and propaganda. Instead of assembly lines, the archetypal eighteenth-century machine was what

Siegfried Giedion has called the "machine of wonder," the wonder-working whistling bird or fluteplayer or fortune teller. Robert de la Chesnaye's hobby in *La Règle du Jeu* of collecting these elaborate and unique machines is an image of Renoir himself, creating each film through the enlisting of the mechanical in the service of a miracle.

Once a viewer has seen several Renoir films, he realizes that there are two basic elements in Renoir's work, with repercussions in theme and method, that predominate at least in first viewing over all others. These are, of course, nature and theater, which, as Roger Greenspun has pointed out, come into the Renoir world with Renoir's two first films as a director: the canal and countryside of *La Fille de l'Eau* (1924) and the theater and artifice of *Nana* (1926). To understand their proper place in his work, one must first assent to their equal importance, and disregard any assumption that the open world of nature is necessarily superior to the closed world of theater. This emphasis on theater must be the first corrective to the usual critical view of Renoir's films, in which it is supposed that his main impulse is to glorify nature, in the supposed manner of his father, Auguste Renoir, the Impressionist painter. In the simplest terms, such critics consider Renoir to be his father's son because they are searching desperately for some critical categories by which to praise the undeniable physical beauty of many of Renoir's films. No terms common to painting and film are invoked. Instead such critics search films like *Le Déjeuner sur l'Herbe* for "renoiresque" frames or color schemes. Painting becomes the source, first and formal cause, of the films. Renoir is subordinated to his father, as though artistic perspective is in the gift of heredity.

Such analysis misses one of the most important elements in Renoir's artistic nature: the way he defines his own point of view and his own artistic perception by including and then going beyond the other arts. The painting that he grew up with is certainly in many of his films, as is the theater, the puppet shows, and the wandering singers of the Parisian streets. But these arts are always included within the larger framework of the total film. Their existence in any individual film partakes of both homage and supercession. From the glimpses of scenes resembling Manet or Auguste Renoir in *Nana* down to the evocation of late nineteenth-century Montmarte in *French Cancan* (1955) and *Elena et les Hommes* (1956), Renoir invariably implies that the world defined by the camera and the director is always a step beyond the briefly framed shots of the painters or their work. They may have captured the moment, but Renoir's film has captured the movement. At its best the moving world of film is superior to the static world of painting; at the least it is something very different.

Since Renoir's films are so often praised by the standard of his father's painting, it is only a short step to assert that when they are not like those paintings they are "theatrical" or "uncinematic." The implication is that not only has Renoir sinned against his impressionist heritage, but he has also betrayed the "basic nature" of film by introducing the atmosphere of the artificial and contrived. Even so generally sympathetic a critic as Andrew Sarris can say of *Chotard & Compagnie* (1933) that it shows too much "the theatrical origins which Renoir was unable to transcend as he had in *La Chienne*" (Renoir's first full-length sound film). The fact that *Chotard* is Renoir's fourth sound film and his eleventh feature does not encourage Sarris to change his categories rather than condemn Renoir's abilities. The film admittedly is a light and charming one; but abrupt dismissal as "theatrical" does little for the viewer's understanding. Like many critical categories, "theatrical" and "uncinematic," or "natural" and "truthful," are value judgments masquerading as descriptive terms. They obscure more than they reveal.

"Deception" is a word often used in French criticism by critics who deplore the theatrical strain in Renoir's films. With such a term they can pick and choose a "false" and a "true" Renoir from the total world of his works. Whatever is alien to their preconceptions about Renoir's aesthetic relation to his father, they can label "alien" and expel. The difficulty with such criticism lies as much in the realm of theory as it does in the appreciation for the individual film. Movies, it is assumed, are by definition supposed to transcend theater. Renoir's nature films succeed in this theoretical venture; his theatrical films just as obviously fail. The aesthetically oriented critics who love nature and the social critics who love documentary embrace this carved-up Renoir, since both kinds of critics believe that the proper end of film is in "true" physical representation. They define Renoir's "best" films as those in which there is an easy transposition of social reality or the beauties of nature into cinematic images. Armed with these precepts, one critic says that Renoir has not made a "real" Renoir since *Diary of a Chambermaid* (1946). For others *Partie de Campagne* (1936) is the summit of his art, with its lovingly photographed evocation of a brief summer encounter. *La Grande Illusion* (1937) first made his international reputation and was considered his greatest until the restored version of *La Règle du Jeu* (1939) was first presented in 1956. And the taste for particular films may change again.

In this book I would like to avoid deciding when Renoir is being true to some predefined personal nature or artistic canon and when he is not. I wish to take an inquiring and expansive view of all his work, without losing sight of the question of relative value. The easy rejection of the theatrical films or theatrical elements in the other films may be the

greatest general barrier to a full appreciation of Renoir.
But just as much confusion is sowed by an uncritical appreciation of his use of nature. And only after the relative
roles of nature and theater have been assessed can an appreciation of Renoir's other major themes be attempted. In
Renoir's world neither the natural perspective nor the
stylized is totally secure. Each is presented through irony.
Like the halves of Milton's apple of the knowledge of good
and evil, they come into the world distinguished but necessarily linked. Like Aristophanes' primitive men and women
constantly trying to merge into one being, nature and art in
the films of Renoir need each other for wholeness. Naturalism
breaks down the limitations of theater; theater brings order
to the chaos of nature and instinct. Depending on which you
hold constant, nature subdues artifice, or artistry absorbs
naïveté.

The complexity and breadth of Renoir's work is therefore
an invitation to place it in the broadest and most sympathetic
critical context. At large there are four possible ways to
organize and discuss films: chronologically, thematically, in
terms of separate films, and in terms of the milieu in which
they were made. To discuss Renoir's films chronologically
would have involved, I believe, an impossible weaving and
reweaving of strands. I have decided instead to talk about all
of Renoir's films—as well as his plays, his novel, *The Notebooks of Captain George,* and his biography of his father—
in terms first of the two great motifs of nature and theater,
then in terms of the definition of society, to which they must
be related, and finally in terms of Renoir's emphasis on actors
and the emergent theme of the artist, who must make the
coherence and resolve the conflicts between art and nature,
individuality and society, instinct and civilization, into a larger
and more comprehensive vision of the world—the contingent
dialectic of Renoir's films. The first two sections—nature and

theater—deal more directly with the major motifs of Renoir's films, while the last two sections—society and the hero— bring these motifs into a discussion of more embracing issues of film structure, as reflected in the social world within a film and the shape given that world by the individual sensibility. Individual films are treated at length under these separate divisions, depending on the strongest elements in their own composition. By accumulated reference to different aspects of especially complex films, I have attempted to give some idea of how their complexities might be discussed. Finally, in the appendix, I have placed a brief account of Renoir's life, as well as the credits for his films.

Naturally, I have my own ideas about what subjects and methods are best suited to films, which are more appropriately "cinematic," or at least which are most interesting. Such issues must arise when one discusses the career of a director who has both exploited and expanded the nature and limits of film. Theory is always changed by the practice of great artists. In this book I would like to define what is rich and compelling about the world of the films of Jean Renoir. Many times, when I have read books about an individual director, I have felt that all had been said within the confines of the covers, or at least that the writer hoped it had all been said. The book I have written here is not by any means a complete appreciation and exposition of Renoir. It sketches some problems and provides some tentative answers. Like the work of all great artists, Renoir's films should be constantly susceptible to new critical approaches. More than almost any other artist today, he has absorbed the great themes and methods of art since the Renaissance and put his own stamp upon them, not by catalogue and allusion but by spirit and understanding. Renoir's films realize the highest nature of art, in their capacity to assimilate, to criticize, to reconcile, and create anew within the confines of his capacious imagination.

CHAPTER TWO

The Necessities of Nature

> My father sulked for an hour or so. But he forgot
> all about it as soon as we got back to the house,
> and started painting some eels, despite the protests of
> mother, who wanted to cook them with wine and
> onions.
>
> —*Renoir My Father*

> I try to work close to nature—but nature is millions
> of things, and there are millions of ways of under-
> standing its propositions.
>
> —JEAN RENOIR, 1970

In the beginnings of film, in the French 1890s, were the two
early giants who divided the world between them: the doc-
umentarian Louis Lumière and the fantasist Georges Méliès.
Lumière went out into the street to record passing human
reality, while Méliès stayed in his studio to create elaborate
supernatural and scientific illusions. In their separate natures
they seem like providential metaphors for the double tendency of films, toward immediate reality and toward timeless
illusion. A character in Jean-Luc Godard's *La Chinoise* can
even whimsically turn them around: Lumière, he argues, is
now the fantasist because his streets and their crowds have
vanished into dust, and their very existence become a bright

hallucination; Méliès, on the other hand, is the true realist because he freely admits the manipulation of reality the film allows, and he then exploits the truth of its illusions.

Despite the presence of both the realistic and the illusionistic orientations at the birth of motion pictures, both the interest of film-makers and film critics have inclined toward Lumière's documentary realism, with its concentration on the concrete fact, the reality the camera—in theory—presents unalloyed to the audience. This tendency is what is usually meant by "naturalism," a key word in film criticism since the beginning of the century, when it was absorbed from literary criticism. The young French film-makers of this period believed that the essence of the new medium was its ability to record and immerse itself in authentic detail. Their theories of film were usually parallel to the precepts of Émile Zola in his *Le Naturalisme au Théâtre,* a polemical blast at the artificialities and limited social viewpoint of nineteenth-century French popular drama. The early film-makers assumed that detail had a truth of its own, which need only be exposed by the film-maker. They had little sense of naturalism in depth, like that technique Zola actually practiced in his novels, which subtly developed the interplay between the natural detail and the narrator's perspective. Zola could balance an assertion of the "higher value" of a fidelity to nature with a self-conscious use of naturalism as a literary device. In films the need for such a balance is more acute, because the viewer senses less artistic mediation between himself and what he sees; a novel contains words, a play has props, but a movie is *there.* Yet many early film-makers blurred the distinction between naturalism as an artistic method and "truth to nature" as a standard for art. They maintained instead that film could "liberate" artistic truth from the artificialities of the stage much more quickly and effectively than Zola's novels or his theories of theatrical naturalism. After rapid technological advances removed the camera from dependence on the tripod, these young enthusiasts immediately went outdoors to free themselves from the closed studio set and the full-figure presentation typical of the audience's view of the stage.

"Location" shooting flourished all over France. Again with literary precedent, the search for "nature" became associated with a general social radicalism. Many of the new film-makers were associated with André Antoine's "Théâtre Libre" group, which had specialized in the naturalistic presentation of plays adapted from Zola's novels. Zola had become the literary godfather of the new French film industry. Ferdinand Zecca and Lucien Nonguet sought natural locations for the two films they made from Zola's *Germinal: La Grève* (1903) and *Au Pays Noir* (1905). To make his version of *Germinal,* entitled *Au Pays des Ténèbres* (1912), Victorin Jasset took his crew to the north of France, where he used blocks of real coal to construct versions of the mining galleries on the ground directly above the real galleries and shafts—as if the location shooting for these sets authenticated their reality. In 1919 Henri Pouctal got permission to use the Creusot factories to shoot *Travail* and in 1921 André Antoine went on location in Beauce for *La Terre*. The American film, which had already moved out into the countryside to make early westerns and comic chases, no doubt strongly influenced these French searches for "real" nature. But Zola remained its patron. The movies, with their ability to present a fully detailed physical reality, seemed to many of these young French directors to have been invented and perfected at precisely the right time to translate the precepts of *Le Roman Expérimental* and *Le Naturalisme au Théâtre* into their purest practice.

The obsession with the role of "nature" in films, on the part of both critics and film-makers, has continued to this day; and its influence has been less than helpful. Its main effect on film criticism has been the tendency of critics to consider each work in terms of its individual elements rather than in terms of the way in which these elements are brought together into a total form. Such criticism has encouraged the impulse of the average viewer to "disintegrate" a film into its surface details. Parker Tyler has written that "Film is the art . . . where the finished 'form' is the most easily soluble into raw 'content' or ingredients of meaning." Thus the inner coherence of a film frequently vanishes because the spectator links its various parts to the discrete realities he knows outside the film: the faces, the streets, the real and fancied objects of daily life. The other side of this disintegration is an obsessive concentration on every detail, not allowing a film to have a richness which, like the world itself, defies total interpretation. In this view, instead of treating a film as a transcript of reality and therefore ridiculing most attempts at critical interpretation, one becomes convinced that *every* detail has an equal weight of meaning. Since a balance between these views is difficult to maintain, many people interested in film hold firmly to the belief that there are great film "moments," but few great or good films. But in fact, this dwelling on detail allows one to abdicate the critic's true responsibility to search for order and form. And film then achieves its importance for these critics not as an art in itself, with its own problems and solutions, but as nothing more than what Siegfried Kracauer (approvingly) has called "the redemption of physical reality," a vehicle for a world outside film that by definition exists more truly and authentically than any film can.

Most of the early film-makers considered the pursuit of natural detail such a basic assumption of film art that they approached their material with little artistic self-consciousness. Their commitment to the naturalistic theory of films

has come down to us as a kind of orthodoxy, now spawning
the pompous theories of *cinéma vérité* put out to publicize
recent films like *Titticut Follies* and *Salesman*. The total
deduction of value from the image alone, the minimizing of
formal qualities almost to the denial that they exist at all,
and the loud trumpeting of the necessary truth of what is
on screen—all are current manifestations of these old fervors.
But, like the early French enthusiasts, when the trappings of
the naturalistic have been shorn away, the new documen-
tarians produce artistic banality and flat moralisms. Although
the frenzied rush to coal mines, factories, and the countryside
may have liberated the early cinema from a total dependence
on studio sets, it also confined them in a net of facts and
crude naturalistic theory from which they rarely freed themselves. Natural details did not make woodenly played scenes
any more authentic or creaky plots any more flowing. Georges
Sadoul, the French film critic, remarks that these film-makers
made the same mistakes as had the bad naturalistic novelists:
". . . a minute description or the reconstruction of dress and
authentic settings aren't enough to achieve the kind of truth
that was the mark of Zola's work. . . ." Instead of truly considering themselves to be at work in a new art form, they
were at work merely trying to trace in a somewhat freer
medium some combination of what they believed to be the
accomplishments of novelistic naturalism and impressionist
painting. Instead of a real evocation of nature, and the
ambiguities of natural forces, their films moved ideally
toward the documentary, with its pretense of accumulative
neutrality. If the only valid role of the film is to collect physical facts, it makes little difference what order the facts are
in, since they are there only to be extracted.

It is this retreat into detail and "physical reality" that often
lies behind the many critical comparisons between the views
of nature held by Jean Renoir and his father, Pierre-Auguste

Renoir. Such critics assume that the "natural" moments in a film exemplify the "true" Renoir. Any analogy between the work of Jean Renoir and that of his father obviously does injustices to both of them. Since this book is about Jean Renoir, I therefore must to an extent hold Auguste Renoir constant, and characterize him more in the way that his work has been used to judge Jean Renoir than as he actually is in himself.

If, for the Zola-influenced film-makers, a fidelity to natural detail was by definition a liberation from the stage, Auguste Renoir, on the other hand, felt a sense of liberation from photographic realism to be at the foundation of his painting. As Jean Renoir says in his biography of his father, "He gave due credit to Nièpce and Daguerre for having 'freed painting from a lot of tiresome chores, starting with family portraits. Now the shopkeeper who wants his portrait has only to go to the photographer. So much the worse for us, but so much the better for the art of painting'" (p. 179). And Auguste Renoir remarks later that "what seems most significant to me about our movement is that we have freed painting from the importance of the subject" (p. 186). Auguste Renoir implies that it is the understanding of different artistic forms and what they can contribute to each other that yields the true artistic freedom. Strict adherence to naturalistic methods can become an enslavement, in itself as tyrannical as the conventions of stage melodrama. The "renoiresque" moments in the films of Jean Renoir exist less as set pieces than as brief eddies in the total structure of the film. The flat foreground of Impressionist painting is granted a brief inclusion in a medium that emphasizes movement and perspective. When we see scenes resembling, say, *Le Moulin de la Galette* in *Nana* (1926) or in *French Cancan* (1955), the critic's responsibility is to see how they fit into Jean Renoir's total vision,

as part homage and part inclusion, instead of mounting
them in some imaginary album of the "true" Jean Renoir,
whose necessary cinematic nature is to recreate endlessly
the artistic world of his father.

From the very first film of his career Jean Renoir seems to
have a complex awareness of the possible ambiguities of
"naturalist freedom." He can appreciate the realistic detail that explodes artificial limits and punctures myths and
fantasies. But he also appreciates the kind of realism that
affirms new myths. As he remarked in 1959 about *La Petite
Marchande d'Allumettes* (1928): "This film embodies a
preoccupation that I have always had and which, I believe,
is the care of everyone who tries to create something in films,
novels, music, or whatever art: it is the conflict between exterior realism and exterior non-realism. If you like, it's the
conflict between the commedia dell'arte and Zola, between
Harlequin and Colombine, who can give us a reality as
great as exterior reality, and, Coupeau and Gervaise in
L'Assommoir, and the dirt and squalor that cover them."
In accord with this felt conflict, Renoir's films, from the
very earliest, even when they are nominally focused on
natural settings, are remarkable for their exploration of the
possibilities of film beyond the mere absorption of objects.

Renoir's first film as a director, *La Fille de l'Eau* (1924),
begins quite firmly in the anti-studio tradition of the early
film-makers. But Renoir does not seem to share their aesthetic prejudices, for the film also relies heavily on dream,
fantasy, and an almost sardonic awareness of the limits of
the natural world as an absolute source of moral or aesthetic
value. In one of the first scenes in *La Fille de l'Eau,* and
therefore one of the first images in Renoir's films, is a medium
shot of a barge slowly moving down a canal, with lazy trees
drooping their branches into the water. On top of the barge
walks Catherine Hessling (Virginie) back to the makeshift

kitchen to cook breakfast for her father and uncle, who are running the barge. The camera moves with her as she walks *against* the movement of the barge down the canal, and sets up a shutter-snapping effect with the stand of poplar trees behind her, curiously reminiscent of that forerunner of the movie projector, Joseph Plateau's phenakistoscope. Nature here therefore is not nature in itself, but nature viewed and rearranged through the medium of film. The camera does not guarantee a clear and unambiguous picture of what lies before it. One must first understand what nature can offer and how it can be used. In the same way the general method of *La Fille de l'Eau* does not rest with an evocation of the Fontainebleau countryside. In fact it goes beyond concrete nature into the dreams of the feverish Virginie: she is pursued by her evil uncle, who tried to rape her after her father fell off the barge and drowned; attempting to rescue her is Georges Raynal, the son of the mill owner, who has been worried about her safety. The atmosphere of the dream is reminiscent of *Alice in Wonderland,* the passage down empty corridors, the waving clothes, the hallucinatory ride on transparent horses in double exposure over the "natural" countryside. Nature is not the only reality; dream also has its demands.

The use of the dream is one way in which Renoir, in his films principally set in nature, can relate to a natural world deeper than the world of lush descriptive detail. *La Fille de l'Eau* also embodies an awareness that appears in Renoir's films, especially those of the 1940s: violence and sexuality is as natural as lyricism and love. Nature can be a place of benevolent expansiveness or malevolent confinement. The canal itself is an image of limits, the barge forever in its one channel. Virginie briefly breaks away from the barge to live with the Ferret and his mother, two gypsy-poachers who teach her about the life of the countryside.

But then the drunk farmers come and burn the gypsies' wagon. Virginie runs away, half-mad and distracted, to fall finally by the river and have her dream of capture and escape. The rain that brings fertility to the fields brings hallucinations to Virginie and takes her to the verge of madness. Twenty years later, Scott Burnett's recurring dream in *Woman on the Beach* (1946), of his near death by drowning aboard the wrecked troopship, invokes again the same fear of drowning that qualifies the natural beauty of the riverside scenes in *La Fille de l'Eau*. Behind the image of the placid river, indiscriminately caressed by the naturalistic camera, is the fear of the drowning river and deaths or near-deaths by water in *La Fille de l'Eau, Boudu Sauvé des Eaux, Toni, Woman on the Beach, The River*—all summoning up the darker side of Renoir's attitude toward nature.

I dwell upon the fear of drowning before making some broader generalizations about Renoir's use of nature because the rivers in Renoir's films are so frequently interpreted as purely positive symbols of the "flow" and "effortlessness" of his films; they serve as combined images of love of nature and proper film-making for the naturalistically oriented critic of Renoir. The models for such an approach are obviously *The River* (1951), his film of the life of an English family who live beside the Ganges, and *Le Déjeuner sur l'Herbe* (1959), a comic pastoral attack against science and artificial insemination in the name of nature and love. But in fact Renoir always uses his rivers as they suit his different ends in a particular film, without accepting any one-sided interpretation of the river as a benevolent image of all nature and man's absolute need to submit to its flow. Neither *The River* nor *Le Déjeuner sur l'Herbe* is in fact unqualified in its evocation of nature and natural values. But before considering these films in any detail, I would like to sketch how the river is used in Renoir's films from *La Fille de l'Eau* on.

The river can function as an obvious symbol of benevolent nature because it is associated with fertility and growth. But it is interesting that these kinds of association are emphasized only comparatively late in Renoir's career. In the earlier films, the use of the river is more ambivalent. At the end of *La Fille de l'Eau,* for example, Jeff, the wicked uncle, who has returned to torment Virginie and disrupt her growing friendship with Georges Raynal, is finally pitched into the river by the young man. But in the last view of him, one of the final shots in the film, Jeff is swimming off, with the stream, shaking his fist at the people on shore. The river, like nature itself, is morally neutral. It can be used for evil purposes as well as good.

The ripple of light on water behind the credits of *Boudu Sauvé des Eaux* (1932) announces Renoir's more elaborate play with the river in that film. Boudu tries to commit suicide in the Seine at the beginning of the film seemingly because the police won't help him look for his only companion, a dog, who has run away. They prefer to help a pretty rich woman instead of Boudu, the bearded tramp. Lestingois, a bourgeois bookstore owner looking out of his telescope at the passing Parisian life, captures Boudu's image within its frame, and exclaims "The archetypal bum." When Lestingois watches further and sees Boudu jumping into the river, he rushes out, dives in, and saves him out of a mingled sense of humanity and propriety. Like the piano in Lestingois' house that no one can play, Boudu will be collected and exhibited.

The Seine of Boudu's attempted drowning is so dank and dirty that one may wonder why both Boudu and Lestingois do not immediately fall sick from some obscure poisoning. At the end of the film is a more photogenic river. Boudu is being married to Anne Marie, the maid, who had been Lestingois' mistress. The wedding party floats down

the Loing in an obviously overloaded boat. Boudu reaches
for a water lily and over the boat goes. All reach the
shore, but Boudu, whom we watch while he floats lazily
down the river on his back until he comes to shore, trades
clothes with a scarecrow, cadges some food from two pic-
nickers, shares it with a goat, and wanders off. Submission
to the river can mean death; for Boudu it has twice been
the way to a change of identity. This time, instead of seeking
death in the river, he has used it to move consciously from
one life into another, just as Lestingois' rescue had brought
him from the life of the clochard to that of a well-dressed
and coiffed bourgeois. As Boudu walks off whistling shrilly,
the camera pans to the river and his floating derby and
then down the river under distant bridges. The other members of the wedding party, looking as though they are
dressed in the togas of some classical farce, wonder what
has happened to him. Says Lestingois, "His fate was to drift."

Boudu may be able to use the river as escape and change,
but generally in Renoir's films of the 1930s it appears painted
in more melancholic tones. Suicide in Renoir's films invariably takes place in rivers. In *Partie de Campagne* there
is no actual suicide, but the river flows through the film
carrying with it brief joys, which must be seized with
Heraclitean awareness before they are lost forever. A Parisian
bourgeois family, the Dufours, are on a day's holiday beside
a river in the country, complete with inn and fishing
poles. They are trying with comic desperation to appreciate
nature fully before returning to Paris. While the father
and the fiancé/shop assistant try to fish, the mother and
daughter go for a trip up river with two local boys, Rodolphe
and Henri: Rodolphe out for a day of fun and romping, Henri
somber and serious, worried that Rodolphe is irresponsible
and will hurt the daughter's feelings. To protect her, Henri
decides to go with her himself. While Rodolphe and Madame

Dufour romp goatishly around a tree, with Rodolphe playing a mock syrinx in imitation of Pan, Henri and Henriette gaze soulfully at each other in a riverside copse, until they finally kiss, with somber and elegiac music surging behind them.

The two couples correspond to two views of nature, pagan exuberance versus a melancholic self-indulgence in emotion. Henri and Henriette, as their names suggest, are easy counterparts. One from the country and the other from the city, they both romantically yearn for and sentimentalize about nature and natural spots. We are told that the cherries of the tree near the inn are bitter, but Henriette eats them with exuberance and pleasure. The idea of nature overcomes the reality. After Henri and Henriette kiss, we return to the boat landing and the inn in the middle of a cloudburst. The rainstorm that has been building up all through the film has finally burst, and the camera pulls us backward across the water, while the pinpricks of the rain, reinforced by the music, sympathetically mourn the dire necessities of Henriette's engagement to the doltish Anatole despite her "true love" for Henri. In the brief afterword, set several years later, after the marriage of Henriette and Anatole, Henri moodily returns to the spot by the river where he and Henriette first embraced. There he finds Henriette and Anatole, Henriette looking appropriately moody and Anatole lying back on the grass, sleeping with his mouth gaping. Henri and Henriette look at each other wordlessly. The music rises again. Anatole awakes with a fatuous stretch. Henri retreats into the woods and we move back with him to watch the couple row off, with Henriette handling the oars. Then our point of view separates from Henri, while he looks dolefully up at the sky. It ought to be raining, he seems to be thinking. Perhaps it should be, if one also believes in the sentimental view of nature shared by Henri and Henriette. But their view of nature is not Renoir's. It

is only one possibility in a total vision. The river, like so
much of nature, seems in *Partie de Campagne* to be what
you can make of it. It offers change and chance. Instead
of being some invariable touchstone of value, it means what
you can make it mean.

The river can therefore be a limit for those characters
who have already limited themselves, while it is a passage
to change for those, like Boudu, who use it properly. Like
many of the more obvious "symbols" in Renoir's films (Rauffenstein's geranium in *La Grande Illusion* comes to mind),
the river is a symbol created by the characters even more than
by the director. An individual character will impose heavy and
absolute meaning, even while Renoir explores ambiguity and
ambivalence. What the river means in a particular film,
then, tells us more about that film, and the ideas of its
characters, than about some general view Renoir has of rivers.
Rivers at most break down limits. They bring the outside
world into both the selected compass of the frame and the
lives of the characters and forces them to collide with it,
as the Seine carries Lestingois and his own humane com-
pulsions out of his quiet quaiside bookstore to rescue Boudu,
and as Boudu himself is carried from his life as a wandering
clochard into the world of bookstore formalisms and the
"bourgeois" orders of neckties and beds. The previously com-
partmentalized lives of both Boudu and Lestingois are swirled
together by the river. The river moves into the film and
opens up cloistered realities. Like the briefly glimpsed streets
in such films as *La Chienne* (1931) or *Madame Bovary*
(1934), the river implies other possibilities it is up to the
characters to act upon. We see no river mouths nor sources
in Renoir's films, only middles. In fact it would be more
accurate to talk of streams in the films of Renoir rather
than rivers. The word most often used in the French dialogue
is *rivière*, a flowing body of water that does not lead to the

sea. *The River* (*Le Fleuve* in French) is the only grand
river in Renoir's films that is viewed positively. The Seine
in *Boudu,* like the vast Étang de Berre in *Toni,* in which
Marie tries to drown herself, is anonymous and immense, an
overbearing, inhuman river, as opposed to the pleasant, personal streams of other films.

The muted force of all these early rivers emerges finally
in the great Ganges of *The River* (1951), and many of
the naturalistic critics have interpreted this film as Renoir's
long-awaited final commitment to the world of nature that
had always been his true heritage. But "nature" can also
mean a commitment to society, and more socially oriented
critics have seen in *The River* a pastoral conservatism of
bland acceptance after the sharp insight of Renoir's political
films of the 1930s. Clément Cartier remarks sarcastically
about *The River* and *Le Déjeuner sur l'Herbe* (1959), "The
official film-maker of the Popular Front today praises the return to the earth and soul."

But two important considerations qualify the lyrical interpretation of *The River* (as well as that of *The Southerner*
(1946), which is often linked to *The River* in this vision
of Renoir returned to soil, nature, and the soul). The first
is Renoir's carefully expressed ambivalence toward nature,
even in the midst of paean; the second is the frame of
aesthetic detachment that qualifies total acceptance. The
Ganges in *The River* in many ways partakes more of the
earlier rivers of gloom than some free-flowing Impressionist
river. Only in this film, instead of dark fatality, Renoir
asserts some special virtue in conforming to the flow of life,
whatever its terrors, some need to submerge the individual
personality that is positive, in contrast to the earlier images
of suicide by drowning. The way to the complexities of
The Southerner and *The River* is paved through Renoir's
other American films, principally *Swamp Water* (1941)

and *Woman on the Beach* (1947). In both films man is isolated in a hostile natural world. The little town in *Swamp Water* stands perched on the edge of Okefenokee swamp, which most men are afraid to enter for fear of getting lost forever. The brief prologue to the film says that the fear of Okefenokee arises more because of its vastness than because of the creatures that live there. Similarly, the cottage of the Butlers in *Woman on the Beach* stands on a windswept and deserted beach, corresponding in its isolation to the isolation of the characters: Tod Butler, the blind former painter; Lieutenant Scott Burnett and Peggy Butler, the self-absorbed lovers. The choices made in adapting the two novels—Vereen Bell's *Swamp Water* and Mitchell Wilson's *None So Blind*—emphasize man's aloneness in the midst of a hostile nature. Peggy's other lover has been removed from the film version of *Woman on the Beach* and a harsh scene of death by quicksand added to *Swamp Water*. In *Swamp Water* when Tom Keefer, the accused murderer who lives in the middle of the swamp, is bitten by a water moccasin, he survives because he knows and respects the world of the swamp. Nature is not an easy benevolence that one can merely choose to ally with; Renoir implies that man's relation to nature must be conscious and deliberate.

In *The Southerner* the positive attitude toward nature again does not disguise the terrors and accidents which that relationship can bring. Sam Tucker leaves his sharecropping cabin with his wife, children, and old mother, to tenant-farm for himself. After troubles with Devers, a grasping nearby neighbor, Sam finally succeeds in planting a good crop. But during the festivities of a wedding party in town, torrential rains destroy all his plantings by making the nearby river overflow. Tucker and his friend Tim, the narrator of the film, stride through the former fields, now turned into low-water marshes, while logs with chickens perched on them and various other debris float by. The boundaries have been broken between the well-planted field and the rushing river. But the boundaries between Tucker's land and Devers' farm have also been broken. The catastrophe of the overflowing river, which could have led to despair, instead sets the scene for a new kind of integration, a mingling of failure and hope rather than the blind faith in the soil and the absolute power of his own will that had earlier characterized Sam Tucker.

Throughout both films natural rhythms are to be understood rather than unconsciously submitted to. Renoir emphasizes the process of such understanding by distancing both stories by narrators, although this detail is usually overlooked because the visual effect is unmediated nature. Yet we are introduced to the Tucker family in *The Southerner* through the static images of a family album. The pages are turned and commentary is supplied by Tim, the city cousin, a character not in the novel. Tim has escaped the arbitrary world of nature for more secure work in a factory. Yet he comes back frequently for renewal. The country for him is a place of nostalgia, and nature is an image of past purity and innocence. His involvement with the life of the Tuckers brings him to a wider appreciation. Tim in fact resembles Renoir himself in his love of food, his general girth, and his mixed detachment and involvement as he views the life of the Tucker family. Like the two couples in *Partie de Campagne*, Tim and Sam appreciate nature from angles so different as to release the film from a simple-minded formulation of its allure.

The River opens with an explicit welcoming of the audience into the film. Within the film itself the distancing consciousness is supplied by the mature Harriet, looking back on her younger self. Marcel Oms has said that in Renoir's treatment of Bogey's funeral in *The River*, there is "something obscene in his aesthetic detachment." The detachment is certainly there; we view the funeral procession from a distance, seemingly still inside the precincts of the house. But the detachment is "obscene" only if one believes that the norm of *The River* is a simple pastoral nature, and that its tone contains no ambiguity, only celebration. But it would in fact not be very difficult to consider *The River* as an attack against the necessities of nature similar to the Squire's refusal to submit to the demands of Death at the end of Bergman's *The Seventh Seal*. Man cannot be kept in his place by the overflowing river in *The Southerner*. Nor can man be defeated by the tragedy of the death of a small child. The blander affirmation after Bogey's death is the fact of the coming new baby; there is always another one waiting. But Renoir's sharper affirmation is in Harriet's understanding and aesthetic control. *The River* ends with the festival of the new spring, whose titular god is Kali, creator and destroyer. But these are gods made by human beings. In the center of the film Harriet tells in a dance dream sequence her own story of Kali. The sense of renewal marked by the festival is inextricably intertwined with its aesthetic nature, principally the spraying of man-made colors on everything and everybody in sight, until the screen becomes an explosion of color—not nature's colors, but man's, reminiscent of the garish and "unnatural" colors, as well as the stylized movement, of Harriet's story of Kali.

In fact the trees in *The River* were painted for greater contrast in the shots. Claude Renoir, Renoir's nephew and director of photography for *The River*, has said that he and Renoir were appalled by the kind of film they were shown at Technicolor studios in London before they made the picture. In the course of the filming, they tinkered endlessly with the make-up, the settings, looking for an elusive gray, until

their work became a "veritable war against color." Renoir's
sense of the technical and aesthetic order he was imposing
on the acceptance of nature in *The River* has therefore
tremendously enriched the final film. The film-maker's war
against color in *The River* is man's war against nature,
half-involved and half-apart. The naturalistic critic may
think he is seeing "pure" nature, but the film-maker's view
of nature can never be so pure, because he knows the
difficulties involved in gaining the transparent effect. It is
a mark of Renoir's ability to absorb and use everything
he knows that he makes this process of "creating nature"
part of his world. Unless one clearly underlines Renoir's self-
consciousness of his own role in mediating between the cinematic "nature" of *The Southerner* and *The River* and the
physical perceptions of his audience, it will be difficult indeed
to explain why after *The River*, Renoir should make three
films—*Le Carrosse d'Or, French Cancan*, and *Elena et les
Hommes*—in which he uses studio sets, carefully controlled
color, and a romantic reconstruction of history.

If there is pantheism in Renoir's films, it is not the
pantheism that critics have linked to Auguste Renoir
and the Impressionists, but a Pan-theism, a worship of the
sardonic and manipulative in nature, the twist in the tail
of benevolence, the goatish side of romantic and lyric love.
Rodolphe capers about with Madame Dufour in *Partie de
Campagne*. In *Les Bas-Fonds*, when Pepel and Natacha
meet after he has taken her away from the gross police
officer, they talk of their love and their desire to leave the
inclosure of the tenament. It is a perfect opportunity for
Renoir to contrast the stifled human potential of the film
with a scene of natural exuberance and openness. The
outdoor café and the trees do provide such a contrast.
But behind Pepel and Natacha spouts a wry faun's fountain. No tenderness is unalloyed with irony. With his

music and his ironic eye, Pan mediates between the world
of nature and the world of artifice. The rushing stream in
Le Déjeuner sur l'Herbe may signal the transformation of
Étienne Alexis from advocate of artificial insemination and
candidate for the presidency of Europe to lover of Nénette,
the country girl who lives with her family in Les Collettes
(the old Renoir family home in Cagnes, Provence). But
the actual director of the transformation is the wandering
Gaspard who with his goat Cabri summons up the panic
wind that destroys the formal order of the official picnic
and tumbles Étienne Alexis into the natural world of
Provence and the arms of Nénette. Unlike the wind of
The River, which toys with the kites of young boys and
strands them in a tree, the wind of Gaspard is man-made,
the result of his playing on the pipes of Pan. The kites
in the trees are a comic presaging of the tragic reversal
of nature that causes Bogey's death by the snake he and
his friend had been half-worshiping and half-tending. Gaspard directs his wind to spill the revelers onto the stage
of a half-ruined Theater of Diana. With this character
Renoir goes beyond the distancing of the Tucker family
album and Harriet's voiceover narration to present an image
of the magical manipulation of nature by art.

The clear understanding of nature in Renoir's films is
reserved not for the person who clearly knows the uses of
rivers, streets, and boundaries, but for a figure like Gaspard,
who knows more secret paths. This is the root of Renoir's
fascination in his films, and in his plays *Orvet* and *Carola
ou les Cabotins*, with the figure of the poacher. In *La Fille
de l'Eau*, Virginie's time with the poachers teaches her about
the world that exists beyond the limits of the canal. The
rescue from court of Cabri, the poacher in *La Marseillaise*
(1938), becomes one of the first events in the French Revolution, because it focuses popular animosity against the limita-

tions of feudal law. Class conflict in nature becomes the conflict between the landowner's fences and poacher blithely leaping over them. The poacher is the man who makes trails of his own, which follow no traditional pattern, who can use nature for his own advantage, instead of being bent to the fatal necessity of rivers and roads and streets. The wisdom of the poacher allows him both to shun the ready-made trails and to find trails where there seem to be none. And other characters may share this knowledge. Tom Keefer in *Swamp Water* knows all the tracks and trails of the trackless impassable swamp. Ben Ragan can find him because like Keefer he has become separated from the life of the town and the life of his own family and has seen an image of his own aloneness in the solitude of the swamp.

But, typically, Renoir cannot leave the poacher so unambiguous a hero. The most important poacher in any Renoir work is Marceau, the poacher in *La Règle du Jeu* (1939). Robert de la Chesnaye, the owner of the estate on which Marceau poaches, admires Marceau's ability to make a world for himself in the wilds of nature, beyond rules, while La Chesnaye must abide by a host of forms and civilized gestures. But Marceau in his turn has a longing for order. He wants to be a servant and be accepted into the house, taken away from his life in the fields.

Tom Keefer, on the other hand, in Renoir's next film after *La Règle du Jeu*, is afraid of coming out of his natural sanctuary and facing the townspeople, even after he has been cleared of the murder. (At the end of the novel Keefer dies, without ever getting out of the swamp.) As *La Règle du Jeu* explores the world of rules for everything, *Swamp Water* exists in a world without rules. Renoir's last French film before the war is obsessed with the overlapping orders of society and its customs and their ability to absorb even the eruptions of passionate nature. In *Swamp Water*,

Renoir's first American film, nature is so pervasive and potentially hostile that the problem is to choose the river from
the endlessly crossing waterways and marshes. What is a
river? What are the clear rights and wrongs, the clear passages from nature to the world of society, from one stage
of life to another—all of these were appropriate questions
to be asked by Renoir, who had only recently arrived in
the United States in the wake of the German occupation.

The undiscriminating critical emphasis on "nature" in Renoir's films usually carries with it an assertion of his "invisible" camera. It is true that he does not usually use the strange
angles that in contemporary films call attention to the existence of the camera and especially to the director's manipulation of the image. But Renoir's camera is far from invisible. It is a kind of poaching camera, making its own paths
through the world of his films. The early French films
broke out into nature but preserved the woodenness of
composition by frame, whatever the subject. Renoir's camera,
on the other hand, can move into and out of a scene, exploring beyond the surface and withdrawing to show that
there is more world than the frame can momentarily delimit.
Like all great artists, Renoir will use conventions, but with
artistic self-consciousness. The silent-film cliché of opening
a scene from a particular detail is used in Renoir's silent
films not to bring the viewer back into a tableau from a
diverting detail, but to expand the world of the frame.
In *Tire-au-flanc* (1928), for example, characters brush off to
the right of the frame as they leave. The camera is another
character, another viewpoint, not a framer forever. *Tire-au-
flanc* in fact begins with the camera pulling back from a
painting over the fireplace in the d'Ombelles house, announcing a cinematic transcendence of the pictorial and
theatrical stasis of the play from which the film was taken.

A thematic complement to the intrusive and expansive ability of the camera in Renoir's films is the breaking down of boundaries and limitations. This is the most positive side of nature on the thematic and visual levels. The theme of boundaries and limits permeates all phases of Renoir's work, in his use of theatrical settings and devices as well as in his examination of society. But nature more traditionally expands man's confines. The river can be the appropriate image for this breaking of limits because no river can ever be contained within the limits of a film, unless it were a film similar to John Banvard's painting of the Mississippi that was three miles long and played to nineteenth-century vaudeville audiences by unrolling before their eyes. Jean Renoir's camera is no gallery observer of paintings by Pierre Auguste Renoir; it seems actually to walk into a renoiresque space.

Movies can preserve and exploit the visual continuity of directed movement, in which the camera leads the eye somewhat below the level of consciousness into the necessary positions for viewing the action. André Bazin has written that the "depth of field," which he believes characterizes Renoir's films, is a "democratic" technique because it allows the spectator to choose the details within the frame he will concentrate on. I will discuss depth of field further in the next chapter. But for now let me mention the actual leading of the eye involved in Renoir's camera work. The camera binds together and makes choices. In comparison with the experience of standing before a painting, something is lost and something is gained. The viewer can no longer partially guide his own eye and partially follow the lines of the painting; his visual choice is less free in the film. But with the aid of the camera he can penetrate some richer reality. The flat painting or tableau of an establishing shot opens up with the movement of the camera to reveal a deeper world. The device of the intruding camera, like any technique, can be used perfunctorily. And stylistic devices in film can be even more easily detached from their meaning than new methods in the other arts. In Fred Zinneman's *From Here to Eternity*, for example, the camera stands in the rain outside the house. Inside, Sergeant Warden (Burt Lancaster) has entered and is embracing Karen Holmes (Deborah Kerr). The camera moves forward in the rain, through the bushes, through the window and the wall to stand next to them inside the house. Perhaps some thematic justification may be found for this movement, but it does not seem to exist on any level beyond embellishment. Renoir's camera movement, on the other hand, whether "invisible" or obtrusive, always serves to express his meaning. And its purported invisibility can be quickly qualified by a look at the very elaborate movement in, say, the scene in *La Grande Illusion* in which we are introduced to the hall in which the preparations for the amateur theatricals are taking place, or the scene of the singing of the "Marseillaise" during the performance, as the camera in one long continuous movement binds together the French prisoners on stage and behind the curtains and watches the reactions of the Germans in the audience.

A scene in *Le Déjeuner sur l'Herbe* presents a further model of Renoir's contrast between film and painting. First there is a strictly framed tableau: Étienne Alexis is marching through the woods, looking for Nénette; he passes a little glade in which a man is asleep beside a tree. The colors and the framing are all reminiscent of some momentary Impressionist painting. When Étienne finally finds Nénette, she has decided to take a nude swim in the river. Critics have attacked this scene because it is voyeuristic rather than an evocation of natural purity. But natural purity and voyeurism cannot be separated. The painting of Nénette bathing would successfully keep the viewer at a distance and allow him to "excuse" his excitement with the detachments of art. But the film must exploit the special point of view. We see Nénette go into the river from the point of view of Étienne Alexis. And, as soon as she comes out, he grabs her hand and pulls her off into the deeper woods. It is hard to imagine a better image of the violation of static natural beauty by the energies and movement of film.

As the track forward opens up the world of flat nature, so the track back can distance the scene. A common camera movement in Renoir's films of the 1920s and 1930s is a movement backward in front of someone walking. This movement can be made for comic effect, for example, in *Tire-au-flanc*, in which a new recruit thinks that he is being saluted by a line of officers when he enters camp; actually it is someone behind him who is receiving the salutes. In *Madame Bovary* (1934) there are strangely evocative shots from a carriage looking out over the road already past, much like the shots from the train in *La Grande Illusion* that show the passing countryside, but not the train itself. Perhaps the most striking of these withdrawals is the one at the end of *Les Bas-Fonds*, in which Jean Gabin and Junie Astor walk along a road, with the camera gradually withdrawing in front of them until they become a small almost indistinguishable image within a broad black frame. All of these sequences seem related by the withdrawing camera which signals the presence of perspective and detachment. In *Tire-au-flanc* it is a comic perspective that the main character is unaware of. In *Madame Bovary* it is the perspective of artifice in the world of nature, for the coach bounces along this road, a baroque object amid the rough and bare countryside, like Madame Bovary herself, an effort to resist by stylization the crushing sameness of this provincial world.

The perspective from the train in *La Grande Illusion* preserves an involuntary detachment from the freedom of the
fields beyond. Many critics have considered the end of *Les
Bas-Fonds* to be an imitation of the final shot of Chaplin's
Modern Times. (Chaplin's shot does not have the same
black border; Vittorio de Sica seems to imitate Renoir rather
than Chaplin in *Two Women*.) But Renoir's image, whether
or not it derives from Chaplin's suggestion, is much more pessimistic. Chaplin and Paulette Goddard walk jauntily down
their road and leave us behind—an image of potentiality and
optimism. Gabin and Astor walk toward us. But we move
backward even faster than they move forward, until they are
caught within the black frame and reduced. By taking to the
road, they are trying to escape the confinements of the tenement, and the static theatrical vision of the film in general,
with its black curtains pulled down between scenes. But the
escape into nature is not such an easy solution. Chaplin's
pastoral faith in the ability of nature to cure the ills of
society is too simplistic for Renoir's more ironic vision.

Renoir may toy with the pastoral solution, the retreat from
reality to romance, as he does in the *Le Déjeuner sur l'Herbe*
by juxtaposing the comic inhumanities of science with the
comic exuberances of Provençal nature. *Le Déjeuner sur
l'Herbe* seems to be a return to the world of natural things,
but without the solemnity and frequently flat profundities of
the script of *The River*. Renoir has said that he did not
treat the subject seriously enough. The contrast between
science and nature remains a comic one. But perhaps it must
be in a film in which Renoir says he frequently used five
cameras to preserve the naturalness of the reactions of the
actors. Nature may yield its secrets only after the most elaborate technical preparations. At the end of the film, the final
image is a wedding bouquet superimposed on a natural

scene, a whimsical image of the marriage of art and nature. Unlike *Le Déjeuner sur l'Herbe*, *The River* finally keeps art and nature too far apart, and its solemnity about the natural world prevents a true dialectic between the two. The purely pastoral in Renoir's works is usually, like pastoral in literature and in art in general, an invention of the jaded city. Étienne Alexis' stand against love and nature seems almost to inspire Nénette and her family to spring up out of the provençal soil. The beginning of *Boudu* is a stagy dance of nymphs and satyrs, with Lestingois playing one of the satyrs and the maid, Anne-Marie, a nymph. It is clumsy and farcical; a column almost falls over in the pseudo-classical countryside the stage is made up to represent. Then immediately Lestingois and Anne-Marie appear in a more "natural" (for them) setting, the inside of the bookstore. But the language of pastoral is still with them. Lestingois whispers pastoral nothings into Anne-Marie's ear: "My pipes shall play a hymn to Eros with my last breath." Like Étienne Alexis and Nénette twenty-five years later, Lestingois is the city man and Anne-Marie the natural woman fascinated by his talk and more swayed by his pseudo-pastoral language than by the real nature she knows. Boudu shatters this holding of nature at a distance by bringing it into the bookstore in his own form. Lestingois' pastoralism is not quite prepared for the natural violence of Boudu. This sense of the expansive side of nature relates Renoir's moving camera to his wandering characters. Both explore the nature beyond pastoral conventions. Like the many street singers and musicians who arrive fortuitously in Renoir's films of the 1930s to comment ironically and obliquely on the main action, this kind of camera implies a world beyond the film's frame that constantly impinges on the more closed world we are observing. When the camera plunges forward, it reveals the human complexity behind

the conventional tableau; when it draws back, it distances
the story in the harmonious coherence of art.[1]

GENRE NOIR

I have spoken mainly until now of the sunny side of
Renoir's view of nature, the exuberance and the bursting of
boundaries. But adherence to the standard of nature, Renoir
always implies, is not a simple thing. Nature in art can
have both optimistic and pessimistic connotations, for there
is a rainy naturalism as well as a sunny naturalism, a naturalism of urban melancholy to balance rural exuberance,
a naturalism of fate to counteract the naturalism of freedom.
The literary naturalism with which Renoir grew up is quite
different from the luxuriant pictorial naturalism with which
he is often associated, and his films exploit both varieties.
Nature is not an absolute release from convention and the
falsehoods of sophistication; it must be qualified by the se-

[1] Renoir's use of the moving camera to plunge into the heart of natural things is certainly not his own invention. Neither is the depth of
focus that complements the movement by showing the possibility of
extension beyond the camera. The documentaries of the Lumière
brothers, although they concentrated on the figures before the camera,
always include the mysterious long shot of the streets on which the
figures move. Renoir's *Toni* (1935) is known as the forerunner of
the Italian neo-realist films of the late 1940s, made by directors such
as Rossellini, de Sica, Visconti, and Antonioni. But they have taken
over from Renoir the dialect language, nonprofessional actors, and
concentration on lower-class life, rather than Renoir's sense, in films
like *La Chienne* or *La Nuit du Carrefour,* of the melancholy of
streets. The street in neo-realist films is still a stage set, in impact, if
not in fact. Everything that the camera wants is there. Only in brief
moments, like the Anna Magnani character's run after the Nazi truck
taking away her husband in *Open City,* is the street more than a
local-color setting. In that moment it moves and becomes a fatality
that drags people away. Otherwise its visual and cinematic potential
is stillborn.

lectivity of art that has in fact chosen to frame this pageant of release.

The dark side of naturalism is Renoir's true heritage from Zola. His first three full-length sound films—*La Chienne* (1931), *La Nuit du Carrefour* (1932), and *Bondu Sauvé des Eaux* (1932)—are explorations of precisely this negative side of nature, which confines rather than liberates the human spirit. While other directors were returning to the studio because of the heaviness of the new sound film equipment, in these three films Renoir took to the streets. He was influenced by Zola's dark cities and perhaps in part by the gloom of German Expressionist films (although the influence here seems to go both ways, from, say, Renoir to Lang, perhaps more than the other way round). Instead of a naturalism that offered nature as antidote to all ills, these films contain a naturalism of perspective, in which the inquisitive camera moves beyond the surfaces of life to reveal the more turbulent nature beneath. The result was the invention of a new atmosphere for films, what might be called the *genre noir*, that could stand in opposition to the bland optimism of the films of directors like René Clair.

Boudu is more familiar in the United States, even though it was not shown here commercially until 1967. *La Chienne* and *La Nuit du Carrefour* are rarely shown, even in the museums. They are both films of darkness, night, and rain. It is no wonder that Renoir is considered to be the director of sunlight, when our view of his films has been so truncated. *La Chienne* is a great film, while *La Nuit du Carrefour* is very good. Renoir had ended his silent career with two expensive and lavish spectacles, the elaborate historical reconstruction of the Middle Ages in *Le Tournoi dans la Cité* (1929) and the paean to the colonization of Algeria in *Le Bled* (1929), in which an army of conquering French soldiers turns into an army of tractors, in

a reminiscence of *spectacle à la russe*. After these lavish
and looming spaces, both *La Chienne* and *La Nuit du
Carrefour* are suddenly intimate, concentrating on the petty
details of crime and the twisting of human lives. In *La
Chienne* the perspective on events is achieved through
several devices: the puppet-show frame that begins and ends
the film; the cold camera that peers in the window of the
apartment Maurice Legrand (Michel Simon) has rented for
his paramour Lulu (Janie Marèze); and those common Renoir props, the street singers. At the climactic scene in the
film, when Legrand is murdering Lulu because he has
caught her the night before with her pimp boyfriend Dédé
(Georges Flamant), the street singers unconcernedly sing of
true love several stories below the murder. Dédé abruptly
pulls his fancy car through them to see Lulu, unaware of
what is going on. As things turn out, Dédé is convicted
of the crime and Legrand gets off—imagistically at least
because Dédé is committed by his car to the authority of
the streets as a way of going places, an invariable line from
one spot to the other, complementing his con man's ability
to use society and dupes like Legrand for his own enrichment. Legrand has only his own nature to deal with and
so he walks away from the apartment house and merges with
the crowd. By the end of the film he has become a clochard
like Boudu, drifting around the city streets, diving after a
spied cigar butt, opening the doors of the rich. The puppet-
show frame falls on his new life, a harsher world, but once
again distanced.

  La Nuit du Carrefour handles the distancing a little less
obtrusively by locating it in the basilisk gaze of Inspector
Maigret, played by Pierre Renoir, Jean's older brother, already at that time a famous French stage actor. His stolid
eye emphasizes the lesson of rainy naturalism that there
must be an observer; the camera eye, or the novelist's per-

spective, is never transparent. The film is adapted from a
Simenon novel titled in English *Maigret at the Crossroads*.
The basic structure of the novel is built on coincidence,
and the murder scene and investigation set at the lonely
crossroads suggests both chance and fate, neither within
the control of the human participants. The only true perspective on the events is that retrospectively allowed to
Maigret. Simenon lightly counterpoints the general gloom
of the novel with a few brief descriptions of singing birds
and green fields around the gloomy crossroads. But Renoir
omits even this small relief. The atmosphere is gray and
drizzly, the almost vacant interiors of the Andersens' house
a hodgepode of dusty and cobwebbed objects, the garage
a confusion of tools and automobile parts. Maigret's office
in Paris is suffused with billowing cigarette and pipe smoke.
Nothing is certain except that which is totally arbitrary. To
underline the absence of natural purity and innocence, the
only stream of water we see is a gutter rivulet in Paris
flowing into a nearby sewer. It is from the perspective of
this gutter that we watch a kiosk whose walls feature news
of the case. As we watch from the gutter, passers-by drop
copies of successive editions into the murky water, Renoir
intercuts scenes of the interrogation, with the room gradually
filling with smoke. *La Nuit du Carrefour* does more with
these images of murkiness than any other film I know.
Brief scenes may be recalled from other films, the steam
of the train station in *Anna Karenina*, the fog of the morning
talk in the park in *On the Waterfront*. But the effect in
La Nuit du Carrefour is more organically related to the
entire structure and meaning of the film. There are only
a few moments of brightness: the lighted interior of a car
in the midst of a gloomy night (an image that reminds
one of *Bonnie and Clyde*). Once a spotlight bursts across
a dark field; shots are fired quickly, and all is dark again.

To complement the murky gutter and the movement
through smoke and fog that characterize the continuity of
La Nuit du Carrefour, the final auto chase of the criminals,
archetype of so many succeeding chases, goes far beyond
its shallow descendants. Instead of the usual clarity with
which the chased car is clearly visible from the pursuers,
and vice versa, the interchange of shots being the main
point, Renoir's chase is just as shrouded in darkness as
the rest of the film. We peer through the rainspecked
windshield, dimly trying to see the other car, which becomes
faintly visible or not at all, after it has made a fast turn.
There is no overview of two cars weaving down a country
road, only a limited point of view, either from within the
pursuer's car or infrequently from outside on the road. Jean-
Luc Godard has perpetuated the story that *La Nuit du
Carrefour* is obscure because Jean Castanier lost three reels
of film from the daily shooting. But the complications of
the plot as Renoir retells it are quite close to Simenon's
story. What Renoir has done is to increase the confinement
and obscurity of the atmosphere of the novel, creating for
these country crossroads a claustrophobic city-oriented naturalism to replace the expansive naturalism of the rural
setting. Renoir has said that he doesn't think any film was
lost in *La Nuit du Carrefour:* "As usual, the money ran out
before the film was over." Raymond Chandler always claimed
that he never understood the plot of *The Big Sleep,* and
Howard Hawks agreed. But the point of *The Big Sleep*
is the character of Marlowe, who holds together even what
is logically unbelievable. In *La Nuit du Carrefour* Renoir
sets up a masterful counterpoint between the confused world
of the film and the penetrating presence of Maigret. We
understand because he explains, not because what happened is objectively explainable. Godard's anecdote of the

lost film is symbolically quite true, even if it is literarily false.

One element that Renoir does add to the original story is an increased emphasis on the sexual theme, an essential part of his dark naturalism, from its beginnings in *La Fille de l'Eau*. Madame Maigret has been removed from the story and a tentative relation between Maigret and Else Andersen enhanced, as well as a subsidiary intrigue between one of the assistants in the garage and the wife of Oscar, the garage owner. In all of Renoir's gloomy films of the 1930s the sexual impulse is seen as a source of confinement and limitation, unless it can be treated lightly as Rodolphe does in *Partie de Campagne*. *La Chienne* (1931), *Toni* (1935), and *La Bête Humaine* (1938) do not contain the kind of freeing and awakening sexuality that is to become the theme of *The River* and *Le Déjeuner sur l'Herbe*. In different ways each of these three films is a tragedy of passion and sexual nature. In *La Nuit du Carrefour* sex is an undercurrent in the general gloom. Only in *The Crime of Monsieur Lange* (1936), *Les Bas-Fonds* (1936), and *La Grande Illusion* (1937) are there relations between men and women with the possibility of tenderness, and in all three the relation can survive only outside the social context that spawned it. In *Lange* we do not know whether Lange and Florelle will be happy or not; in *Les Bas-Fonds* the dark frame reduces our optimism about the future life of Pepel and Natacha; and in *La Grande Illusion* the idyll of Maréchal and Elsa must finally be left behind for the demands of the war outside. Even the heroic artistry of Christine in *La Règle du Jeu* is not enough to bring anything from the chaos of emotions and relations made and unmade throughout that film.

Renoir's insight in these dark films is that one can be just as trapped by a narrow image of the natural world as by the

city, and that nature defined simply in contrast to the city
and bourgeois life is a naïve kind of freedom, suitable for the
whimsical satyr play of *Le Déjeuner sur l'Herbe,* but not for
films that attempt some serious understanding of the relations between men and women. Both *Toni* and *La Bête
Humaine* are films in which nature is the handmaiden of
fate and death. In *Toni* the action of the film is framed at
the beginning by the arrival of Toni in the mining town,
filled with expectations, and at the end by the arrival of the
new immigrants after Toni has been shot next to the railroad tracks for taking the responsibility for a crime he did
not commit.

As in *Partie de Campagne,* the serious-minded romantics
suffer, while the gay manipulators and passionate asserters
get what they want. While Toni dawdles romantically after
Josefa, the gross Albert takes her by force and marries her.
Gaby, Josefa's cousin, who has done more than Toni to egg
on Josefa's murder of Albert, blithely borrows Toni's motor-
cycle to go off to Marseilles, after telling Toni he's been
sleeping with Josefa for two years. Toni meanwhile has been
pining away in an unhappy marriage to Marie, waiting for
some obscurely defined chance to take Josefa away from Albert. But, like Henri in *Partie de Campagne,* he has been
more confined by his romantic view of Josefa and himself
than by chance itself. When he first met Josefa, he had sucked
the wasp poison from her shoulder, but never spit it out. His
image of nature controls him instead of the other way
around, and again like Henri in *Partie de Campagne,* he
consoles himself with his gloomy world. The true romantics
are the worst victims of nature's fate because they have ideals
to be crushed. Rodolphe takes his pleasure with Madame
Dufour, Gaby takes his with Josefa, and neither is the
worse, while Henri mopes endlessly at the riverside and Toni
dies meaninglessly by the railroad track.

The railroad in *Toni* crosses the river, suggesting the rigid fatalities to which Toni has committed himself because he can envision nothing beyond it. The wasp poison has bred in him both a fatal love for Josefa and a fatal submission to the demands of nature. The overwhelming walls of the quarry where he works appear as images of nature's pressure on the details of his life. Renoir seems to feel for Toni both compassion and detachment, even verging on a kind of disdain. When Toni is shot by the nervous hunter, we watch the shooting, not from the side, but from the hunter's point of view. Perhaps this is the "obscene" detachment with which we watch Bogey's funeral procession in *The River,* saddened but neutral observers in a situation where the anguish seems more worked up by the characters than authentic. Like Toni, Bogey has too readily embraced the snake in nature, with too little consciousness that nature is not always benevolent. His death is less an event in itself than part of the passage to adulthood of the girls, in which birth, love, and death must all play a part. Harriet supplies the understanding that Bogey lacks. The confinements that destroy Toni, in which he so willingly acquiesces, in the same way should invite us to see beyond them to a larger world.

Jacques Lantier in *La Bête Humaine* has even less choice than Toni in his relations with the dark possibilities of nature, for his own nature, as the brief prologue emphasizes, has been poisoned by the alcoholic generations of his heritage. Like Toni, Jacques does live within a society more vital and more direct than the effete life of the city middle classes. But the depth of his immersion in this world is the depth of his confinement. *La Bête Humaine* shares with *Toni* the image of the train and the track it runs on. In early films the railroad train frequently functioned as an image of freedom and movement. A. Nicholas Vardac has described how turn-of-the-century theaters began using train backdrops

and elaborately staged chases to imitate the cinematic sense
of movement. And in Méliès' *Voyage à Travers l'Impossible*
the space travelers leave the earth by train.

In contrast to other films of the 1930s, like Hitchcock's *The Lady Vanishes* (1938), in which the train and
freedom equation of the early years of films expands to allow
a release from conventional identity and character, *La Bête
Humaine*, like *Toni*, makes the train an image of limitation.
The much-imitated tour de force of the Le Havre-Paris run
with which Renoir begins the film reverberates throughout
the remainder of the film as an image of the determinism
and fatality that controls the lives of the characters. The
transient railroad men's apartment in Paris, where Séverine
first confesses her affair with Grandmorin to her husband,
Roubaud, and where Séverine and Lautier have their first
trysts, looks down upon the railroad yard tracks—an image
of the rigidities of their lives. To enrich the theme of fatality,
the setting of many scenes in the cab of the locomotive emphasizes a mechanistic explanation of human nature: Lantier's heredity, the greed and sexuality of Séverine, the greed
and vengeance of Roubaud. Paradoxically enough, Lantier,
the most determined—through inheritance—of all the characters in *La Bête Humaine*, is perhaps the most selfless and
most manipulated by others. His blind rages are as much
provoked by his surroundings as they are by some internal
dynamic. The rhythmic alternation of enclosure and release
when the train goes through the tunnels and across the rivers
reflects the conflicts within his own nature. Even when he attacks his innocent cousin Flore, it is within the shadow of the
railroad track, not the easy symbol of sexuality that it becomes in films like Antonioni's *L'Avventura*, but the form of
Lantier's personal fatality. Lantier loves his locomotive like a
man who believes his only destiny is to fit himself in with
movements larger than himself. So he allies himself with the

aims of Séverine until he finally destroys both her and himself.

All of the images of *La Bête Humaine* are images of entrapment: by heredity, by the weakness of personal will, by uncontrollable emotion, by the mechanical forces of society. In the face of these pressures, Lantier's final act at the end of the film, when he jumps off the train after knocking out Pecqueux, the fireman, who has been trying to stop him, is an attempt to tear himself away from the nature that has in so many ways pressed him into an inescapable mold. Renoir shrouds the dialogue before the jump in roars and clashes of train equipment so that nothing rational emerges from the action. Just a desperate cry of rage and freedom from a Toni who can finally no longer be submissive and romantic.

The nature that traps instead of freeing is underlined in *La Bête Humaine* by the presence of many mirrors, more mirrors than Renoir generally uses in his films. Although mirrors are a common cinematic device, they usually function to give some illusionistic effect. In Renoir's films they signal a kind of self-involvement, understood simply enough, in a film like *Nana*, for example, as narcissism and stylization. But in *La Bête Humaine* the mirrors reflect a constant turning inward and, conversely, an inability to get outside the self or to be free of the demon self revealed by the mirror. Séverine reveals her affair with Grandmorin to Roubaud while they stand in front of a mirror. In front of another mirror Lantier gives himself up to the rage that will bring him to kill Séverine; his eyes look at his reflection while his hand reaches unconsciously for the knife. But environment and nature need not have this fatal effect. Tom Keefer, trapped within the wild nature of the Okefenokee Swamp, is a kind of self-conscious Lantier, who cannot leave his confinement because of a hostile society, but who at least has tried to understand its workings. There is no understanding for Lantier, and his only freedom is the freedom of death. The only remotely free character in the entire film, like a breath of fresh air from Renoir's other films, is the simple poacher Cabuche, played by Renoir himself; and he is being prosecuted for the murder of Grandmorin (actually killed by Roubaud in Séverine's presence) by a zealous examining magistrate.

La Bête Humaine is Renoir's deepest statement of the theme of the fatality of nature. In *Swamp Water* he has already changed to a different point of view. Fate is more neutral than actively malevolent in *The Southerner* and *The River*, although the intensities of female passion strongly preoccupy Renoir in *Woman on the Beach* (1947). By the time of *Le Déjeuner sur l'Herbe* nature has become once again the liberator, the reasserter of youth and innocence, *rajeunir sur l'herbe*. But something has been resolved in Renoir's contemplation of the theme of nature. The opposition between the nature that confines and the nature that liberates has been reconciled by an appeal to other imperatives in Renoir's world. I would like to discuss these other imperatives in the following chapters. But for now I want to consider how Renoir reconciles these two seemingly opposed attitudes to the image of nature.

In the harshly lit interiors of *Toni* we see clearly the contrast between these cramped ugly spaces and the freedom of the outside world, although the characters themselves may be just as manipulated outside as inside. In *La Grande Illusion* Maréchal and Rosenthal escape from the confines of the prison camp to a world of open fields and sparse woods. When they find an Eden in the home of Elsa, the German peasant woman who lost her husband at Verdun, they can rest for the moment. But the tiny house is only a partial refuge from both the freedom and oppression of what lies outside. The scene in which they decide to leave begins with Rosenthal opening a window to see Maréchal standing outside. In some unstated way they both feel they must make some connection with the world outside the house. This silent commitment then forms the basis for the tremulous optimism of the final shot of the film, the two men knee-deep in snow, dark figures totally vulnerable in the immense blankness of nature, moving forward to some obscure destiny.

Pastoral retreat is usually a static ideal in Renoir's films of the 1930s and 1940s. Only in *Diary of a Chambermaid* (1946) is there a journey in and out, and there the journey is into an artificial world from a natural world. In *Woman on the Beach* the refuge in nature, the beach house built by Tod Butler as a retreat from the world, finally burns at the end of the film. Butler burns his paintings along with it. He must do new work. Isolation on the beach, at the verge of nature, is more detrimental to his growth and life than the shocks of the world would be. *Woman on the Beach* was Renoir's last American film.

The River, which was Renoir's next film, resolves this separation between inner and outer worlds because it contains within it a countryside in which the outer and the inner world are not so absolutely divided. The invitation into the film imitates the Indian ritual invitation into the home. The family house itself preserves no strict distinction between its outside and its inside; many scenes take place on the wide verandah, with the trees waving their branches into the area of the house. Since the film deals basically with initiation, the movement from the protected house to the possibly hostile world outside is greatly emphasized. Harriet must finally leave the "Secret Hole" behind the stairs, where she meditates and writes. Ram Singh, the most Indian of the members of the household, is appropriately enough the gatekeeper. He wordlessly mediates for the children between the assurances of the family and the strangeness and fascination of the India beyond its walls. *The River* in fact may be less appealing than many other Renoir films because it has resolved so many earlier problems with too little conflict, subsuming what had been dark fate into the natural cycles of life, growth, death, and rebirth. The death of Bogey from the snake is merely another cautionary note in the symphony of natural movement—a brief waystation to prepare us for Harriet's renewal after slipping into the river, born again into maturity. At the end of the film the camera swoops up over the heads of the three girls, posed stiffly on the verandah, and goes into the sky. Perhaps this is a mime of Harriet's own detachment in reviewing her childhood through the voracious perspective of art. Harriet's narrative voice is another step toward the absolutely moralistic narrator of *The Testament of Dr. Cordelier* (1959) in which the Jekyll-Hyde creator is totally condemned. *The River* may at one level too simply praise the acceptance of the natural rhythms of success and defeat. But in terms of Renoir's later career, what remains most compelling about the film are its stylized and anti-natural scenes, such as Rahda's dance of the gods and goddesses and the Holi festival. In the more theatrical world of Renoir's films of the 1950s, he returns to a turn-of-the century world much like that in which *Diary of a Chambermaid* is set. But instead of the studio set being an image of provincial isolation, after the purgation of nature's demands in *The River,* Renoir finds a renewed vigor in the closed world that a total commitment to nature too frequently ignores.

Renoir's use of nature in his films therefore cannot be totally separated from his development of other, even anti-natural, elements in his method and interests. The many variables involved in a particular film might be ordered and properly subordinated by someone interested in a clear schema. But what is more fascinating is the way these themes meld, change, and emerge reformed. Nature means

certain things to Renoir, both as theme and setting, which I
have tried to sketch in this chapter. He never makes the
kind of commitment to its purity, innocence, and necessity
to the film that the early French film directors or his own
naturalistically oriented critics would want him to. Already
in his first film, *La Fille de l'Eau,* he can juxtapose and try
to integrate the demands of natural setting and semi-surrealist
dream. The darker films of the 1930s, with their interest in
the social world, then turn the simple hues of pastoral nature
into the darker tones of natural passion. The American films
of the 1940s in part continue this trend, but introduce in
figures like Tom Keefer in *Swamp Water* and Sam Tucker in
The Southerner some possibility of dealing with nature's
hostility and capriciousness. *The River* becomes a prelude to
the emphasis on artistic perspective in the 1950s, which will
bind together all of Renoir's interests, nature, theater, and
society, into the episodic structure of his final film, *Le Petit
Théâtre de Jean Renoir,* in 1970.

Throughout these mutations, Renoir retains his involved
detachment and his sense of irony. His refusal to define the
cinematic use of nature solely in terms of detail and physical
setting is underlined in a fascinating film made by Eric
Rohmer and Jean-Pierre Abont, made for French educational
television, in which Renoir and Henri Langlois, the director
of the Cinémathèque Française, discuss the films of Louis
Lumière, while the films are intercut with their discussion.
Langlois' approach to Lumière is aesthetic and social. He
constantly refers to Lumière's "plastic art," his feeling for
the multitude of things in the world. By extension Langlois
asserts that the proper end of film is to record these things.
The only difference between us and Lumière, says Langlois,
is social, not technical or aesthetic. Lumière records bourgeois
events alone, but all film-makers concentrate on "les impon-
derables de la vie." Film is essentially a plastic art; even with

sound it is still preoccupied with objects. Its grandeur is the
precision of the image.

Throughout the film Renoir quietly objects to all of
Langlois' formulations. Although he too admires Lumière
tremendously, he finds totally different things in his films.
Instead of a halting at the surface, Renoir sees in Lumière
a searching after depth. We do not, he says, stop at the surface of Lumière's images; instead they fill us with curiosity
about the interior of his characters and open the doors of
our imagination to other possibilities, other worlds. Langlois
agrees, calling this depth "l'espèce profond," perhaps in
analogy to Bazin's discussion of Renoir's "depth of field." But
Renoir does not really mean such a casual look into things
upstage. Realistic props, he says, do not make a realistic impression. He objects to Langlois' belief that film deals in
tableau, because it implies that the camera must stop at the
surface of character and remain a mere physiognomist. Lumière, says Renoir, fills us with uncertainty rather than with
facts and satisfaction. Film, says Renoir, does not show us a
world of objects alone, but two worlds, a world that exists
in reality and one that exists in the mind of the cameraman
and the director. Like the natural world of the painter Henri
Rousseau, nature in films exists both in reality and in the
mind of the perceiver, whether the creator or the audience.
In the same way, Renoir's naturalistic heritage serves through
all his films to enrich his perspective rather than to restrict
it to the surface of things. And one remark he makes about
Auguste Renoir in his biography of his father may be applied
with equal justice to him:

> Now I know that great men have no other function in
> life than to help us see beyond appearances; to relieve
> us of some of the burden of matter—to "disencumber" us
> as the Hindus would say.

CHAPTER THREE

The Freedom of Theater

Puis, enfin, la réalité est toujours féerique.
—JEAN RENOIR, 1962

I like films or books which give me the feeling of a frame too narrow for the content.
—JEAN RENOIR, 1969

It was not until I was three years old that I was allowed to see a puppet show with Gabrielle. Renoir advised against going to the one in the Champs Élysées because the puppets wore cheap, overly shiny silk costumes, but sent us instead to the Tuileries "Guignol," which had kept to the best tradition of the city of Lyon. The first performance I saw was an experience I shall never forget. To start with, I was positively hypnotized by the drop curtain, painted as an imitation of red and gold draperies. What dreadful mysteries lay behind it?
—Renoir My Father (317)

One of the most constant rallying cries in the history of film commentary, whether by critics or film-makers themselves, has been the "cinematic," that essence, however it is defined, that separates film from other arts and gives it a

unique aesthetic nature of its own. Since the beginning of
film theory, the "theatrical" has been considered the worst
enemy of the "cinematic," although lately the "literary" and
the "painterly" have gotten their quota of sneers. Such animosity toward the "theatrical" usually springs from the commitment to cinematic naturalism briefly discussed in the last
chapter, although, as A. Nicholas Vardac has pointed out
in his book *From Garrick to Griffith,* the early film merely
expanded and perfected the fantasy realism that the nineteenth-century stage was already attempting to achieve with
less tractable technical methods. The condemnation of the
"theatrical" in films may be a proper way to condemn the
film director who believes that his only role in adapting
a play for the screen is to "open it up" with a few outdoor
scenes, as, for example, Fred Coe in *A Thousand Clowns,*
or many other recent films that can be easily recalled.
Usually, however, the standard of the "cinematic" is waved
too indiscriminately. When there is any larger understanding
behind its use, it generally involves the assumption that the
ends of film and the ends of theater are naturally and necessarily opposed. Theater contaminates film, it is argued (although not the other way around—that's avant-garde). The
cultivation of its unique technical nature is the proper end
of any artistic form. The theorists of "pure" film, like the
theorists of the "pure" novel, want to take a form especially
able to be enriched by contact with the other arts and make
it into an "uncontaminated" aesthetic object. Fiction ought
to be purged of description, it has been argued; and much
of the same assumptions are behind the belief that film art
was ruined by sound or stylized sets and movement.

Such a definition of film, or the arts in general for that
matter, is alluring because it involves a meditation on the
significance of technical methods and mannerisms, a meditation that in fact should always be part of one's critical

method. What such a definition omits is the reflective and absorptive relation between the arts, the way painting feeds on literature, or literature on theater, or many other, always changing, combinations.

Theater was in many ways an albatross to the early film-makers which they threw off in their rush to nature. In Renoir's films it is from the start a principle of vitality, because it is dealt with rather than jettisoned. No film made today that pretends to be avant-garde even in a narrowly commercial way would dare to use anything resembling theatrical method or setting. ("Operatic" films like Visconti's *The Damned* and Ken Russell's *The Music Lovers* may be exceptions.) In their search for nature and truth, however, many contemporary film-makers make mistakes similar to those of the naturalistic film-makers in the early years of the cinema. They believe that authentic setting and allusion to contemporary events make up for the woodenness of characterization and plot. As Vardac has pointed out, the early film ignored interior realism for exterior realism, and exterior realism could be just as easily in the service of fantasy and romance as a tool of everyday truth. Natural setting was no cachet of truth. In one sense, the choice for the critic seems to be between an art of purity and an art of eclectic inclusion, between a concentration on the total supremacy of the image on the one hand and a desire to integrate image, words, and music into a total design.

The film career of Jean Renoir stares boldly into the face of any pure definitions of what film is and is not. As I indicated in the last chapter, his films are frequently attacked for their "impure" theatrical elements. Either he is chastised for his lapses from the naturalist faith, or the theatrical elements in his films are conveniently ignored. Bernard Chardère says that in *French Cancan* (1954) Renoir has lost his sense of the cinema because he plants his camera directly in front of the dancers. He compares the method unfavorably to the way a director of American westerns would describe a saloon and its denizens: "Such a return to the theatrical point of view is completely unbearable. The objects lose their dramatic role. . . . This kind of cinema is regressive; it is boring." But regressing to what? To Renoir's first interest in the theater in *Nana,* his other backstage film? Regressing after the great sociological naturalist films of the 1930s? Henri Langlois in 1937 said that *Les Bas-Fonds* was too psychological and theatrical for Renoir's "talent d'extériorisation." No one has ignored the obvious preoccupation with the world of the theater Renoir displays in late films like *Le Carrosse d'Or* and *French Cancan.* But the theatrical films of Renoir tend to be discussed in isolation from the more "natural" films, even though Renoir himself links the two when he says, "This exterior realism has always been for me a way to begin to reach an interior realism."

The relation between theater and nature in Renoir's films obviously cannot be resolved by picking and choosing. Some effort must first be made to emphasize the continuing importance of theater throughout his career, and the way in which it interweaves with and strengthens the strand of nature, so that in a film as late as *Le Déjeuner sur l'Herbe* Renoir can employ movement strictly parallel to the horizontals of the frame, pure stage movement in the midst of nature. Such a juxtaposition of natural setting and theatrical movement should be a challenge to the viewer, since it strikes deep at one's assumptions about the separate spheres of the arts, and in the process could bring one to a richer understanding of each. Renoir's world of theater and his world of nature do not exist in mutually exclusive categories, and in fact more of the unique quality of film can be illuminated if one examines their interaction than if one keeps them totally separate.

I wish to use "theater" here to mean two related things: the forms and methods usually associated with the theater, such as the proscenium frame and the obviously constructed set; and the sense of style and artifice that is sometimes related by Renoir to traditional theater, as it is in *Nana*, and sometimes not, as in *La Marseillaise*. I relate these two categories because I believe they are related in Renoir's work. Neither theater nor nature is merely a setting for the action of a film, although setting is certainly important; both also imply a complex of feelings and action that go beyond the momentary truth of detail, whether a real or a painted tree. The themes of Renoir's later films are clearly the fruits of a preoccupation with both theatrical method and theatrical metaphor that begins with his first films. To understand his use of theater would be to understand, say, why films with as different content as *La Chienne* (1931), *Le Carrosse d'Or* (1953), and *Le Petit Théâtre de Jean Renoir* (1970) are all framed by a red-and-gold-draped puppet-show stage.

Of course, every art, whatever its artless protestations, is a realignment, a reconstruction, and a reharmonization of reality. One merely must retreat far enough to find the frame. But Renoir's use of theater goes beyond the artifice that every art possesses. In almost all of Renoir's films, even in those most committed to the image and method of nature, there is a conscious evocation of the theatrical and the stylized, all the way from simple inclusion of theatrical props and methods to the most elaborate exploration of the Elizabethan metaphor of the world as stage. Throughout Renoir's films there is a flirtation between naturalism and illusion that in large part accounts for the richness and complexity of these films and Renoir's achievement as an artist. The cinematic self-consciousness of the New Wave and other contemporary film-makers is usually confined to allusions to other films (of which Renoir's films form a large bulk; *The Crime of*

Monsieur Lange may be the most alluded to film ever made, just as *La Grande Illusion* is probably the one most stolen from). Renoir's self-consciousness is directed to the other arts, especially painting and theater. Allusion within one art form to other works in the same form can expand meaning. For example, Shakespeare's introduction of a Marlovian character within one of his plays enriches the meaning of the play, through allusion rather than straight exposition. But film allusion is frequently hermetic, at least at its most notorious. Unlike Renoir's involvement with theater and painting, one does not grasp the relation and turn back to the film with a sharpened awareness. Instead of being hermetically sealed within films, Renoir explores the possibilities of film by tracing that strange aesthetic frontier where the arts mingle, his sight basically unclouded by any artistic theory that equates artifice with constriction and nature with freedom.

Susan Sontag, in a wonderfully destructive essay entitled "Film and Theatre," has shown the deficiencies of all theories that purport to separate the two definitively. André Bazin, in his two articles on "Theatre and Cinema," collected in *What Is Cinema?*, has argued that a film adapted from a play should in fact emphasize its theatrical elements more strongly: "The more the cinema intends to be faithful to the text and to its theatrical requirements, the more of necessity must it delve into its own language" (pp. 116–17). The result, says Bazin, is "a dialectical enriching of pictorial technique" through the need to define what exactly would be a cinematic treatment. Olivier's *Henry V*, he says, is both a particular performance and the play itself. "One is no longer adapting a subject. One is staging a play by means of cinema" (p. 93). Behind Bazin's gnomic prose is the idea that the play transformed into a film must be appreciated in terms of its artifice. Perhaps certain plays can never be made into films, because their particular artifice is so delicate that it is immediately compromised by the overlay of physical reality the screen necessarily gives. The detachment from the hero possible in a play, implies Bazin, is difficult to transfer to the more intimate screen. The obvious need is not a mere resetting, but an analysis of the elements of the naturalistic and the theatrical in the material itself. Transferring *Boudu* from stage to screen necessarily involved a shift in the center of gravity from the enclosed world of Lestingois, the bookstore proprietor, to the more open world of Boudu the clochard. René Fauchois, the author of the play, who had also played Lestingois in the stage production, was outraged at what had happened and threatened to sue Renoir. But, as I shall discuss later, it was Renoir's achievement to exploit the natural shift of sympathy that occurred because of the change of artistic medium.

When we think of a theatrical film now, we tend to think of a film adapted from a play. But Renoir's theatrical films come from a variety of sources. *Chotard* may be from a successful play, but *Madame Bovary*, which is often singled out as the worst example of "theater" in Renoir's films of the 1930s, is of course drawn from a novel that is the ornament of the realist tradition. Still other theatrical films, like *French Cancan* and *Elena et les Hommes*, are original scripts. Renoir implies in fact that film is the proper place to explore such differences between source and treatment because film is potentially suprageneric, a commodious form within which to include and learn from the other arts. His interest in the theater goes beyond mere formal considerations to a world where form and content are inseparable, and he can indulge his more general concerns with the dialectic between freedom and limitation, the outside world and the prison camp, the urban society and the country house, daily work and festivity, history and private life, the trail and the river, the exceptions and the rules, the camera that moves inward and the camera that draws away. The metaphor of the theater becomes mingled with the matter of nature, and the theme of theater is presented through the realism of film. Theater then becomes for Renoir a constantly renewing concern that has repercussions in visual technique, narrative structure, delineation of character, and dominant themes.

It is difficult to make a strict division between the different stages of Renoir's interest in theater because it is such a constant element in his artistic personality that it is apt to appear in different ways at different times. In any case Renoir's "maturing" is definitely not expressed as a moving away from the theatrical to the naturalistic, nor vice versa. Some of Renoir's latest films are among the most theatrical. Consider, for example, the theatrical frames of *La Chienne* (1931) and *Le Carrosse d'Or* (1953). *La Chienne* opens with puppets giving an analysis of the story to come; the three main characters appear on the stage in double exposure. Then the curtain rises and we are on a real Parisian street. At the end of the film, after comedy, pathos, farce, murder, and melancholy, the camera draws back from the action to show once again the puppet-show enclosure for this "real" life. The clash between stylization and naturalism in *La Chienne* is in fact much more acute (although perhaps more schematic) than that in *Le Carrosse d'Or*, which is in fact about theatrical people who even in nontheatrical scenes continue to posture. In *Le Carrosse d'Or* the theatrical presentation of the film, with it opulence and stylization, complements the theme. In *La Chienne* the naturalistic observation of milieu and the Zolaesque plot of illicit romance and murder contrast strikingly not only with the puppet show frame but also with the subplot attempts of the hero, Maurice Legrand, to obliterate his everyday life by becoming

La Fille de l'Eau. Falling asleep in the rain, Virginie (Catherine Hessling) dreams that she is being carried off by Georges Raynal (Harold Lewingston). In the midst of a naturalistic setting, Renoir experiments with the technology of dreams.

La Fille de l'Eau. Above, Uncle Jeff on the barge sneers at the offer of breakfast. Behind him is the stand of poplars that gives the effect of a phenakistoscope to the early scenes. Below left, the dreaded Uncle Jeff (Pierre Lestringuez) hangs on a tree in Virginie's dream of escape from his influence. Below right, Virginie and Georges embrace after Georges has pushed Uncle Jeff into the river.

Nana. Above, Bordenave (Pierre Lestringuez), the theater manager, peers typically through a peephole to watch Nana (Catherine Hessling) charm Count Muffat (Werner Krauss) and Georges Hugon (Raymond Guérin-Catelain), whom he hopes will help finance his theater. Below, Muffat confesses his love for Nana. Even in this more natural backstage setting, the camera sits back at a footlights position to emphasize the theatricality of Nana's reaction.

Nana. Nana shows how she will play the part of the "Little Duchess" to prove she is more than a mere comedienne.

Sur un Air de Charleston. Catherine Hessling in slow motion making the Charleston into a ballet of sensuality. Below, Johnny Higgins, the black explorer, meets Catherine Hessling, the last representative of European civilization.

Sur un Air de Charleston. Catherine Hessling's pet monkey is outraged because she is leaving Paris.

La Petite Marchande d'Allumettes. Below, the Little Match Girl (Catherine Hessling) peers into the window of the heated restaurant. Above right, in the dream world of huge toys the Little Match Girl meets a military man (Jean Storm) who resembles the rich young man she has longed for before she fell asleep in the snow. Below right, the large ball will soon come crashing down on the pins; the world of toys is not such an easy refuge from the world outside.

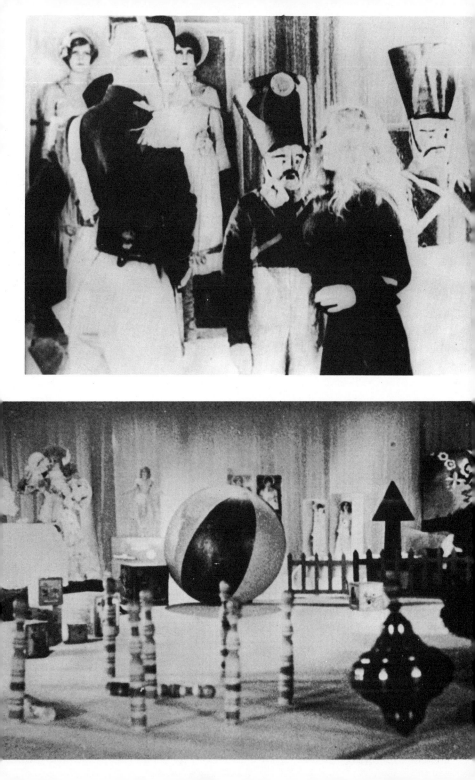

Tire-au-flanc. Joseph (Michel Simon) and Georgette (Fridette Faton) kiss while setting the d'Ombelles's dinner table. Overhead is the eighteenth-century pastoral scene with which the film opens. Below, Joseph demonstrates his own brand of bayonetry.

Tire-au-flanc. Jean Dubois d'Ombelles (Georges Pomiès) is released from prison where he had been confined for fighting with the regimental bully.

Le Tournoi dans la Cité. François de Baynes (Aldo Naldi), the head of the Protestant faction, and Count Ginori (Manuel Raaby) duel beside a rampart wall in Carcassonne.

Le Tournoi dans la Cité. The courtiers assemble in their elaborate
costumes during an interval in the tournament honoring the visit of
Catherine de Médicis and Charles IX to Carcassonne.

Marquitta. Prince Vlasco (Jean Angelo) (with cigar) has taken Marquitta
(Marie-Louise Iribe), a street singer, away from Paris to live in the high society
of the Riviera. His chamberlain (Henri Debain) (at left) disapproves. The
architectural framing here is reminiscent of German expressionist films.

Le Bled. Above, the dinner table at the farm of Christian Hoffer (Arquillière) (wearing the hat). Second on the right is Jacques Becker. Middle, Manuel Duvernet (Manuel Raaby) and his sister Diane Duvernet (Diana Hart) about to hatch a plot against Claudie Duvernet (Jackie Monier) (not shown), who has inherited a rich house and land in Sidi-Ferruch they believe should be theirs. The gloom of the shot presages the darker naturalism of Renoir's films of the early 1930s like *La Chienne* and *La Nuit du Carrefour*. Below, Christian Hoffer shows his nephew Pierre (Enrique Rivero), recently arrived from Paris, where the French troops landed to conquer Algeria in 1830. Behind him spring up the troops themselves, shortly to be transformed into tractors.

On Purge Bébé. M. and Mme. Follavine (Louvigny, Marguerite Pierry) discuss the problems of administering a purge to their recalcitrant child. Note the obviously painted view through the windows. Below, Chouilloux (Michel Simon) attempts to demonstrate his unbreakable chamber pots. But they break.

an amateur painter. His girl friend Lulu and her boyfriend Dédé sell Legrand's paintings for high prices as the work of a "famous American woman painter, Clara Wood." In the final scenes of the film, after Lulu's murder and Dédé's execution, Legrand has lost his job for embezzling and wanders the Paris streets as a clochard. He pauses in front of an art-shop window to look at a painting by Auguste Renoir (which Renoir says just happened to be there). Down the street we watch a shop assistant emerge from a door with the "Wood" painting, actually Legrand's self-portrait, and load it onto a truck, obviously bound for a rich buyer. Legrand and a clochard friend go off to buy some wine, while the camera pulls back to reveal the same puppet-show frame that introduced the film, now that the "grand guignol" is over. By this reassertion of the puppet-show frame Renoir wryly mocks the order of art that is so totally separate from human anguish, while at the same time he enhances the striving for art that constitutes a kind of salvation by its perspective.

The theater is by definition an enclosed world. Depending on the context, its enclosure can be a tyranny or a refuge. The little world of art and illusion can be an escape from the larger world of buffeting reality. Juxtaposing "open" natural scenes with "closed" theatrical scenes allows both to have an effect greater than each might have alone. It may be puzzling to see a beautifully "real" scene juxtaposed with one extreme in its artificiality, but the puzzlement should be recognized as a false reaction based on the assumption that the proper progression of film, or art in general, is from its artificial and theatrical youth to its naturalist and realist maturity.

In many of his early films Renoir will use an unobstrusive framing in scenes that suggests the frame of the proscenium arch without emphasizing it excessively. In *La Fille de l'Eau,* for example, a mask over the camera lens frames the eyes of Virginie's uncle Jeff in the scene of attempted rape. In later films, with the disappearance of the masking conventions of early silent films, the proscenium arch may appear in the architecture of the scene itself, in the doorways or windows with draped sides characteristic of films like *Chotard* and *Madame Bovary*, in the groined vault ceilings of the castle rooms in *La Grande Illusion*, and in the arches of the ruined Temple of Diana in *Le Déjeuner sur l'Herbe*. As André Bazin remarks, there is "no theater without architecture" because of the "essentially theatrical notion, that of the dramatic place" (p. 104). Renoir often enhances the theatrical effect by placing the camera back at a midfootlights position. The camera eye then becomes the eye of the spectator at a theatrical performance. In this simplest sense, the effect of theater is caused by the sight of the actors' feet. In *Nana*, for example, there are many closeups, but for one entire scene, the camera sits back at footlights center while Muffat and Nana complete their transactions at a simple stage table, with a stage window behind. The masking frame in *La Fille de l'Eau* tries to make theatrical sense of a closeup. In this first film Renoir has begun to play more freely with the varying assumptions and methods of film and theater. He alternately enforces and breaks down the audiences' sense of being at a performance. Escaping by night, Virginie in *La Fille de l'Eau* runs before a black background and then falls into a natural quarry. Muffat sits on a parkbench in *Nana* as if he were before the curtains in an *entracte*. *Nana* goes behind the stage to show the reality and then the artifice in the natural world. Renoir's interest in the backstage story is perfectly complemented by the naturalism and theatricality that tug at each other in his cinematic method.

Perhaps because of his appreciation of fantasy and dream, Renoir is also fascinated from the first by the theatrical character, the character who "plays" himself, from Nana to Madame Bovary to Boeldieu in *La Grande Illusion* to Camilla in *Le Carrosse d'Or*. Gaston Modot once recalled that during the filming of *La Règle du Jeu* he and Julien Carette were actually mistaken for a gamekeeper and a poacher, the parts they were playing. He takes this to be great praise for Renoir's method, but in fact it is only part of Renoir's interest. He can appreciate the naturalistic character, in which the actor is so submerged that he is invisible. But he also explores the theatrical character, who is always putting on a show. This kind of character frequently makes himself the center of a highly articulated and artificial world, either the theater (*Nana*) or the aristocracy (*La Marseillaise*, where there are many); by *La Grande Illusion* and *La Règle du Jeu*, the race has almost died out.

The depth of Renoir's early interest in the way characters stylize themselves may explain in part his later reputation as a director of actors, although that praise is usually accorded in situations like that described by Gaston Modot. Renoir says that acting is possible only if his actors are part of a little world, and so he keeps visitors away when he is shooting a film. But in larger terms Renoir also implies that the naturalist assumptions about the transparency of character often ignore the extent to which everyone manufactures a theatrical self to manipulate even in daily life. The full conception of character demands an interplay between the two. Within *Nana,* for example, there is a delicate dialectic between the natural emotion of Muffat and the eyebrow-raising artifice of Nana that extends even to a difference between their styles of make-up; Muffat's is rough and natural, Nana's has stylized contrasts of black lines and white surfaces. When Nana plays emotional scenes, the camera in mock admiration pulls back to the footlights position to appreciate, but then moves abruptly forward to peer in closeup just when she doesn't want to be revealed. With these considerations in mind, the broad acting style of many of the actors in *Nana* becomes part of the fabric of theater and illusion that is the subject of the film. Even in her death Nana cannot resist the grand sweeping gesture. Bordenave, the theater manager, is always peeping through keyholes and eavesdropping, just as if he were checking on the opening-night crowd. Muffat's fumbling but honest emotions are swept up and tumbled unmercifully in this swirl of illusion.

In *Tire-au-flanc* (1928) and *Chotard & Compagnie* (1933) Georges Pomiès plays a more lighthearted version of the stylized character. Pomiès had been a dancer and Renoir cast him in *Tire-au-flanc* because he was fascinated by the way Pomiès moved. In *Tire-au-flanc* (*The Goldbrick* might be an English equivalent), Pomiès is the rich young poet faced with the comic brutality of life in an army camp; in *Chotard* he is the ne'er-do-well son-in-law who doesn't fit in with the stolidities of bourgeois business practice. The character has since become a familiar one, although in these films we see what obviously lies behind the role played by Jean-Pierre Cassel in films by Philippe de Broca like *The Love Game* (1960) and *The Five-Day Lover* (1961). (Cassel even looks somewhat like Pomiès, a resemblance that may have moved Renoir to choose Cassel for the lead in *Le Caporal Épinglé* (1962), that strange combination of the breezy *Tire-au-flanc* and the somber *La Grande Illusion*. Paradoxically then, Cassel in *Le Caporal Épinglé* plays a role for a director who thirty-five years before had helped create his own screen personality.)

Jean Dubois d'Ombelles, the hero of *Tire-au-flanc*, both wins the girl and confounds his tormentors in the barracks. Julien Collinet, the hero of *Chotard*, has somewhat more difficult a time of it. He is rejected by his wife's parents until he wins the Prix Goncourt for his poetry. Then they set him up in his own workroom and keep asking if he has written anything yet. The business of poetry is more demanding than the business of business, and Julien descends from his writer's room to become a partner in his father-in-law's grocery store. Both films are neatly resolved. The end of *Tire-au-flanc* is a double cake-cutting celebrating the double marriage of Jean in the dining room and Joseph, his servant, in the kitchen; instead of a curtain being rung down on *Chotard*, the metal screen of the storefront comes down and the name "Chotard" changes to "Chotard et Cie." Both worlds can stay theatrical and enclosed because there are no pressures on them. *Tire-au-flanc* and *Chotard* also both display a "social security" with respect to all classes, which suits their comic tone. Pomiès plays a comic, stylized hero, mugging and leaping about in an unthreatening world of social stability. The theatrical elements in *Tire-au-flanc* and the enclosed theatrical setting in *Chotard* constitute the stylistic image of this security.

But when the society is actively hostile, or when its instabilities are apparent, the stylization of character is a last desperate refuge from its harshness. It seems absurd that *Madame Bovary* should have been so ferociously attacked for its theatricality when it directly concerns Emma Bovary's attempts to fend off the barrenness of her life by making herself into a romantic heroine with a life of consuming passions. Stylizing the self is the psychological analogy to the retreat to a closed society. This theme preoccupies Renoir in other films of the 1930s, such as *Le Crime de Monsieur Lange, La Grande Illusion,* and *La Règle du Jeu.* But the critics of *Madame Bovary* consider that theater destroys truth. Pierre Leprohon, for example, complains that the scenes are set up too woodenly: "Renoir often substitutes isolated characters and closeups with dialogue for a true depth

of field" (p. 53). Leprophon fails to perceive that the isolation of the characters in the individual shot imagistically
strengthens the theme of provincial isolation. He relies on
some absolute distinction between the spontaneous "cinematic" film and the rehearsed theatrical film and ignores the
possibility of consciously chosen stylization. Renoir, he as-
sumes, is not only a naturalist in method, but he is also a
naturalist in his sense of character, viewing them only from
outside: "For Renoir, the truth of characters is not psychological but visual" (p. 54).

In fact, the theatrical character, as it develops from its
beginnings in *Nana* through the films of the 1930s, leads
Renoir to a richer understanding of character in general.
It certainly seems true that films cannot so easily as fiction
imply the richness of a character. They do dwell on the
surface of things. Their ability to give some glimpse into the
inner life of a person must be conveyed through action,
or the stilted technique of a voiceover narration. But the
theatrical character, who erects a façade of self in society,
is one type about which films can make a subtle psychological
point, where novels must be content with affected dialogue
and description. By the adjustments of character and milieu,
the film can, and Renoir does, achieve an interplay between
the artificialities of an individual character and the nature
of his environment. When Nana is emotionally moved, the
visual effect is much stronger because of the normal stylization of her character. And Bovary's death, clutching a crucifix, summons up the twin specter of the limited roman-
ticized world she lives in and the pressures that have
brought her to create this world. In this complex portrait,
this interplay between naturalness and stylization, Renoir
preserves both a sympathy for Bovary and an understanding
of her limits.

The natural heirs of Bovary in the films of the 1930s

are the two aristocratic heroes: Boeldieu in *La Grande Illusion* and La Chesnaye in *La Règle du Jeu*. Both preserve
themselves in a hostile world by paying attention to forms
and style. Boeldieu finally commits a kind of suicide of style.
He distracts Rauffenstein and his troops from the escaping
Maréchal and Rosenthal by playing his fife in odd places
around the castle, the searchlight following him like a spotlight, the metal tiles on the roof reminiscent of footlights.
The old world that he and Rauffenstein represent is a world
of style and manners; in this new world it has become mere
theater and each performance must be played as if it were
the last. Rauffenstein does not quite admit that his day has
past. But Boeldieu organizes his own character around principles of style. He will not take part in the amateur theatricals because, he says, "I am a realist." Yet his grandest
gesture is a gesture of theater.

Like the court society of *La Marseillaise*, the aristocracy,
whether eighteenth-century or twentieth, is frozen into attitudes that are visually presented by Renoir in terms of
theatrical style. Marie Antoinette sees herself as an actor
in a tragedy and is impatient for the curtain to be rung
up. The palace doors open symmetrically and shots are
framed by guards and drapes. Outside the palace similar
order must be imposed. When the king's soldiers march, they
march in regular file; when the Marseillais march toward
Paris, they look like they are on a hike in the country.
The court characters are enclosed by their rituals, their
heavy costumes, and their ordered lives. When they speak,
they are centered in the camera's eye, unlike the more
varied composition in the views of the revolutionary characters. Two aristocratic characters are sympathetically presented in *La Marseillaise*: Louis XVI and Saint-Laurent. Our
sympathy for Louis XVI results not only from the fine performance by Pierre Renoir, but also from the character's in-

cessant interest in domestic detail, whether he is worrying
about Brunswick's inadequacies as a hunter or praising the
newly introduced tomato. Saint-Laurent, on the other hand,
is sympathetic not because of some relation to the nature beyond artifice, but because he, like Boeldieu and La Chesnaye,
sees clearly the passing of his class. In *La Marseillaise* the
revolution is visually expressed as a descent from the moun-
tains to reform the town, a movement from nature to explode
the artificialities of theater. But the consolations of theater
and the warmth of its closed world are preserved in Renoir's
portraits of Louis XVI and Saint-Laurent. Only those characters who do not realize they are making themselves into
theatrical personalities are condemned, as Emma and Nana
may be condemned (although that is a strong word to use to
describe Renoir's attitude toward any character). Yet self-
conscious theatricality does emerge as a better choice, for
Boeldieu, for Louis XVI, and for Robert de La Chesnaye, who
leads his guests back into the house after the "accidental"
murder at the end of *La Règle du Jeu*. As Louis XVI says in
La Marseillaise, when Marie Antoinette refers to the tragedy
they are playing, "Unfortunately, we are the actors in this
drama, which is obviously less convenient than being the
spectators."

Throughout his career Renoir's visual method implies that
the freedom and uniqueness in film is less the existence of
real detail than it is film's potential third dimension. Films
that choose to exploit this third dimension can imply to the
viewer that there is something more to be discovered, which
neither theater nor painting can find. This kind of exploration
is technically achieved by the interrogative camera that moves
into a scene. In terms of plot it appears as an interest
in the backstage life of the theater, as in *Nana* and *French
Cancan*. But in many films that have neither a theatrical
setting, nor that feeling that a studio-set is being used, the

sense of the third dimension also involves the placement of actors and the setting of scenes. The symmetry of the physical relation between the court characters in *La Marseillaise* is one expression of this method. A major Renoir prop that helps the illusion is the doorway, which in many films plays momentarily the function of a proscenium. When the camera does not enter, the doorway frames; when it does enter, the door, or the wooden frame of the window, functions as an opening into space that the theater cannot enter. While Renoir's camera, sometimes whimsically and sometimes seriously, recalls the limitations inherent in the theatrical separation of audience and action, it also exploits the physical freedom that movies can allow.

In a typical Renoir scene, there exist layers of action, a Chinese box of frames, that finally extend into the audience itself. The effect seems especially calculated to toy with the expectations we have from the conventions of the stage. In *Madame Bovary*, for example, Emma stands alone, framed in a doorway, and opens Rodolphe's letter of separation. Then, in a startling but appropriate movement, a door we have already glimpsed through this first door opens to reveal Charles Bovary, who wonders why Emma is so upset. Emma then runs upstairs and hangs half out of a window in anguish, potentially suicidal, but still framed, now by the window. In terms of nature, the window can be an opening to freedom; in terms of theater, it freezes and stylizes. In its ambivalence, it resembles the mirror, which can either intensify the superficial or reveal the inner world. The mock-heroic solipsism of Emma Bovary's emotion is imagistically expressed by the many frames, in which, we cannot help feeling, she purposely places herself.

The character usually makes the window or doorway a frame; the camera tends to announce that it is a passage. In a setup that Renoir uses until the 1950s, two actors

speak in a room with either a window or a doorway behind
and between them. We perceive them first as stage actors
in a conventional setting; the only element that announces
a film is the closeness of the camera, although in earlier
films the camera might even be footlight distance away.
Then either we gradually realize that there are important
occurrences going on outside the window, or the door opens
and we look into another room. The background has
abruptly stopped being merely the illusionistic perspective of
the stage flat, painted to look like fields stretching into the
horizon, or a disappearing city street. After the existence of
the significant background is noted, we then watch the
layers begin to interact. The deeper world is not merely
local color: someone shouts at the principal actors through
the window; someone in the rear room appears and walks
forward.

Madame Bovary furnishes another good example. Emma
and Charles are seated at a table at the end of a garden
path; the path and its surroundings, for all the role they seem
to play at first, may as well be painted on a backdrop.
But then a character walks away down the path. Renoir
has enforced the reality of the scene at least in part by
denying our expectations of a theatrical convention. This
method is not accurately described by André Bazin's invo-
cation of "profondeur de champ," depth of field, which
Bazin says asserts the ambiguity of reality and allows the
spectator to choose what he will watch in a scene. In fact,
it is in the theater that the spectator really chooses what
to watch; anyone at a bad play or even a good one can
choose to let his eye wander from the playing area to take
in the rest of the stage. In this cinematic kind of opening
to the third dimension, Renoir is directing the viewer's eye
toward his reverse apron stage. The first plane of the presentation has opened backward to reveal, certainly in *Bovary*,

a reality beyond the theatrical that is part of the meaning of the picture. In films like *Forty-second Street,* Busby Berkeley's camera tracks forward to reveal the limitlessness of his stages, the total absorption of reality by theater. In films like *Bovary,* Renoir's moving camera and the opening perspective allow the viewer to perceive a world larger than the one the characters inhabit. Like Boudu standing on his head in Lestingois' house, the moving camera can ignore conventional architecture and symmetry to assert the virtues of spontaneity and movement.

But camera movement, like any other method in Renoir's work, is never a value in itself. It only reveals value, and the value it reveals cannot be easily categorized. To complement those scenes, like those described above, in which movement inward breaks down the theatrical frame, there are many occasions, often in the same films, in which the camera withdraws to discover some separation between the audience and the action—a balustrade, a porch railing, a series of columns, a low wall, a row of bushes or trees —all Renoir's equivalent for the footlights and the raised and therefore separated stage. Such a shot is frequently used when the theatricality of the scene itself calls for it, especially in scenes of special occasions. In *Chotard* this kind of camera movement occurs in the scenes of the charity ball. In *Madame Bovary* Renoir's use of the figure is even more elaborate. We enter the scene of the count's ball through the orchestra. Through columns we watch Emma dancing, while Charles sits uncomfortably alone in a closer shot. Then the camera pulls back from our view of Charles and we discover not only columns but also a balustrade and the entire orchestra again between us and what we were watching. All of these movements have their place in the meaning of the individual film. *Bovary* is so replete with them because Renoir draws on it throughout the 1930s as a

personal touchstone for the idea of the theatrical personality
and the role of theater in films.

Films and theater and perhaps all art may be accused of
the potential to thwart action and defeat involvement. But
in films at least one is implicated through sight. The camera
sees things that we would rather not, and it impresses
its vision on us no matter how we struggle. In most of
Renoir's films people use doors and cameras use windows,
although they do not also enter, but more often peer
through. The impulse of the Renoir films of the 1920s is
voyeuristic, with its model the eavesdropping theater manager Bordenave, in *Nana.* The theater frame of *La Chienne*
preserves the voyeur's distance and detachment, and the
camera movement corresponds to this separation. In one
shot in *La Chienne,* which has since become a film cliché,
the camera rises outside a building to the appropriate window, while the character climbs the stairs inside. This
camera is a witness, not a judicial witness to the murder
that will follow, but, in the light of the puppet-show frame,
a witness from a theater audience, lured in by whimsy, who
finds himself watching lust and murder and wondering how
to react. Such invocations of the theatrical frame per se
appear less and less in Renoir's films of the 1930s. When
he uses a raised and lowered darkness in *Les Bas-Fonds*
to parody a kind of act-scene division, it invokes the similar
raising and lowering of the window shade of the Chotards'
dining room in *Chotard,* through which we watch much of
the action. By the time of *Les Bas-Fonds* the device is a
bit irritating; it seems used for mere wit, to contrast with
the sordid world of the tenement, or perhaps to comment
wryly on the incompatibles involved in the attempt to create
a naturalistic play.

In the films of the 1920s theater could be interpreted as

an archaic mode of artistic representation, whose only continuing life could be in its allusive use in the cinema. In
the Renoir films of the later 1930s, to which *La Chienne*
and *Bovary* form a transition, the enclosed world of theater
has become a model of the society to which nature must
give way. The opening to the possibility of relations with
others in a society is expressed through the image of theater.
In the Renoir films of the 1930s theater frequently represents an older and socially more aristocratic past that
must energize by sacrifice this new democratic art of cinema
before it loses its roots in artistic tradition. The Renoir films
of the 1920s, which invoked theatrical methods in order to
comment upon them, give way to films in the later 1930s
that include theatrical situations or entire scenes that take
place in a theater. The greater total realistic illusion allowed
by the introduction of sound seems paradoxically to impel
Renoir to revaluate the relevance and energy of theater.

To come upon the scenes of theater and style in the
films of the 1930s is like walking through a modern house
and coming on well-furnished rooms in an older style, perfectly integrated with the rest of the house, but exposing
more fully the ancestry of the contemporary portions and
offering a kind of haven from them. A precursor of this
new mutation of Renoir's interest in the theater can be
found in the importance that almost every Renoir film, from
La Fille de l'Eau to *Le Petit Théâtre de Jean Renoir*,
gives to social occasions, especially the community of the
dinner table. The sense of social occasion that is focused
every day on the dinner hour is the natural equivalent of
the sense of special occasion that is indissolubly linked with
the idea of theater. The social occasion makes its special demands in the articulation of class (the two wedding cakes
at the end of *Tire-au-flanc*), proper dress (a running gag in
Le Bled), the choice of food (*La Marseillaise*), and most

of all in manners appropriate to the moment (*La Grande Illusion, La Règle du Jeu*). Even in a milieu like that of *Toni*, which is presented with extreme naturalistic fidelity, the daily life of the people must be defined against and in terms of the special occasions of Toni's marriage and Sebastien's funeral.

In direct analogy to such scenes of social occasion are those scenes in Renoir's films of the 1930s in which the theater becomes a microcosm within the larger world of the entire picture: the prison camp theatricals in *La Grande Illusion*, the shadow play in *La Marseillaise*, and the weekend theatricals in *La Règle du Jeu*. In all three films, but especially in *La Grande Illusion* and *La Règle du Jeu*, certainly two of Renoir's greatest, the world of the theater becomes both a refuge from the larger world, as well as a replica of it, whether a prison camp during World War I or a country house isolated from a world of inquisitive reporters and surging crowds. The gentle tones of aesthetic archaicism that accompany the image of theater in film now lend it an air of moral affirmation. One thinks of the photo of the publishing commune in *Le Crime de Monsieur Lange* (1936), in which all the members pose in cowboy costumes before a painted backdrop. It is obviously artificial and mugged up, like the cowboy trappings Lange keeps on his wall to inspire him in the writing of the "Arizona Jim" series of pulp novels. But it also projects a vision of social order more humane and vital than the nominal "realities" of the world outside the little Parisian court where the commune is located. The rhythms of nature are not so obviously preferable to the orders of theater and style. In *La Petite Marchande d'Allumettes* (1928) Renoir juxtaposes fuzzily focused scenes of the Little Match Girl's sordid life on the street with the sharp clarities of her fantasy world. In this film reality is sentimental, while art can be witty and ironic, and paradoxically, therefore more engaged in the complexities of the world it seems to be trying to escape from. The "illusion" and the "game" that is society is only truly exposed and revitalized by the "illusion" and "game" of art.

After the simple evocations of theatrical method in *Les Bas-Fonds* (1936), Renoir in *La Grande Illusion* (1937) explores aspects of theater that have a more vital relation to his basic themes. Within the German prison camp the French soldiers prepare a show. The costumes they are sent from Paris remind them of an outside world that is slipping away from them, in which girls' hair and dresses are both getting shorter. During their rehearsal they receive news that the town of Douaumont has been captured by the Germans. In the middle of the show itself Maréchal bursts on stage to tell the audience that the French have recaptured Douaumont. This news relates the prisoners to the war outside in a way they have been longing for. They stop their show to sing "La Marseillaise" uproariously in the faces of the prison camp officials. The camera moves from its center-stage position and sweeps majestically around the room, coming to rest on the female impersonator, who has taken off his wig to sing. Reality seems to assert its rights over illusion. But the next scene shows Maréchal locked in a cell for what he has done. His action has really accomplished nothing. In fact it has also meant nothing. The camera looks through his cell window at a poster telling of the recapture of Douaumont by the Germans. Maréchal has broken the salving and cohesive frame of theater in order to assert an illusion less worthwhile and less enduring. It is a pattern which repeats itself throughout the film. Boeldieu first insists on the reconnaissance flight because he wants to see what that gray smudge on the aerial photograph "really is." The incessant escapes are images of the same attempt to engage reality beyond enclosure. Maréchal and Rosenthal finally escape from the castle prison and leave behind the most cohesive community they have ever been a part of. And they must also leave Elsa's cottage for some undefined reality beyond the frontier. "Lucky bastards," says the German patrol leader, who orders his men to stop firing on them. But what illusions are they trading their own for now?

The prison society, like the theater it contains, is not really a microcosm of the outside world of war; it is an alternative to it. In a world of vicious nationalisms, military and aristocratic honor, as embodied in the relation between Boeldieu and Rauffenstein, promise the only possibility of international community. But the world of Boeldieu and Rauffenstein is obviously doomed. No social order seems able to replace its breadth of sympathy. Only the order of art can contain the bursting potentials and rivalries of the world, as La Grande Illusion itself contains the various characters with their separate languages and social origins. The theatrical in La Grande Illusion defines an isolated but self-sufficient community, which attempts to preserve some standard of value in a valueless world. Only by making a total commitment to the stylized theatrical gesture can Boeldieu help Maréchal and Rosenthal escape. On his deathbed the frailty of his bare arm contrasts with the continued stiffness of Rauffenstein, sewn forever into his uniform and gloves, kept upright by his chin cup and back brace. Before Boeldieu went out to his fife-playing he had carefully put on white gloves, much to Maréchal's confusion. But this conscious commitment to style has allowed him to enter a reality unavailable to Rauffenstein.

La Marseillaise (1938), made a year after La Grande Il-

lusion and a year before *La Règle du Jeu*, preserves a more
negative attitude toward the virtues of the theatrical and
aristocratic perspective, perhaps because it was sponsored by
the Confédération Générale du Travail, the French trade
union. After the Marseillais soldiers get to Paris, during a
night on the town, they enjoy a shadow play about contemporary politics, applauding exuberantly as the cutout figures of King and Nation discuss their differences. Later,
whimsical emphasis is given to the decision that the members
of the Théâtre Française will give the signal for the attack
on the Tuileries. By entering into the Revolution, Bomier,
Arnaud, and their friends have descended from the Provençal hill where they were hiding out to renew a world of
outmoded forms. But even the Revolution is theater of a
sort, perhaps a new kind, to replace the old aristocratic
form, but theater nevertheless. Toward the end of the film,
Bomier lies dying in a courtyard, shot by the Swiss guards
during the attack on the palace. In a beautiful shot we
stand in the courtyard and see Bomier and the others in
the courtyard, while outside in the street, framed by the
proscenium of the gateway, the victorious Revolutionary
soldiers march by. In a film that styles itself "a chronicle
of several facts contributing to the downfall of the Monarchy," the perspective of the theater, of the artist, remains
just outside the doorway of history.

La Règle du Jeu makes the retreat into theater its main
subject. Robert de la Chesnaye tries to preserve his world
from chaos by an elaborate structure of style and theater.
His collection of eighteenth-century mechanical birds and
music boxes evokes a world when society was a vital moving
thing, in which every part contributed its share to the harmony. Through the costume party and theatricals at his
country home La Colinière, La Chesnaye tries to smooth over

the warring emotions of his guests. The costumes work for a
while; the audience sits calmly through the songs and clown-
ing. When Schumacher the gamekeeper chases Marceau the
poacher through the party, threatening to kill him because
Marceau has been poaching Schumacher's wife, and waving his gun, the guests think it is still part of the festivities.
But then the gun goes off, and the feelings that the theater
has been so preoccupied to channel and calm proceed to
explode. Octave, the failed musician, who tries to play the
reconciler in the same way as La Chesnaye, keeps asking
people to help him off with his bear costume. But Octave's
refusal to accept his own emotions (in his love for Christine,
La Chesnaye's wife) and his desire to avoid conflict at all
costs as yet keeps him metaphorically in costume, even when
he finally succeeds in getting it off. With chaos shuddering
through the rooms about him La Chesnaye opens the stage
curtains to show his newest and proudest possession, an
enormous and elaborate calliope that elaborately makes music
and harmony from its mechanical parts. The calliope recalls
a society in which all the rules worked, but which is now
accessible only as an artifact, an archaic reminder of a lost
past, enclosed within the frame of theater. Theater and its
distancing frame have become a dead end rather than a
refuge. The momentary lightheartedness and distancing,
even in the face of violence, murder, and social upheaval,
has turned sour. La Chesnaye fails to control and conduct,
and his major-domo, suitably named Corneille, cleans up the
broken glass and drags away the fallen after La Chesnaye's
command: "Arrêtez cette comédie." Emotion has erupted
through style and rules. At the end of *La Règle du Jeu* La
Chesnaye shepherds the gaunt shadows of his guests back
into his house, while Marceau and Octave leave La Chesnaye
and his world forever. Like a melancholic Prospero, La
Chesnaye makes order of the useless fragments that re-

main, because it is his destiny to follow the rules, even
when they are hopelessly outmoded.

After *La Règle du Jeu,* there is in some sense no new place
for Renoir to go in his evocation of theater. The film does set
an end to many of his themes of the 1930s, especially in
its somber acceptance of the inadequacy of the theatrical
retreat while it holds out little hope for any opening
to nature. With the beginning of Renoir's career in the
United States, his personal isolation contributes to a further
development in his films of the contrast between the artificial
and the natural, the interior and the exterior, the limited and
the expansive. In films like *This Land Is Mine* (1943)
and *The Diary of a Chambermaid* (1946), the studio set,
with its artificial vistas and clean-swept backdrops, becomes
an image of confinement. The swamp in *Swamp Water*
(1941) is a confining world, but a rich one; Tom Keefer
relishes his refuge in the same way that Maréchal and
Rosenthal relish for a time the camaraderie of the prison
camp, in which the class divisions of the outside world have
been sloughed away. But the provincial world of the anti-
Republican Lanlaires in *Diary of a Chambermaid* must be
broken down because it is a tyranny of the enclosed rather
than an authentic retreat. Provinciality itself does not seem
to be condemned in *Diary of a Chambermaid,* in the same
way that the Nazi Occupation of the small French town
in *This Land Is Mine* is of less central importance than
the efforts of Albert Mory to break out of the stranglehold
his mother has on every aspect of his life. Interestingly
enough, *This Land Is Mine* and *Diary of a Chambermaid*
are the only Renoir films in which an oppressive mother is
an important character. Personal oppression focuses the op-
pressiveness of the enclosed society. Unlike the totally
naturalistic presentation of *Diary of a Chambermaid* that

Luis Buñuel makes in his 1964 film adaptation of the Mirbeau novel, Renoir's obvious sets emphasize the artificiality
and entrapment of the world of the Lanlaires, just as Renoir
scants the perverse aspects of the novel (which so intrigue
Buñuel) to concentrate instead on those aspects of character
that interact with environment. Buñuel's naturalistic setting
trivializes the pressures on Celestine: why, for example,
doesn't she just walk away? But Renoir's sets emphasize a
world of enclosures: the town itself, the shuttered house of
the Lanlaires, and the inner vault that holds the treasured
family silver that appears once a year, to help Madame
Lanlaire protest the Bastille Day festivities of the town by
celebrating the Monarchy. Finally, toward the end of the
film, the tight seal of the house is momentarily broken
when the songs of the crowd impel Lanlaire to rebel against
his wife and open the windows. She quickly regains control,
but the damage has been done. In the next scene, Georges
Lanlaire, the previously weak (and Republican) son, fights
Joseph, the militarist-monarchist valet who has coolly murdered a neighbor and now has been bribed with the family
silver to take Celestine away from Georges. The fight takes
place in the greenhouse, in front of Celestine, and the
glass windows frame the emergence of conflict from the
shroudings of class and society into a new visibility; for
Georges anger and love have for once made class irrelevant.
As in the greenhouse scenes in La Règle du Jeu, some new
openness in personal relations has been achieved.

The scope of the achievement is clearer in Diary of a
Chambermaid, and the finale more optimistic. In La Règle
du Jeu, the moment in the greenhouse reveals their mutual
love to Octave and Christine. But clarity stops there. The
observers of the greenhouse scene, Marceau the poacher and
Schumacher the gamekeeper, mistake the identities of the
lovers, despite their visibility. And later André Jurieu, dressed

in Octave's coat and running to meet Christine, is shot by Schumacher, who thinks Jurieu is Octave going to meet Lisette. No such confusion exists for Celestine, who is the observer in *Diary of a Chambermaid*. Georges's hands burst through the glass of the greenhouse, and even though Joseph momentarily wins both Celestine and the fight, Georges's new sense of connection enables him to enlist the Bastille Day crowd in attacking Joseph and distributing the silver to the community. In the final scene Georges and Celestine ride away from the provincial world in a train. Outside the window is what appears to be a real countryside.

Tom Keefer in *Swamp Water* is finally ambivalent about returning to the world from which he came; Celestine is pleased to be on the way back to Paris. One journeyed into a natural world that was a possible refuge; the other has escaped from an enclosed world of the exiled and the provincial, in which a ritual and theatrical celebration of the past attempted to hold back time. Inside the train compartment Celestine continues to write in her diary, including even the wedding service for herself and Georges. The relative values of the natural and the theatrical can be explored more thoroughly once the frame of art has been asserted—with the diary of Celestine, the family album in *The Southerner*, or the memories of Harriet in *The River*.

With *Le Carrosse d'Or* (1953), *French Cancan* (1955), and *Elena et les Hommes* (1956), Renoir returns to a conception of the theatrical image more vital than either the darkly enclosed social world or the exuberant nature of the American films would have allowed. In these films the theater becomes an image of renewal rather than refuge and separation, perhaps as a result of the the distancing devices first formulated in *Diary of a Chambermaid* and *The Southerner* and more subtly developed in *The River*. Like some of the

films of the 1920s, these theater films of the 1950s distinguish between those characters who imprison themselves unconsciously and those who find a greater freedom in conscious enclosure and stylization. A character like Camilla in
Le Carrosse d'Or is a more direct descendant of the lighthearted characters played by Georges Pomiès in *Tire-au-
flanc* and *Chotard* than of the melancholically theatrical
Madame Bovary. Instead of pessimistically accepting the
limits of theater like Boeldieu and La Chesnaye, she is an
actress who delights in her profession. Unlike the theatrical
characters of earlier films, who tended to be victims, the
three theater films of the 1950s present theatrical characters
whose control is based on their understanding of the frame
in which they are caught. If there is an edge of sadness,
these films are dark comedies rather than tragedies mingled
with farce. Although Renoir's American films are usually
considered to be the work of a period of isolation away from
his "roots" in France, they in fact directly presage his concerns in the first films made after his return to Europe in the
early 1950s. The key to the change is the way in which the
fatal implications of the theatrical frame that had been enforced in the 1930s, even when the frame itself was viewed
positively, has been transformed into an image of freedom
through theater. The change occurs because the emphasis
falls on the aesthetic freedom within the frame rather than
the human constriction, which, as films like *Toni* and *La
Bête Humaine* imply, can occur just as easily in nature as in
theater. Although both nature and theater can be tyrannical,
nature offers no order and theater no inner energy. The way
to the theater films of the 1950s is paved by *The Southerner*
and *The River*, in which Renoir comes to terms with and
deals with the energies of nature. In the former, in the spirit
of the title of the book from which the film is adapted—

Hold Autumn in Your Hand—nature is controlled through understanding; in *The River*, through art.

Both methods are used in the theater films of the 1950s. All three of the films are free reconstructions of the past; no fatality of time or nature inhibits their vision. And all three deal in some way with artistry. *Le Carrosse d'Or* involves a *commedia dell'arte* troupe in eighteenth-century Peru, while *French Cancan* deals with the efforts of the entrepreneur Danglard to found the Moulin Rouge and revive the cancan. *Elena et les Hommes* absorbs this positive view of artistic order and intermingles love and politics amid the intrigues of the early years of the Third Republic.

Pauline Kael has called *Le Carrosse d'Or* "a comedy of love and appearances," and the framing of its action within the curtains and proscenium of a stage emphasizes the primacy of the theatrical view of reality that dominates the film. Unlike the puppet-show frame of *La Chienne,* which served to emphasize detachment and contrast between the security of art and the chaos of life, the frame in *Le Carrosse d'Or* defines a perspective that dominates the film, with its sets within sets, and their elaborate and obvious ceilings. The given of the film is enclosure; when the troupe moves into the courtyard of the inn, they immediately begin varying its inner space with curtains and hangings. When they play, the footlights appear at the bottom of the screen. All characters fall into postures naturally, framing themselves in windows or stopping in mid-gesture. The camera sits back from them in their settings and again shows their feet, in the process miniaturizing them and for a moment making their world a precious and intricate bauble, like Pope's "moving toy-shop of the heart."

The romances of Camilla (Anna Magnani) with her three lovers form a delicate counterpoint to the main theme of the ownership of the coach, this awesomely grotesque and gilded

monster, which, like La Chesnaye's mechanical birds in *La
Règle du Jeu,* is an image of the art of film itself. Each of
the lovers represents an aspect of the world that Camilla
must include. Ramon the bullfighter participates in a kind of
theater that is directly competitive with her own. When he
comes into the audience of the troupe's show, he must divert
all the attention away from the actors to himself. Don
Antonio, the Viceroy, comes to the performance disguised,
and his daily life of elaborate wigs and conferences is the
public world's equivalent of the formalities of theater. Only
Felipe, Camilla's lover within the troupe, asserts the values
of what he calls reality. But these values are in this context
attenuated and unbelievable. It may be idle to speculate on
Renoir's casting, but in fact Paul Campbell, who plays Felipe,
is the most wooden actor in the entire film, most so when
he tells Camilla he loves her for herself and not for the
characters she plays. In *Le Carrosse d'Or* the would-be actor
must fail. Don Antonio loves Camilla for the relief from
the orders of his public life she can give, while Ramon
sees in her a worthy companion in the public eye. No one,
indeed, loves Camilla for what she thinks is most authentic
in her nature, her theatrical self.

Like the coach, Camilla is the object of every one's demands and possessive assertions. She must elude the forms
of the various worlds that try to entrap her to assert her own
form and her own world. In a more seriously weighted film
the implied questions could be harsh: does the coach belong
to the state or to the actress? where, in short, can art survive?
But this is a comedy. "The coach doesn't belong to any of
us. It's a symbol," says one of the characters. The world is a
stage, the state is staffed with comic fools, and the theatrical
can absorb the rest of the world into itself. The separate
demands of politics and art are easily reconciled by the
archbishop, that master of baroque ritual. *Le Carrosse d'Or*

rides through a world of ormolu fantasy, happily protected
from the rhythms of a world outside art. One exception may
occur when Ramon the matador tells Camilla about his adventures among a tribe of Indians, a simple, natural people
who live by a river. For a moment Camilla's face looks lined
and older. But she quickly reassumes the style and glitter
of art. Art is a balm for the pains of life. At the end of the
film, when the proscenium frame has reasserted itself, Camilla stands alone at stage center, without her three lovers.
Does she miss them, she is asked. "A little," she answers.
Art may be self-sufficient, but it is also lonely and self-absorbed.

In *French Cancan* and *Elena et les Hommes* the separation
between theater and history is more acute because history has
become a more oppressive force than it was in the purer
theatrical world of *Le Carrosse d'Or*. In these two films the
aristocratic detachment from history that furnished the
pathos in the court scenes of *La Marseillaise* has become a
way of understanding history from the outside. In *French
Cancan* there are wry analogies between the founding of the
Moulin Rouge and the founding of the Third Republic; in
Elena, also set in these early years of the Third Republic, the
shift of value from history to theater seems to have become
complete. The outside world of politics impinges comically
and cryptically on *French Cancan*, more oppressively on
Elena. The central focus has shifted from Camilla, the
actress and role player, to Danglard, the producer and impresario. Instead of merely being within the theater, the
main character now constructs and invents the entire theater,
presenting *l'illusion de grande vie* for the public, like the
illusions manufactured by the ministers who arrive for the
dedication of the Moulin Rouge. But Danglard's role is not
defined in the social terms of politics and governments. Like
Camilla, he is alone at the end of the film. As he tells his

jealous mistress, Nini, he exists not for her but for the audience. Backstage he sits in a large prop chair and swings his foot to the music, while on the other side of the curtain the crowds cheer and the camera sits firmly before the dancers, enjoying their performance as a good spectator should. With the film's end we are outside the new glittering Moulin Rouge and the camera pulls back until it has a long shot like those we have seen in the course of the cabaret's construction. A momentary stasis, and then a drunk reels by, dances a bit, and takes a bow.

Toward the beginning of *Elena et les Hommes* Elena (Ingrid Bergman) and her fiancé, Martin-Michaud the shoe manufacturer, take a coach to the Bastille Day celebrations. The first view of the crowd we get is from the inside of the coach, a totally black background with one window cut in it, through which we see the surging crowd while someone tells them through the window that they can't proceed any further. The door opens. Elena gets out, and is immediately swallowed up by the surging, exuberant crowd. She seems to have moved from the interior of her apartment in the first scene, through the enclosed coach, to be finally pulled outside into the crowd. But in fact the crowd is only a larger version of the theater of her own life. In the first scene she remarks that she dismissed her last lover because she had succeeded in inspiring his opera *Héloise and Abelard* and need not do any more. In the rest of the film she similarly inspires the political world, as she is enlisted to use her wiles to convince General Rollan (Jean Marais), a Boulanger-like figure, to take over the government of France. Like Lisbonne, the journalist "who gave Sarah Bernhardt her start," now a publicist in Rollan's shadow cabinet, Elena moves easily from art to politics.

But the point of the film is that her values are actually reversed. It is politics that are reducible to mere theater, while love and art are the real world. And the world of *Elena* is filled with theatrical allusions and situations that emphasize its own commitment to the reconstruction and replacement of politics by theater and what it has come to represent for Renoir. A street singer comes in to sing choruses of the song "Méfiez à Paris" and hands out broadsheets of the song announcing that it was written by Jean Renoir and Joseph Kosma. Two women appear as a kind of chorus commenting on events and talking up the good old days, not in terms of politics, but in terms of the attitude toward women. Like the man and woman chorus in *French Cancan,* who sit in a sidewalk café and watch the construction of the Moulin Rouge, these women whimsically allude to the past when things were better. Yet these comments are part of a film that asserts its own vision of a real past, transmuted by art.

Elena herself is diverted from these values because she believes it is her "duty" to France to take part in the Rollan intrigue. She rejects Henri (Mel Ferrer) and goes off to Martin-Michaud's country home, where the complaisant shoe manufacturer, who is basically worried only about tariff control, allows her time and space for her mission. The house is a maze of rooms strung together by farce, with people running in and out, reminiscent physically of the movement through rooms in *La Règle du Jeu,* but without the sinister overtones of disruption and chaos. In Martin-Michaud's house, theater makes social and political uneasiness comfortable. The battle-front of the Franco-Prussian War is actually only a few miles and at one point Elena and Henri are arrested as German spies. But within the house itself farce reigns, and the camera, instead of looking through the rooms at eye level, as it tended to in *La Règle du Jeu,* takes the position of cinematic theater, about eight or ten feet above the floor, so that it can see into more than one room at once, emphasize the background, and in one shot include

the various artificialities of form that surround Elena's attempt to bring Rollan to politics through love.

André Bazin has said that "all the work of Jean Renoir
is a quest for the realism of the end of the nineteenth-century." But in the light of *French Cancan* and *Elena* this
realism cannot be said to have any direct relation to the
actual public world of that time. Theater triumphs in both
films because it offers an alternate and better world to the
world of politics and patriotism. It is a deeper "patriotism,"
like the international order of art that is asserted amid the
warring languages of *La Grande Illusion*. When the observation balloon breaks loose in *Elena* and lands in Germany, we are shown the French and German newspapers,
which each react in their own chauvinist way; there is no
difference between them. And perhaps we are meant to re-
member that Gambetta escaped from the siege of Paris by
balloon.

Renoir's world of art, expressed in these films as theater, has
taken over history for its own, and made it into something
quite different. As Henri says to Elena toward the end of the
film, the greatest gift of French civilization to the world is
love, not politics or anything else. Elena still thinks of
theater only in terms of play-acting. They must stand before
a window and pretend to the crowd below that it is Elena
and Rollan rather than Elena and Henri, so that Rollan
can make his escape. Elena is upset at having to perform this
charade with Henri and she uses the theatrical metaphors
of Marie Antoinette in *La Marseillaise:* "Je propose un entracte." But through this particular bit of theater she discovers that she has been submerging her real love for Henri.
Through pretending they have come to reality. And the
agents of their reconciliation have been the gypsies, who
appear abruptly in the world of *Elena et les Hommes,* like
fugitive prophets from beyond the world of political maneu-

ver. The head of the gypsy troupe calls himself its artistic director; and while Henri talks to them, tumbling and juggling go on in the background. Like the *commedia dell'arte* troupe of *Le Carrosse d'Or*, the gypsies have magically appeared to redress the balance of politics and art. They turn bad theater into good theater. "La comédie est terminée," says Miarka (Juliette Greco), the gypsy girl who has wandered through the scenes, mainly unnoticed by the self-absorbed principles. She sits on the windowsill, watching Elena and Henri leave together, and she sings them away from this world. They have gone, and the crowd in the street has gone. Like Camilla at the end of *Le Carrosse d'Or*, Danglard backstage in *French Cancan*, Miarka, the singer and reconciler, is finally left alone. But she is not the last image in the film. Instead we see a newspaper account of the marriage of Henri and Elena, in which a parenthesis identifies Elena as Ingrid Bergman. Theater has done its work, even to the extent of restoring "reality."

Most critics have considered these three films of the 1950s to be Renoir's recommitment to a sense of spectacle in cinema after the social consciousness of the 1930s. But what is striking about his own remarks about them is the frequency with which minimizing words appear, words like *croquis, pochade, esquisse,* and *divertissement*. In fact Renoir seems to believe that the time of spectacle has come to an end, that the world is suited only for briefer epics that contain rather than expand. The image that he constantly invokes for such limitation is the image of theater, for theater is conscious limitation that enriches what lies within its boundaries. In this way, the constantly escaping prisoners of *Le Caporal Épinglé* (1962), a film with little theatrical allusion beyond some framing shots, reflect the theme of theater. The prisoners escape, but they are never quite sure what they are escaping from: some find a brief solace in imprisonment;

others constantly escape and find no solace at all. In *Le Testament du Docteur Cordelier* (1959), where the visual allusions to theater are also very sparse, the same mood of pessimism is present. Theater in *Le Déjeuner sur l'Herbe* (1959), in the person of Gaspard, the panic flutist, can bring together the worlds of science and nature under the shadow of the proscenium arch of the Temple of Diana; and it is part of Renoir's whimsy to have traveled from Corneille, the major-domo in *La Règle du Jeu*, to Rousseau, the major-domo in *Le Déjeuner sur l'Herbe*. But in *Cordelier* and *Le Caporal Épinglé*, the mood is not so exuberant or conciliatory. Their themes are those of limitation that the theatrical allusion has helped Renoir to nurture, but the mood is more reminiscent of the gloom of the *genre noir* films of the 1930s.

Le Carrosse d'Or, French Cancan, and *Elena et les Hommes* in no way settle the issue of the uses of theater. They form instead an artistic counterpoint to the social and psychological issues of limit and confinement Renoir explores in *Cordelier* and *Le Caporal Épinglé*. It is worth remarking that Renoir's use of theater departs totally from the use of theater in two other notable theater films, Marcel Carné's *Les Enfants du Paradis* (1944–45) and Max Ophuls' *Lola Montès* (1955). Both combine a plot that occurs in a theatrical context with some reconstruction of a historical period. But in neither is the theatrical more than an extra mask. In *Les Enfants du Paradis*, the relation between the characters and the theater is the usual "vesti la giubba" laughing on the inside/crying on the outside melodrama. Any "metaphysic of theater," defining what theater means in relation to the world of film, seems lacking.

Les Enfants du Paradis, even though a theater film, is very crowded. But the crowds have little meaning. The crowd at the end of that film, for example, into which Baptiste loses Garance, could just as well be the crowd at the end of *The Bicycle Thief,* which anonymously swallows up the characters. Renoir's sense of crowds and the violation of theatrical space they imply, for example in the Bastille Day scene of *Elena,* is totally lacking from Carné's film. Theater is mere varying artifice or exotic milieu to Carné; he sees neither its limitations nor its potentials. Perhaps under the influence of Renoir's theater films, Ophuls uses the theatrical as a metaphor of Lola's life in society, through a series of circus tableaux, complete with artificial scenery and cardboard balustrades. But his treatment displays primarily the charming "world is a movie set" sentimentality of his earlier films, like *La Ronde.* Ophuls does exploit a relation between social and theatrical artifice, but the last shot in *Lola,* that long track backward (with which Andrew Sarris was perhaps so rightly entranced) fuzzes over with glib irony the actual need of an artist to be paid for his work. Renoir's own attitude toward theater and the place of the artist, actress or entrepreneur, within it, is at once more magical and more hard-edged. His understanding of the vitality of artifice perhaps owes something to the lessons of American musical comedy, and works like Vincente Minnelli's *The Pirate* (1947). Instead of either the disdain for theater of the "cinematically" oriented directors, or the crippling respect for theater of the wordy scriptwriters and posturing actors, Renoir pre-eminently knows how to use theater. In its many mutations of theme and method, from the start of his career, it has furnished an ever-replenishing refuge of order amid the freedoms of nature.

CHAPTER FOUR

The Search for Society

"French Cancan" embodied for me a great desire to make a film in a totally French spirit, a film that might be an easy and comfortable contact, a pleasant bridge, between myself and the French public. I believed that this public was very close to me, but I wanted to verify the contact."

—JEAN RENOIR, 1962

The twin worlds of nature and theater, as they exist on both thematic, imagistic, and structural levels in Renoir's films, are brought together and reconciled by Renoir's fascination with society, its possibilities and its failings. Whether the emphasis in a particular film is on nature or theater, the social orientation of Renoir's grasp of the issues becomes the principal means of expression. Society is the standard against which films of nature, like, for example, *Swamp Water*, or films of theater, like *Le Carrosse d'Or*, measure themselves. Society offers a thematic context within which the rival claims of natural exuberance and formal structure may be brought together, and their excesses controlled.

When Renoir invokes the motifs of society, he again reveals his assumptions about the ways film is often technically and formally distinct from the other arts. The film experi-

ence involves depths of solitude and sociability more complex than those called forth by any other art form. More
than any other art form, film exploits and elaborates the
idea of community. From the simplest war film, with its
ethnically mixed squad, to the theatrical world of a film like
Les Enfants du Paradis, films seem peculiarly obsessed
by the mysteries of groups in confined spaces or limited
situations. The number of times, for example, the scenes
and situations of *La Grande Illusion* have been imitated, is as
much a tribute to the fascination with groups as it is to the
special qualities of that particular film.

Renoir's own preoccupation with the social theme in his
films may spring in part from a heightened sense of the
collaborative process of film-making. In the films of the
1930s, in which Renoir makes his most elaborate exploration
of the nature of social reality, we must be as often aware of
the increasing importance of the community of film-makers
behind the camera as we are of the possible community
before the camera. As the characters in the film search for a
society that brings together energy and order, the technicians
and Renoir himself, behind the camera, are searching for
some natural flow, some spontaneity, in the film they are
making, amid the fantastic technological apparatus of the
film-making process. Throughout the 1930s Renoir relates
the forming societies before his camera to the *équipe* of
artistic associates, with their political, social, and cultural
relations, behind the camera. *Le Crime de Monsieur Lange*
(1936) draws substantially on the "Groupe Octobre," a radical cultural group formed to support the Popular Front, for
its *équipe; La Vie Est à Nous* (1936) is a film made
by Renoir for the French Communist Party, using the talents
of many of the same actors and technicians who worked
on his other films; *La Marseillaise* (1938) was produced by
the French trade union group, the Confédération Générale du

Travail (C.G.T.), and financed at least in part by two-franc contributions from union members. These are only the most obvious examples of the collaborative process in the films of the middle and late 1930s. In these films the social themes that had always been present but never emphasized in Renoir's work now come into their own.

Renoir's sensitivity to the theme of the social or communal group in his films must derive not only from a sense of the community behind the camera, but also from a sense of a community in the audience that he wishes to reach and half-create. The novel in the twentieth century has increasingly become the art form within which to explore the theme of rebellion, separation, and self-definition; film has meanwhile taken up the traditional novelistic exploration of political and social community. This process might be related at least tentatively to an increased awareness of the solitary processes of composition in the novel and the solitary attention given to a novel by the reader. The novel is born in a sense of lost community. To some extent in the eighteenth and nineteenth centuries it tries to reconstitute the old community; by the twentieth century it tends to direct its attention at the individual in its audience. The movies, on the other hand, reach out to an audience of solitary viewers and, at least in these social films of Renoir, try to mold them into a community as vital as the one that has produced the film. This extension into the audience is as much a general characteristic of films as it is of Renoir's work.

Film, to give just one example, is a more effective propaganda vehicle, precisely because of these potentialities for creating a communal cohesion, secreted within the nature of the film experience. More than any other medium, films are fascinated with defining their own audience. Renoir has remarked that he has always tried to make commercial films, but his interests and methods never quite corresponded to those of the audience. It is easy to dismiss this preoccupation with the audience as mere commercialization, that is, catering to an audience that already exists. But with the great directors as well as to the worst, the reaching toward the audience is a necessary part of the director's attitude toward his medium. The theater experience already carries with it a sense of occasion, of dressing up, that can substitute for the recreation of social order within a particular play. Because the film experience is so casual, so much a part of daily life, it often strives more coherently and in a more complex manner to create its own ideal society from the darkened individuals of its audience. Northrop Frye has remarked about popular art that

> The structure of a work of art makes it the focus of a community. It does not act on people; it pulls people into it. An audience with varied backgrounds, associations and habitual preferences is drawn together by something that says the same thing to each of them. (*A Natural Perspective,* p. 49)

Renoir's interest in the social theme goes beyond this mere mirroring to present a recreation of society, sometimes better than the society of the audience, like the commune in *Lange;* sometimes more fallible, like the tenement in *Les Bas-Fonds;* and sometimes involving a grimmer truth, like the country house La Colinière of *La Règle du Jeu.*

Renoir has said that it was only after he had seen Erich von Stroheim's *Foolish Wives* in 1924 that he was convinced that a truly French cinema was possible. Before this, the only possibility was to imitate American or Russian films. But the revelation of *Foolish Wives* was a revelation of the social context of cinema and how a French director, "living in France, drinking red wine and eating Brie before the *grisailles* of Parisian vistas, could accomplish quality work only if he applied himself to the traditions of people who lived the way he did. . . . I began to appreciate that the gestures of a woman washing clothes, or those of one making herself up before a mirror, or a man selling vegetables from a cart, often had an incomparable quality of palpable life." This need to be rooted in an existing society continues through the films of the 1920s. There is little sense in these films of any questioning of society. Society is a given, and the characters are observed working within its framework. The satire of masters and servants in a film like *Tire-au-flanc* (1928), for example, is tempered by unquestioned assumptions about the framework of society, despite the caricatured views of army life and upper-class pomposity.

The interest in society is, of course, balanced by an interest in the individual. In these films, one of the most typical themes is the absorption of a young man into a social framework. *Tire-au-flanc* deals with the process by which Jean Dubois d'Ombelles, the poetry-writing upper-class hero, is turned into a "real man" and good soldier after being drafted into the army. The masters and the servants in Jean's house always have their meals separately, and the camera moves with nervous egalitarianism back and forth between kitchen and dining room, to observe Jean in one place and Joseph, his friend and butler, in the other. When they both are drafted, they eat together in the army barracks. But Joseph cuts a much better figure than Jean, who immediately becomes the butt of every joke. Jean does finally prove himself, in military affairs as well as love. At the end of the film, we have returned to the kitchen and dining room. Nothing has changed. Jean and Joseph are separately celebrating their engagements, with identical cakes. The social order has reasserted itself after the brief egalitarianism of the army, as if that interlude had never existed. In some sense it never really did exist; it was only a farcical setting for the change in Jean. Its larger implications for society are not explored, although they surface again in films like *La Grande Illusion*.

Le Bled (1929) similarly asserts the need to integrate the youthful hero into an ongoing and uncritically accepted society. Renoir made *Le Bled* (equivalent to *The Sticks* in English) with French government aid to commemorate the one hundredth anniversary of the conquest of Algeria. Yet the issue of colonialism is never raised. The point of the film is the socialization of the individual rather than the exploration of possibilities for a better society. Pierre Hoffer, a city-bred young man, comes to Algeria because it is a condition of his potential inheritance from his uncle, Christian Hoffer, a colonist, that he live and work there for six months. In the course of the film Pierre is won over to the hard life of battling the land on Christian Hoffer's farm. His own progress represents a kind of symbolic commitment of urban France to rural Algeria. This theme is underlined when Uncle Christian takes Pierre to a rise near the sea and tells the history of the French in Algeria, while nineteenth-century soldiers rise behind them and are transformed into tractors. For society to be strong, the strong individual must be absorbed into its larger goals. The only questioning of these larger goals comes, if at all, during a gazelle hunt in which the camera bounds along with a fluidity and movement that contrasts with the rigid inhumanity of the hunt itself. But this hunt has none of the satiric force of the scenes of a corrupt society imposing itself on nature in *La Règle du Jeu*. In *Le Bled* the villainous roles are conventionally filled by two cousins of Pierre's, who want to get the inheritance away from him. They exercise their villainy during the hunt and receive their just deserts. The hunt, like the army camp in *Tire-au-flanc*, merely serves as a setting for more conventional plot action, instead of being itself integrated into the total meaning of the film.

With Renoir's sound films comes a greater awareness of the pressure of society upon the world of the film. Perhaps the movement from the image alone to sound plus image is responsible for Renoir's greater sensitivity. But a more apparent parallel to the new interest is Renoir's changed attitude toward the uses of theater. Because theater so obviously invokes the special social occasion, it can serve as a convenient shorthand for society itself. Renoir's assumption in most of his silent films that society is a given seems closely related to his implication in these films that theater is an archaic form, only to be superseded. Theater comes into its own in Renoir's films when he is looking for ways of more closely examining society. *Tire-au-flanc* and *Le Bled* are both films that are basically naturalistic in style. The forests of *Tire-au-flanc* and the deserts of *Le Bled* are natural settings that can connect with a real world beyond the film, because the societies that inhabit them need not be scrutinized. *Chotard & Compagnie* (1933) involves much the same theme of social assimilation as *Tire-au-flanc* and *Le Bled*. Julien Collinet, the lighthearted poet, becomes a part of his father-in-law's grocery business after he discovers that winning the Prix Goncourt is more trouble than it was worth. But the pressures of the world outside *Chotard* have become too strong for it to exist, like *Tire-au-Flanc* or *Le Bled*, in the open. *Chotard* takes place only within the confines of a studio set. Society itself is basically just as unexamined as it was in the earlier films, but the limitation of the physical world of *Chotard* implies the limitation of its social perspective. *Chotard* defines a world of bourgeois fantasy through enclosure and artifice, in the same way that Emma Bovary in Renoir's next film will define herself theatrically in the midst of the oppressive society of Normandy.

The precedent of theater is also responsible for the most pervasive images of society and community in Renoir's films, from the first to the last. As the prologue to *Tire-au-flanc* remarks "les grands circonstances de la vie du baptême à l'enterrement sont marqué par un repas." This Tolstoyan emphasis on the family and the family festivity in Renoir's films of the 1920s leads directly into his interest in the relations between society and community in the films of the 1930s. One could do worse in looking for a key to Renoir's films to observe first the place given to meals in the film, or the role played by a table in visually binding characters together. Muffat bursts in upon Nana's servants when he has heard that she is dying and finds them all drunk and glutted around the long kitchen table, one girl sitting on the butler's lap and revealing for a moment the only fully seen bare breast in any Renoir film. Ritual has been reversed. The servants are now in command and the sense of cabaret or bedroom has been illegitimately brought to the table. In better circumstances the table would have been a symbol of harmony; now it is an image of disruption and chaos. To suit this imagery, Pierre Hoffer's change from Parisian to colonist is directly related to the dinner table. At the beginning of the film, he dresses in evening clothes while his uncle and all the hired men are in their work clothes. At the end of the film, at his own wedding, when Christian and all the guests are dressed for a special occasion, Pierre is still wearing the clothes in which he came in from the field. His sense of the society he has joined is related directly to the daily life of toil.

The dinner table specifically highlights the social relations between characters. It appears through the films of the 1920s and 1930s until it culminates in the servants' table, presided over by Lisette, in *La Règle du Jeu*. The masters do not eat in *La Règle du Jeu*; only the servants have that kind of cohesion. The masters are too involved in the theater of their lives, which has separated them from any vital sense of social ritual. In this more melancholic and incisive use of theater as a metaphor for limit, Renoir has a supple imagistic tool to set forth the harmonious control that must merge with natural energy in order to form a worthy society. Unlike Godard, whose Flaubert is the author of *Bouvard and Pécuchet,* that fabric of verbal wit and incantation, Renoir admires the Flaubert who wrote *Madame Bovary,* with its drama of the individual caught in a fatal frame of social ritual.

The dinner table is potentially a symbol of stability. At mealtimes the family group defines itself and its relations. In the absence of a family, the new community defines itself in the same way. In *La Grande Illusion,* for example, the prisoners prepare for the amateur theatrical around a table, each sewing a costume or contributing in some way. Boeldieu's inability to take part in this preparation, his active desire not to ("I am a realist"), indicates his isolation from the possible community that can replace the crumbling society of which he is a part. In terms of the preparation for a theatrical presentation, it emphasizes that he takes his personal style so seriously that he cannot suspend it even for a moment, while the others can participate in the theatricals to demonstrate the social cohesion they have made for themselves.

Chotard & Compagnie, with its atmosphere of comic reconciliation to society, follows the more "anarchistic" and anti-social *Boudu Sauvé des Eaux* by only a few months in Renoir's career. Its social quietism is probably as responsible for the critical hostility toward it, as is the theatricality deplored by Andrew Sarris or the triviality mentioned by other critics. But through these films made at the beginning of his career in sound film, Renoir is re-evaluating the attitude toward society he expressed in his silent films. *Chotard* remains in the studio set world, the enclosed sound stage.

La Chienne, La Nuit du Carrefour, and *Boudu Sauvé des Eaux* venture out into a social world viewed more hostilely, filled with rigid moralisms, dark criminality, and repressed natural impulses. Society is not a seamless fabric in any of these three films the way it tends to be in *Chotard.* In that world of fantasy, the reintegration of the poet Julien into society can take place because the society defined by *Chotard* stands calmly outside history. It is a limited world, more community than society, determined by the natural rhythms of the day and the digestion.

There are no such natural social rhythms in *La Chienne* or *La Nuit du Carrefour;* so much of their action takes place in the hostile and asocial hours of the night. One may even feel that the imposition of the puppet-show frame on *La Chienne* is Renoir's antidote for the sense of lost social form. From *On Purge Bébé,* Renoir's first sound film, with its manic bourgeois family and games with sound, to *Toni,* with its malevolent nature pressing the characters into the ground, Renoir's films from 1930 to 1935 revolve around the problem of the social world and how it might combine the energy of nature with the theater's benevolent control. Julien Collinet of *Chotard* and Boudu are in some ways very similar; they both swing through the bourgeois houses they inhabit with little regard for the normal paths of stairways and the normal functions of furniture. Julien swings over banisters and makes this structured studio world a kind of jungle gym for his sensibility. Boudu stands on his head in the hallways and will not sleep on a bed, even though Lestingois the bookstore owner tells him that the bed is a marvelous invention. Both characters disrupt the complacencies of the bourgeois house. The difference, of course, is that Julien finally accepts the house, while Boudu leaves it behind. In some sense, coming after *Boudu, Chotard* is archaic. But in fact, like *Bovary,* made shortly afterward,

Chotard merely explores another way of looking at the problem. In contrast to Julien's acceptance of the safe placidities of bourgeois life, *Boudu* concentrates on the un-assimilated man, who defines society by being in such opposition to it. Boudu escapes society by being more natural; Emma Bovary by being more theatrical. Neither nature nor theater then remains an absolute or even a constant in these films. Both are defined in terms of the role they play in the explication and nature of society. Both complexes of value they represent prepare the way for Renoir's attempts in the films of the middle and late 1930s to focus more on the creation of a new community than on the societies that already exist.

Boudu scorns the empty forms of social conventions, just as his frank lust contrasts with the pastoral love talk of Lestingois and Anne-Marie. When Boudu spills wine on the tablecloth, Madame Lestingois pours salt on top to stop the stain. Boudu then pours wine on top of the salt, reversing the process. This gesture represents the larger threat of Boudu to Lestingois' world: he owns a piano because all bourgeois families must have one, and Anne-Marie carefully dusts the artificial flowers on the piano top just before Lestingois spots Boudu through his telescope. Lestingois invites Boudu into his world because he thinks that he can contain Boudu's energy and probably because he thinks that natural energy is basically benevolent. Lestingois thinks of nature in terms of the literary pastoral, and tries both to use and distance nature when he plays the pastoral lover to Anne-Marie in the love duet that begins the film. But nature is more raw and violent than Lestingois will admit. Lestingois' world of silence and books is only a step from the rage and noise of the quais and the possibilities of suicide and drowning while crowds gawk from their safe vantage on the Pont des Arts.

In *Boudu* the studio world is continually threatened by the world of natural energy outside, just as Lestingois' peace is threatened by the anarchic energies of Boudu. There is more than a touch of the nasty and violent about Boudu in his lack of feeling for others; he not only upends social conventions, but also refuses social and human relations altogether. Nature is not totally benevolent or else the acceptance of nature would be easily accomplished in the form of packaged pastoral or the confectionary use to which people put their prints of Renoir paintings. Lestingois tries to make a place for nature and its energies in his world and fails, despite his own benevolence; it is as if an older Julien Collinet or Jean Dubois d'Ombelles decided to take in some replica of a self that they believed was inside them, only to discover that that self was totally disrupting their lives. The closed world of *Chotard* is as much Renoir as the rough edges of *Boudu*. Both show his preoccupation with the problem of limitation and energy within the context of society. If anything, *Chotard* is more prophetic in terms of Renoir's own career, for its closed little community presages the momentarily closed communities of films like *Lange, La Grande Illusion*, and *La Règle du Jeu*. And its theatrical definition of the world looks forward to the theatrical worlds of *Le Carrosse d'Or, French Cancan*, and *Elena et les Hommes*.

Between 1934 and 1939 Renoir had his most sustained period of creativity and exploration. In almost every film, from *Toni* to *La Règle du Jeu*, the explorations of the early years of the 1930s produced increasingly complex and vital achievements. Not all of these films deal directly with the problem of society; *Toni, Partie de Campagne, La Bête Humaine*, as I have already discussed, emphasize instead the influence of nature and passion on the individual. But most of Renoir's other films put society at the center of their preoccupations. In *Le Crime de Monsieur Lange, La Vie Est à Nous, Les Bas-Fonds, La Grande Illusion, La Marseillaise,* and *La Règle du Jeu,* Renoir explores the need to build within the pre-existing society a newly formed and vital community, based on more authentic standards and closer relations between people. That this period is the great period of the *équipe* behind the camera, before its disintegration with World War II and Renoir's passage to America, adds to the intensity of Renoir's search. And to complement the ideal of an *équipe* that produces something socially valuable through artistic talent, the films themselves express their fledgling societies mainly in terms of limits—the boundaries of nations and the frontiers of war, the prosceniums and artifice of theater, the classlines and vocations of society. *Boudu* may prove that society cannot be reinvigorated by massive injections of natural passion. The way in which Renoir's camera moves around Lestingois' house may be reminiscent of the free swooping use Boudu himself makes of the house. But in the light of Renoir's later interests it seems clear that the freedom is only part of the meaning. Ideally the camera moves with the freedom of Boudu, as well as the insight of the more sympathetic and benevolent Lestingois. Nature is not enough, without sympathetic order. All the enclosed worlds of the films of the middle and late 1930s—the Parisian courtyard of *Lange,* the prison camp in *La Grande Illusion,* the tenement in *Les Bas-Fonds,* the country house in *La Règle du Jeu*—are confines within which to explore the possibilities of energy and exuberance.

The touchstone for the possibilities of community in Renoir's films of the second half of the 1930s is, as I have said, *Le Crime de Monsieur Lange.* Society for Renoir seems made up of day-to-day things, perhaps tedious and oppressive, as they are to Emma Bovary, but potentially renewable through understanding and perhaps even able to be formed

into a new vision of community. Bovary defines herself
against an oppressive provincial society by extreme stylization,
just as Boeldieu and Rauffenstein in *La Grande Illusion*
try to define themselves in a world to which they feel they
no longer belong. Lange, on the other hand, does not separate himself from his world, but tries instead to give it some
new meaning. Lange is a lowly assistant writer at the pulp-
novel publishing firm owned by Batala, a crook, womanizer,
and the most archly stylized character in the whole film.
The firm is located on the second floor of a court in Paris,
behind one of those large wooden doors that opens into a
total world, with its laundresses, concierges, and employees
in the publishing firm. Batala goes on a trip to Italy, the
train is wrecked, he is reported dead, and the employees,
in consort with the owner's young son decide to make the
firm a co-operative and to publish Lange's *Arizona Jim*
novels.

The world of the court (Jean Castanier's original title
for his idea was *Sur la Cour*) totally defines the world of
the film, except for three intrusions or scenes outside the
court: Charles's bicycle accident, Batala's departure and arrival, and the final escape of Lange and his girl-friend
Florelle, the owner of the laundry. All three scenes disrupt
the tone of the film because they draw the spectator outside
the comfort and conviviality of the court, where some kind
of utopian community has been achieved. Charles's accident
does serve to bring the people of the court even more closely
together because it resolves the problem of Lange's attraction for Edith, with whom Charles is also in love. But
Batala is a force that can disrupt the community. His passions (for example, his seduction of Edith) and his greed
are the kind of values the co-operative of laundresses and
literary workers are trying to wall out. Even the visual
style of these separate episodes disrupts the viewer's com-

fort. Inside the court the camera movement is fluid, weaving through the windows and up the stairs, a visual web which strengthens the social web the characters are trying to create. The camera explores the confines of the set and makes its little world almost self-sufficient. The final obstacle to the co-operative is symbolically removed when the billboard that Batala has placed over Charles's window is ripped down. We have in fact already seen its destruction, in the previous scene of Lange's talk with Charles, when the camera entered the window from the court, the billboard disappearing by a kind of animation.

The most important impingement of the life outside the court occurs when Batala returns, in the disguise of a priest (who had actually died in the train wreck, dressed in Batala's clothes). Charles's bicycle accident had been a preview of this disruption, but that event could be absorbed and the court community was actually strengthened by it. The threat of Batala cannot be taken care of so easily. He comes appropriately enough during a celebratory meal, in which all the inhabitants of the court are looking forward to a prosperous co-operative life together. Batala draws Lange away to tell him that he will take the business back. Lange decides that he must kill Batala and tells him to meet him at the fountain diagonally across the court from the room where the other court residents, all oblivious, are celebrating. The camera focuses on Lange as he emerges. Then, in a virtuoso camera movement without parallel in Renoir's other films, while Lange goes to the viewer's right to meet Batala, the camera turns to the left and finishes describing its half of the circle with the sight of Batala lying dead on the ground. In terms of *Toni*, the film made just before *Lange*, this circle would be the circle of natural fatality; but in Lange it is both more and less. It is a statement of the wholeness of the court life that moves Lange to commit himself in such irrevocable terms to the murder of Batala. It shows the whole court. But at the same time it shows the limits of the court, which can keep out what is alien to itself only for a brief moment. After this "360°" shot, Lange must leave the court before the police come. Although Lange may be right to murder Batala in order to preserve the life of the court, he must flee. When he and Florelle escape, their car makes an abrupt right turn almost in front of us. In contrast to the fluid camera of the court, the camera outside the court sits awkwardly reporting the action. Outside the court the only fluidity is in Batala's line of conning patter.[1]

The seemingly self-sufficient world of the court is ultimately too utopian to last. After the social and aesthetic economy of the court, the car speeding down the road away from Paris is a disruption that makes us re-evaluate the merits of enclosure. The convivial life inside the court must finally be left behind, but with little certainty about what the outside world can offer. Batala's return is not an unhappy accident. It is a necessary impingement of the world on ideals. After their escape Florelle tells Lange's story to another small community in a small village café. She convinces them of the rightness of Lange's action and they help the two escape. But the end of the film is gloomy. The world of the court basically no longer exists. Florelle's narrative to the men in the bar is the film itself. It encircles the life of the court the way Renoir's camera did, but the unity is achieved perhaps only within the world

[1] André Bazin, who has traced the circular shot in a diagram, generally emphasizes its technical virtuosity rather than its meaning: ". . . it gives an impression of vertigo, of madness, it creates suspense . . . but its *raison d'etre* is more essential; it is the spatial expression of the entire setting (*mise-en-scène*) of the film." (Bazin, André: *Jean Renoir*, edited and introduced by François Truffaut. Paris: Editions Champ Libre, 1971, p. 46.)

of the film and not really a workable ideal. The camera goes
one way around the court and Lange goes the other. Together they move through 360 degrees. Like Boudu and Lestingois, each needs the other to make a total statement. Within
a blooming ideal community, Renoir has raised the question
of the validity of its limits. Can one in fact found a utopian
community within the larger society? *Lange* remains ambiguous. There is the barest hint of potential for Lange
and Florelle. Their footsteps on the wet sand at the end
of the film, and the final setting by what seems to be
the sea and the Franco-Belgian border, may imply a need
to cross frontiers and achieve a sense of expansiveness—possibilities the court lacked.

In *La Vie Est à Nous*, made by Renoir for the French
Communist Party and employing many of the same actors
and technicians who made *Lange,* the ideal of the renewed
community is projected onto the French nation as a whole.
Renoir shows us vignettes of the decay of the present society
and the possibility of a new society through the Popular
Front, which would be both politically and humanly vital.
Each vignette—whether the story of the factory speed-up, the
thwarting of a farm auction, or the unemployed young man
whose education has done him no good—ends with a scene
of a group solidarity. The Communist message is "you're not
alone in your troubles," and Renoir absorbs it into his own
concerns. The speeches of French Communist leaders, such
as Jacques Duclos and Maurice Thorez, which are included
in the film, are addressed almost solely to workers and farmers. But Renoir's film finally embraces all parts of society.
The crowds that sing "L'Internationale" at the end of the
film are made up of rich as well as poor, soldiers as well as
intellectuals, businessmen and clochards. But these larger
aspirations for the ideal of community remain more muted in
Renoir's work in general. *La Marseillaise* will pick up the

Le Petit Chaperon Rouge. Renoir as the Wolf.

La Chienne. Above, Maurice Legrand (Michel Simon) escorts Lulu (Janie Marèze) down a dark street in Montmartre after he has intervened while she was being beaten up by her boy friend. Below, Legrand looks at his paintings, which he considers as much a failure as the rest of his life. Above right, Legrand (in pajamas) pretends that he has been caught with the wife of Alexis Godard (Gaillard) (emerging from the kitchen), actually his wife's first husband, who had been thought lost in the war. The composition leads us back across the bare dinner table to the hapless Godard.

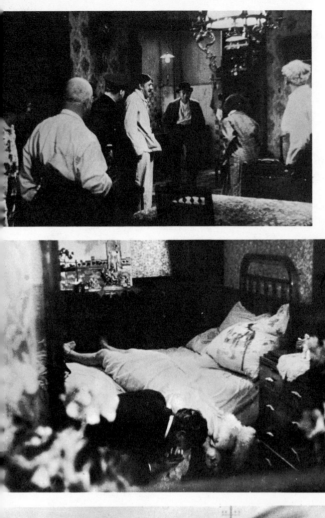

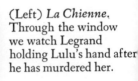

(Left) *La Chienne*.
Through the window
we watch Legrand
holding Lulu's hand after
he has murdered her.

La Nuit du Carrefour.
The crossroads themselves
with Oscar's garage on
the right, in an atmosphere
of grayness and rain.

La Nuit du Carrefour. The car chase by night. Below, Inspector Maigret (Pierre Renoir) with his cold eye stands before Else Andersen (Winna Winfried), a prime suspect in the murder.

Renoir on the set of *Boudu Sauvé des Eaux*, his face visible just beyond the man on the right. On the left is Marguerite Renoir, the editor, and in the center Michel Simon, as the recently cleaned, pressed, and coiffed Boudu.

Boudu Sauvé des Eaux. A policeman tells the Clochard Boudu (Michel Simon) to move on, after Boudu has asked him for help to find his lost dog. Left, Lestingois picks Boudu up in his telescope and observes him until Boudu jumps into the Seine and Lestingois drops the telescope to rush out and save him.

Chotard et Cie. Julien Collinet (Georges Pomiès) pledges poetic love to Reine Chotard (Jeanne Boitel), the daughter of a prosperous grocery store owner, during a pause in a charity ball. Below, Chotard (Fernand Charpin) ecstatic that his new son-in-law has won the Prix Goncourt.

(Left) *Boudu Sauvé des Eaux.* Wearing his benefactor's clothes, Boudu enjoys the comforts of bourgeois life. Anne-Marie the maid (Séverine Lerczinska) and Lestingois's mistress smile, Mme. Lestingois (Marcelle Hainia) is aloof, and Lestingois himself (Charles Granval) is dubious about what he has done.

Madame Bovary. In another shot that opens into the background
Emma Bovary (Valentine Tessier) looks out of the confines of her
home into luxuriant nature beyond. Below, a little gypsy girl stands
amid the glass-enclosed nature of the Bovary household.

Madame Bovary. Emma Bovary meets Rodolphe (Fernand Fabre) in a setting draped for theater. Below right, the little girl tries to comfort Charles Bovary (Pierre Renoir) after his operation on the boy with the clubfoot has failed. Below left, yet another variety of framing. Emma Bovary, once again limited after she has been rejected by Rodolphe, talks with her maid, while her daughter holds a single flower.

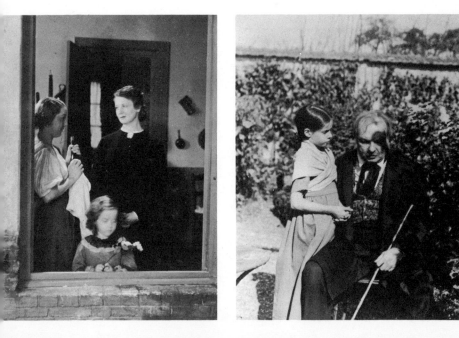

Toni. Toni (Charles Blavette) and his friend Fernand (Edouard Delmont) push a gondola filled with rocks in the quarry where they work. Below, the double marriage feast of Albert (Max Dalban) (second from left) and Josefa (Célia Montalvan) (on his left), Toni (looking disconsolate) and Marie (Jenny Hélia) (on his right). Fernand and Josefa's cousin Gaby (Andrex) (both on Toni's left) look on. Above right, in the harsh lighting of their home Josefa murders Albert.

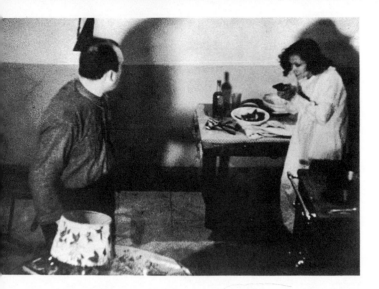

Le Crime de Monsieur Lange. Charles (Maurice Baquet) and Estelle (Nadia Sibirskaïa) embrace quietly in the seemingly protected world of the court.

Le Crime de Monsieur Lange. The members of the "Arizona Jim" publishing commune pose for a group picture before a backdrop in the courtyard. On the horse are Estelle and Lange (René Lefèvre); on the left is the concierge (Maurice Levesque). Below, over a table in a café near the border Valentine (Florelle) tells the story of Lange's murder of Batala and tries to convince the habitués to help them escape. Lange waits in the background.

same themes of the new society two years later, but that film sets them at a time—the French Revolution—when the new unity existed more in fact than it would in the propaganda of the Popular Front. In the revolutionary past of *La Marseillaise* the visionary desire for national unity that suffuses the end of *La Vie Est à Nous* is figured in scenes like the one in which Arnaud, the citizen-lawyer-soldier, and Saint-Laurent, the perplexed aristocrat, walk the battlements of the Marseilles fort and discuss the meaning of the new word "nation." But most of Renoir's social films of this period avoid the heroic road of the revolutionary nostalgia of *La Marseillaise* as well as the semi-documentary Popular Front idealism of *La Vie Est à Nous*. They concentrate instead on an attempt to explore and reformulate the problem stated by *Lange*: what is the best relation between the small community and the large society? how does one sort out the relation between the manageable world of the proscenium and the oppressive reality of political events, hostile nature, and venal individuals?

After the tenuously preserved success of the *Lange* community, the degraded community of *Les Bas-Fonds* (*The Lower Depths,* 1936), living and wrangling in a rotted tenement beside the Seine, seems obviously failed. But it does not require too great a stretch of the imagination to envision the inhabitants of Kostylev's boarding house once having had the social optimism of the co-operative in *Lange*. Now all their hopes are gone, and the normal coin of their conversation is self-involved despair and nostalgic dreams of power and beauty. In *Lange* the true virtue remained in developing the community, and the departure of Lange and Florelle seemed a fatal necessity. The sense of possibility in *Les Bas-Fonds* is through the individuals who can escape. The relationship between Pepel and the Baron invites a glimpse into the possibility of human relations outside a social order that otherwise seems fatally determined. While they sit together on the bank of the Seine, the Baron says that his comedown in the world doesn't bother him because everything is a dream, which changes when we change clothes. The Baron can give Pepel a sense of possibility and change that the tenement would otherwise inhibit. The life of the tenement is basically self-involved theater, dramatized by the confinement of the sets, the way the camera has to dodge around posts and board separations, and the histrionic speeches of the inhabitants.

Akira Kurosawa's version of the Gorki play emphasizes theatrical confinement at the expense of anything outside and becomes finally claustrophobic in its concentration. But Renoir looks in this enclosure for the window that opens onto the yard. Nothing can grow in the tenement but the memory of once-human relations. Pepel can strike against the oppression of Kostylev and for the first time galvanize the individuals, with their stereotyped roles (the Actor, the Drunk), into something resembling a community. But Pepel and Natacha must, like Lange and Florelle, leave this world behind and take to the road. They are distanced from us in the last shot as much by sentiment as by cynicism. There is the possibility of vitality in their relation, but none of Chaplin's blithe sentimentality in *Modern Times* about the individual's ability to understand and reform society. When Pepel and Natacha leave the tenement, the Actor commits suicide. But the value of their acceptance of openness and the world of nature is ambiguous. The community cohesion effected by Pepel's accidental murder of Kostylev is only momentary, and the potentiality for the future life of Pepel and Natacha is dim, like the fleeting footsteps of Lange and Florelle on the wet beach sand.

Both *La Grande Illusion* and *La Règle du Jeu* also end with the isolation of two people. In *La Grande Illusion* we see the tiny black figures of Maréchal and Rosenthal crossing the invisible line of the German-Swiss border, vulnerable but potentially hopeful against the vast whiteness of the snow; in *La Règle du Jeu* Octave and Marceau leave the country house of La Colinière, one going back to Paris, the other to the woods, while Robert de la Chesnaye ushers his guests back inside. This kind of tentativeness, which grows more pessimistic, I would say, as Renoir moves toward *La Règle du Jeu* (and Europe moves toward World War II), grows from Renoir's uneasiness with quick formulas to improve society. Leaving aside revolutionary apocalypse, there are two places to work, if one feels that society is in trouble: one can either try to build a new community within the shell of the old, or one can look toward some international order that will go beyond the petty nationalisms that threaten the vitality of the social order. Renoir does concentrate on the French nation and its potential, in *Lange*, *La Vie Est à Nous*, and *La Marseillaise*. Even *La Bête Humaine*, with its basic emphasis on private human passions, also partakes of both the curious inconclusiveness of the other films and their preoccupation with national self-definition. Protesting against the fatality that has ruled his actions, Jacques Lantier at the end of the film leaps off the Paris-Havre train. In Zola's novel, the final rushing train, with Lantier's and Pecqueux's decapitated bodies left behind, is an image of France headed blindly toward the Franco-Prussian War. In Renoir's film, with the historical setting omitted, the rushing train becomes an anonymous national society worshiped by Lantier for its mechanical perfection but ultimately his destroyer. His personal passions cannot be integrated into a larger society, and they find no outlet in his own community.

Amid the international confusion of war in *La Grande Illusion* every man is looking first for some kind of personal definition, and then for some group definition, to which to relate that personal definition. Imagistically, almost everyone in the film is in a kind of box, either consciously or unconsciously assumed. The near-suffocation of the Actor (Julien Carette) in the escape tunnel symbolically represents both the need for and the dangers of narrow passages. The theatrical impulses of Boeldieu and Rauffenstein, in contrast to the actual theater of the Actor and the other men, help them define themselves and their class within what they believe is a crumbling social order. Their rigidity, articulated by Rauffenstein, whimsically assented to by Boeldieu, contrasts with the "natural" impulses that binds men together, like Maréchal and Rosenthal, who can curse each other in the accents of their classes, then embrace as individuals.

Maréchal and Rosenthal, the two prisoners who escape, might be a potential core for a revitalized community—the stolid, dependable Frenchman and the witty, cosmopolitan Jew. But the time of vitality has passed for the community that Boeldieu and Rauffenstein represent. Rauffenstein refuses to acknowledge its passing and spins out a web of amenities and manners to preserve it. But Boeldieu sees the void of substance that the form tries to hide. Renoir ironically underlines the fact that such "natural" relations apart from the artificial structures of society come to the surface only in the artificially limited environment of the prison camp, in which class matters not so much as what a man can do to help the group. Therefore Rosenthal, the nouveau-riche Jew, performs the important Renoir film task of furnishing the food for all the members of the little prison community. The momentary theatricals for which all work at the dinner table represent a more vital order than the stylizations of society to which Rauffenstein and Boeldieu owe their allegiance.

Renoir does not in fact rest with a simple contrast between the communal group formed in the prison camp, on the one hand, and the archaic rigidities of the aristocracy, on the other. In fact the upper-class and international unities that Rauffenstein wishes to assert with his nominal enemy Boeldieu are presented by Renoir with a kind of nostalgia, for they are the last flowerings of a tradition that could have crossed the barriers of nationality and language that now divide up the world. The way Boeldieu and Rauffenstein easily converse in French, German, and English is favorably contrasted with the way Maréchal fruitlessly tries to tell the English officer of the French escape tunnel. Playing with languages is not a new element in Renoir's work; the prologue to *Toni* announces "The action takes place in the south of France, where nature, in her destruction of the spirit of the Tower of Babel, knows full well how to bring about the blending of the races." And there is a definite interplay in these films of the middle and late 1930s between the nationalistic French-language films and the international films that include many languages. Four languages are spoken by the characters in *La Grande Illusion*—French, German, English, and Russian. The different languages so flow in and out of each other that the first time one sees the film without subtitles one is unsure who is speaking what. Immediately after *La Grande Illusion* Renoir makes *La Marseillaise,* which, in order to realize its paean to the birth of the French nation, takes special care to preserve the native accents of all the characters, whether the Marseillais themselves, the Swiss guards, or the Parisian Court. The vitality of the nation is in its social complexity, and Boeldieu rejects Rauffenstein's pleas in English to stop what he is doing, when he is helping Maréchal and Rosenthal to escape by diverting the Germans. After he shoots Boeldieu, Rauffenstein invents his own symbol for what has happened.

He goes deliberately over to the window of his room and cuts the single geranium, the only flower in the castle, with a self-conscious movement. The blatancy of the symbol may be disturbing; it is certainly a rarity in Renoir's films. But the point is clearly that the geranium is Rauffenstein's symbol, not Renoir's. The rigidity of its significance mirrors the rigidity of his own understanding.

Just as Renoir does not totally reject the style of the aristocrats in *La Grande Illusion,* so he also does not present the society of the prison camp as a total success. Even though each man does contribute to the group effort, each is also isolated in his own interests and profession, until there is some arbitrary pressure from without, like the common enemy or the need to escape. One of Renoir's subtlest balances is precisely between the forces of social camaraderie and the forces of individual isolation in the film. In one scene, for example, Maréchal is looking at a map when the Senegalese announces with a flourish that he has finished his wood carving, which he has been working on in the background of previous scenes. He takes it over and shows it to Maréchal, who glances at it and then away, with a singular lack of interest. The Senegalese with this wood carving, the actor with his bits from old cabaret acts, the teacher with his Pindar—each man has a self-involvement that walls out the other members of the group almost as definitely as the wall of class between Maréchal and Boeldieu, or the wall of nationality between Boeldieu and Rauffenstein, that occupies the foreground of the film. When we are reminded that Renoir in World War I was both cavalry lieutenant (Boeldieu) and aerial reconnaissance pilot (Maréchal) and that in fact his rank in the cavalry was *"maréchal,"* a simple division of the values of *La Grande Illusion* between national camaraderie and upperclass snobbishness is impossible. Each has more complex qualities to offer to the film's total statement.

After Boeldieu's death, the film concentrates on the two escapees, Maréchal and Rosenthal. To complement the world of prison and theater in the first part of the film, the second part of the film presents a more edenic world, in which Maréchal and Rosenthal fill out the dinner table of the widow of a German soldier killed at Verdun. They milk the cows, celebrate Christmas, and generally participate in the life of a family. In one of the few uses of religious symbolism in Renoir's films, we have moved from the grim crucifix that looks down on Rauffenstein's bedroom to the joyous Christmas celebration that Maréchal and Rosenthal make for Elsa and her little daughter. The celebration itself becomes another refuge within the refuge of the cottage. Maréchal and Rosenthal stand at the sides of the door while Elsa goes inside to awaken her daughter. Unlike the framed series of doorways from which Rauffenstein so often emerges, this is a frame not of worked-up style but of natural harmony. At the end of the scene, almost the same shot recurs, but this time Maréchal and Elsa are beside the bed, while Rosenthal remains outside, as both Jew and man.

Both the prison and the cottage are ideal in different ways. The world of men in the prison prepares the way for the possibilities of family in the cottage. Yet both enclosed worlds are equally limiting to the self in its search for the less certain satisfactions of society, which pull both Maréchal and Rosenthal away from the cottage and toward the war and the public, political world. They leave with resignation, not knowing what will happen, expecting only that they will be posted back to their old units. But in that evocative last shot in the snow, they are a society of two, distant like Pepel and Natacha, or Lange and Florelle, but with some faint hope that the understanding they achieved in the smaller world has some possibility of being integrated into the larger, more anonymous society, to which they are returning. War is international political relations that have destroyed the once more benevolent internationality of social class. Only a new kind of nationalism, symbolized by the mechanic and the Jew, may be able to stand against it.

It is fitting that *La Grande Illusion* was Renoir's first international success, for its own themes involve the search for some vital relationship between the best that defines a nation and the best that binds nations together. With the arrival of the sound film came a great internationalization of the movie business, larger companies and more co-productions. But, of course, the sound film also brought the awareness of separation between national cinemas, since the "common language" of the pure image had to give way to the separate national languages and the imposed internationality of subtitles. It is typical of Renoir's awareness of the process of movie-making that such international themes should echo on levels of both production and theme in a film like *La Grande Illusion*. Not until the 1950s will Renoir elaborate this theme further, but his later interests are presaged in *La Grande Illusion* by the inescapable reference to the artistic brotherhood between nations that the film can play host to, not the least indication of which is the presence of Eric von Stroheim in the film. Stroheim's story of Renoir greeting him in German is a capsule form of what most of the characters in *La Grande Illusion* cannot achieve.

In the films of the 1950s Renoir develops the possibility that movies can invite the isolated national viewer into a new community of internationality in art, not necessarily better morally or socially, but more whole and more benevolent. The society of the films that he made before World War II is finally more centered on the French national scene, the ideals of the Popular Front, and the realities of French society. He asks basically whether the separate interest groups and individuals of society, divided by class, profession, and personal nature, be somehow galvanized into a national community. The credits of *La Marseillaise* detail the separate groups of the *ancien régime*—the Court, the civil and military authorities, the aristocrats, the citizens of Marseilles, and the people—as if one of the main goals of Renoir's French Revolution might be to break down these social separations. Murder, in *Lange* and *Les Bas-Fonds* is both a preservative and catalyst for community. But *La Marseillaise* deals with the early years of the Revolution, before the Terror sanctioned scapegoat execution as a means of national unity. The process of the film moves through the journey of the Marseillais troops from their home in the south all the way to Paris and the attack on the Tuileries. This loosely organized army, so unlike the comely hierarchies of the Court guards, is bound together by the growing popularity of the song "La Marseillaise." Perhaps to underscore the subliminal relations in the community, the song itself is sung mainly in snatches in the course of the film, unlike the full-dress singing of "La Marseillaise" in *La Grande Illusion* (made barely six months before), when Maréchal disrupts the amateur theatricals to announce the retaking of Douaumont. In fact, the one time the song is heard at any length in *La Marseillaise,* when it is sung by the Marseillais about to leave for Paris, its effect is undercut by the dislike for it comically expressed by Bomier, one of the principal characters.

At one point in *La Grande Illusion* the group of prison-camp friends look out a window into the courtyard and hear martial music. One remarks that such music is always moving. But Maréchal says, "No, it is the sound of marching feet." If *La Grande Illusion* is to keep its status as an anti-war movie, how does this scene bear on Renoir's very next film, *La Marseillaise,* which takes its title from a nationalist

song, is filled with martial music presented positively, and
ends with the tramp of marching feet, as the soldiers prepare
for the Battle of Valmy? Is war bad only when it is recent,
and good when it is viewed through the distance of history?
Are eighteenth-century French aristocrats more culpable
than early twentieth-century Germans? In fact, these basically
political questions are curiously irrelevant to *La Grande Illusion* and *La Marseillaise*. Both films are less about war than
about society. Like Georg Lukács, Renoir indicates that in
the French Revolution public history had become a mass
experience. But it is the world of politics and history viewed
from the human level that preoccupies and fascinates Renoir.
Political events have a greater importance in *La Marseillaise*
than does the shadowy World War I of *La Grande Illusion*.
But still the main focus of *La Marseillaise* is on the personal
impact these political events have on individuals, from the
inhabitants of Marseilles to the King himself. Renoir has remarked that one of his favorite touches in *La Marseillaise*
is the moment when Louis XVI is being told to flee the
palace and he pauses to muse about the qualities of tomatoes,
which he has just discovered for himself. Historical films
are faced with the aesthetic necessity to express large, frequently abstract themes, through human characters. Usually
the effect reduces history to a hash of personal motivations:
Henry VIII brings about the English Reformation because he
wants to marry Anne Boleyn; Oliver Cromwell decides to
combat Charles I actively when he discovers some soldiers
of the King harassing men of his parish. But since Renoir's
theme is the nature of community and what kinds of action
can achieve a good community, he is not trapped by the need
to find images for political forces. He does use such images,
but mainly to counterpoint the personal story of his characters, for each has his own image of the Revolution, and each

sees the political world they have joined through a somewhat different perspective.

Renoir's optimism about the unity of the French nation that arose from the Revolution never finally reaches an absolute belief in the easy integration of personal impulse with political action. The shadow theater that the friends from Marseilles go to visit in the midst of their revolutionary activities in Paris mimes the world of politics and historical revolution. These political cartoons are mere shadows, while the actual lives of these soldiers (and the actual life of Louis XVI, for that matter) are more central to the values of community that Renoir is trying to emphasize. If it were not for politics and the machinations of the political people on both sides of the Revolution (if it has only two sides at this point), the sympathetic characters in all classes might easily converse. Once again the agent of community is food. Louis XVI's discourse on the tomato and the artist Javel's encomium of the potato shows a community between them that transcends the historical accidents of politics and class. Like so many of Renoir's other films of this period, *La Marseillaise* is basically inconclusive about the ability of men to form a humane society. Bomier dies in a courtyard, finally separated from the street marches and soldiers of the Revolution. Next to him is a mother nursing a baby, a conventional symbol of renewal. But the film ends with his friends leaving him behind as they go to become absorbed into the larger French Army in its campaign against the Grand Alliance. For a few moments perhaps the movements of history could bring to the surface the best human motives, but they are just as quickly submerged. *La Marseillaise* does not end; it is cut off. We know of the successes of the Revolution, but we also know of its failures. And in retrospect the most important figure in the film is not the energetic Bomier, or the lawyer Arnaud, or the officious Roederer, or the pro-Revolu-

tionary aristocrat Saint-Laurent, or the tremendously sympathetic Louis XVI, but the briefly glimpsed poacher, Cabri,
who at the beginning of the film blesses the impulses behind the Revolution (he himself has just escaped from feudal
justice), but says that the young must fight, while he stays on
his mountain.

After the elaborate social order of *La Marseillaise,* the
fatal passions of *La Bête Humaine* (1938) mask Renoir's
larger social concerns with a concentration on the demands
of nature and the limitations of lower class society. In *La
Règle du Jeu* (1939) the problems of what constitutes an
ideal community and what defines a society are placed once
again in the forefront of Renoir's interests. The film begins
with the crush of the present: the radio reporter pushes
her way through the crowd at the airport, where André
Jurieu has just completed a heroic airplane flight, and demands that he say a few words to her listeners. This society
hungers for heroes to define itself and its best nature. *La
Règle du Jeu* embodies a social world in which there are
rules but no values. If you don't know the rules, you are
crushed; but if you do know the rules, you are cut off from
your own nature. Poised on the edge of World War II and
coming at the end of Renoir's increasingly pessimistic explorations of the relation of individuals to society, *La Règle du Jeu*
presents a society that has refined feelings to the utmost, in
order to stave off the demands of time and history and the
potentially disruptive crowds that surge through the first few
minutes of the film. In an early scene Robert de la Chesnaye
and his mistress, Geneviève, each momentarily stand beside
statues of serene and stylized buddhas, expressions of their
own feelings for the orderly rules of their society. La Chesnaye's love of eighteenth-century mechanical toys relates him
to a society just on the edge of the industrial revolution and
the technological complications and identity-destroying mul-

tiplications of the modern world. He wishes the world were like his prize possession, the elaborate calliope he shows his guests at the climax of the nighttime entertainments. He wishes to impose what he believes to be a benevolent order of style on his world, and his archly painted eyebrows, dark sockets, and languid movements, show that he has begun with himself.

But what La Chesnaye tries to preserve as a society of harmonious aesthetic style is in fact a congeries of isolated individuals, each in his or her own world, the masters separated from the servants, the aware from the unaware, the passionate from the unmoved. During the dance of the ghosts and skeletons in the nighttime entertainment, the camera moves around the room and observes the isolated individuals standing alone in the dark. Jurieu rages at Christine de la Chesnaye's responses to Saint-Aubin; Schumacher searches for Marceau and Lisette. In the face of La Chesnaye's social style, individual human nature becomes a force of passion that regards itself as more authentic than the stylized and civilized world it is forced to take part in. Jurieu wants Christine for himself totally and will not agree to any kind of compromise either with her or with La Chesnaye. Schumacher the gamekeeper chases Marceau the poacher-turned-house servant all around the house to kill him for making advances to Schumacher's wife. As Christine runs off through the maze of rooms with Saint-Aubin, she turns to speak to Octave, who wants her to help him off with his bear costume: "I've had enough of this theater." In the beginning of the film she has asked Lisette if friendship, that last community between two people, is ever possible. *La Règle du Jeu* illustrates the impossibility of any authentic society, no matter how small, in this world of isolated egos. Robert de la Chesnaye has tried to orchestrate the weekend the way he has rebuilt his birds and his calliope. When he ushers his guests back into his house at the end of the film after Jurieu's murder by Schumacher, he preserves a hollow victory.

Beside La Chesnaye there are two other characters in *La Règle du Jeu* who attempt to bring the other characters together: Corneille, the major-domo, and Octave, the failed musician, played by Renoir himself. The character of Corneille, as I have mentioned above, helps expand the theme of theatrical control of recalcitrant reality; Octave is a more complex creation. La Chesnaye and Corneille represent on the level of master and servant the forces that attempt to unify the disparate individuals of the house. Octave is a character from outside the usual social order; he can joke as easily with Christine the mistress as with Lisette the maid. Like La Chesnaye, Octave thinks of himself as a coward. All his life, he says, he has been too cowardly to dare any responsibility or difficulty, but has been content instead to float along with the social tide. "If my friends didn't feed me," he says to Christine, "I would starve." Octave is the last person in the hallway at night, shaking hands and making jokes until everyone else has gone to bed. In his biography of his father, Jean Renoir frequently refers to *la théorie du bouchon*, the theory of the cork, which floats with the movements of what is around it. The character of Octave, with his substitution of social stability for personal feelings, subtly criticizes this idea of total accessibility to all experience. Octave has taken openness too far, into placidity and nonentity. "I'd like to bury myself," he tells La Chesnaye. He arranges the weekend for Jurieu to get together with Christine without once allowing his own feelings for Christine to intervene; we don't even hear of these feelings until near the end of the film. If La Chesnaye is the benevolent imposer of order, Octave is the go-between, subordinating his own nature for the fancied good of others and the "harmony" of his little world. La Chesnaye, on the other hand, has a greater appreciation of both the realities of society and what values ought to be preserved than do characters like the General, with their inherited wealth and tradition. La Chesnaye is almost a nouveau riche, and he slyly alludes to the fact that all his wealth was accumulated by an ancestor named Rosenthal. (Marcel Dalio plays both parts.) Like Rosenthal, La Chesnaye is Jewish, a fact that is discussed briefly by the servants; with a typical Renoirian touch the cook finally enters the conversation to say that La Chesnaye, whatever his religion, is a real aristocrat because he knows how to make potato salad properly. La Chesnaye's values, like Rosenthal's, define the Jewish character in terms of a saving internationalism of the spirit that can hopefully mute the worst and realize the best in the French tradition. (It is no doubt this kind of implication that is responsible for Louis-Ferdinand Céline's screed against Rosenthal in his polemic *Bagatelles pour un Massacre*.) But Renoir has already come a distance from the tentative hope of the end of *La Grande Illusion*. Gaston Modot as Schumacher races through La Colinière, firing his gun and disrupting the card games and dances of social order in much the same way that Modot had disrupted the party in Buñuel's *L'Âge d'Or*. Renoir uses Modot both to allude to and to deepen the Buñuelian attitude toward society. The end of *La Règle du Jeu* is a seeming reassertion of order, unlike Buñuel's image of total disintegration. Renoir's point is more complex. Only a bloodless and temporary order has been restored. La Chesnaye leads shadows back into La Colinière. Like Boeldieu, he has accepted a kind of death in order to preserve the last possible harmony for society. As the General says in litany throughout the film, "He is the last of a disappearing race."

Renoir also tried to preserve something from *La Règle du Jeu*. The audiences hated it, and he tells how he frantically cut out scene after scene only to meet renewed hissing and commotion at still other scenes during every screening. The exhibitors insisted on a cut of thirteen minutes to begin with, and Renoir finally cut twenty minutes more himself, in an effort to relate the film to the audience for whom he believed it was made. Says Octave to Christine, "Contact with the public, you see . . . that's the thing I would have liked to experience. That, that must be . . . it must be shattering, eh? When I think that it's passed me by . . . well, it does something to me." This was in fact one of the first scenes cut. There is little sense of potential or renewal in the society of *La Règle du Jeu;* Octave and Marceau go their separate ways, and La Chesnaye closes himself and his guests into the house. Bomier's death in *La Marseillaise* is absorbed into the march of the victorious Revolutionary armies; Lantier's suicide in *La Bête Humaine* breaks from the rigid mechanics of society and his own nature. All that is promised in *La Règle du Jeu* is a funeral the next day for André Jurieu, "this wonderful friend, this excellent companion who knew so well how to make us forget he was a famous man."

Renoir's own separation from French society, first to Italy for the abortive *La Tosca* project and then to the United States, is foretold and almost necessitated by his view of society in *La Règle du Jeu* and the films leading up to it. In 1936, the year of the cautious optimism of *Lange,* and the assertiveness of *La Vie Est à Nous,* he also makes *Partie de Campagne,* with its half-mocking, half-idealized view of late nineteenth-century countryside, and *Les Bas-Fonds,* with its tone of only partially relieved pessimism. *La Grande Illusion* is a conflation of *Lange* and *Partie,* with its small world and edenic idyll. *La Marseillaise* mirrors *La Vie Est à Nous* in its search for values through some kind of national social and political cohesion. But nature is no antidote to the ills of society in either *La Bête Humaine* or *La Règle du Jeu*. It is a force that disrupts without humanizing. *La Tosca* would have taken Renoir back again into a stylized past. But instead he goes to America and, after he has refused to do any back-lot "European" films, he insists on totally natural locations for *Swamp Water*.

In Vereen Bell's 1941 novel from which the film is taken, Tom Keefer, who lives alone in the Okefenokee Swamp until Ben Ragan finds him, has actually committed the murder for which he was sought. In Renoir's and Dudley Nichols' version, Keefer has been falsely accused and the film focuses its attention on his struggle to survive in the swamp and Ben's parallel problem with the world of the small town on the swamp's edge. The character of Keefer's daughter Julie is introduced, a wild almost mute girl, who similarly does not fit into the community. She is contrasted with Ben's nominal girl friend, Mabel McKenzie. Mabel filled with coy wiles, is so permeated with the town ethic that she reveals the secret of Keefer's existence out of pique and brings about the mob action in which Ben is almost drowned in an effort to make him tell Keefer's whereabouts. The humane potentials of the galvanized tenement dwellers in *Les Bas-Fonds* have been transformed into the potential lynch mob of *Swamp Water* (and, later, *Diary of a Chambermaid*). Instead of exploring the community as an image of a possible new society, Renoir shows it to be a violent protector of its traditional privileges and prejudices.

Renoir's post-1939 cynicism about the possibilities for society reforms the episodic local-color attempts of an undistinguished novel into a dark image of the relation of man to society. Keefer is stuck in the swamp; he is separated from society and he thrives on his separation. The society outside is basically venal and greedy. Even if Keefer does go back, what are the greater benefits of society beyond the community of two he has struck up with Ben Ragan as they trap together? The Georgia small-town world is filled with petty jealousies and avarice. The death of one of the skulking Watson brothers in the quicksand is an image of malevolent absorption and internalization in society, which contrasts with Keefer's willed and vital separation from it. To a certain extent one might even parallel Keefer's situation with Renoir's own in America, cut off from the traditions and history he knew most of his life (Renoir was forty-eight when he came to the United States), in a land where he was barely beginning to know the language, a world more rough-edged than the sophisticated society he had left, possibly more vicious. In terms of the development of Renoir's social themes, Tom Keefer's inability to decide whether or not to leave the swamp becomes part of Renoir's rejection of the belief that the social order contains any good at all, a view that characterizes his American films. For the most part they concentrate on people who are separated from the normal processes and traditions of society.

I must quickly qualify this observation by pointing out that Renoir's next American film, *This Land Is Mine* (1943) attempts to portray a man who can make a heroic gesture to affirm the best in a society under foreign occupation. Yet the hollowness of this affirmation supports my general point about Renoir's now more pessimistic attitude toward social cohesion and vitality. Albert Mory (Charles Laughton), the "hero" of *This Land Is Mine*, like Octave and La Chesnaye, considers himself to be a coward. But he takes the blame for the murder of the collaborator Georges Lambert in order to assert some relation to the people around him as well as to the vital traditions of his country. At the end of the film he is taken away by the Nazis, while Louise Martin (Maureen O'Hara), whom he has ineffectually loved, reads to his class the first paragraphs of the Declaration of the Rights of Man. The setting is supposed to be France during the Occupation, and Renoir has said that the film was made primarily for American audiences to show the difficulties of acting heroically in an occupied country. But the film was more the air of parable than reality; the theatricality of the sets in *This Land Is Mine* reflects the stylization of its morality instead of giving it a framework in which to develop vitally. The setpiece of the film is Albert Mory's speech to the courtroom, an assertion, rather than a creation, of character. It is drawn-out and static. However impassioned and forceful Laughton's delivery may be, Albert Mory is a man orating in a locked room. His speech belongs to the theater of high seriousness, not to a vital motion picture. The theme of *This Land Is Mine* is so "important" that only a wooden miming is finally achieved. In the entire film the single touch that one associates with Renoir's better work is the character of the Nazi Major von Keller, a curious blend of humanistic upbringing and totalitarian principles. Birthed in a histrionic optimism, the bare sets of *This Land Is Mine* breathe only futility. Although Renoir's intention, and the intention of Dudley Nichols' script may have been to portray the spirit of a society under occupation, *This Land Is Mine* rises only occasionally above hollow message.

Renoir's three other American films—*The Southerner, Diary of a Chambermaid,* and *The Woman on the Beach* —continue the study of the isolated individual who defines himself against, or at least apart from, the social order. In *The Southerner* Sam Tucker leaves his sharecropping life to become a tenant farmer. This is perhaps not much of a step, but it is nonetheless a step on his own, far from supervision and the boss over him. Sam and his family must go it alone on the farm, as Tom Keefer had to succeed alone in *Swamp Water.* Keefer must merely survive; Sam and his family have to bring in a crop of cotton. Storms and heat disrupt their work, but nature is at least impersonal in her attacks, and only the occasion for recommitment. The real attack comes whenever Sam goes to town. The fight in the bar is blown up from the exuberant anecdote of the novel into a statement of what life in the town is like. Tim's benevolence to the Tuckers when they are in need replaces the kindness of the character in the novel who owns the general store. In the film nothing good can come from the town. Even in this community dedicated to the land, organization beyond the individual and the family automatically brings corruption in its wake. The individual is better off away from society. Sam Tucker may have his troubles with the weather, and Tom Keefer is bitten severely by a cottonmouth moccasin; but they survive, strengthened rather than depleted.

Diary of a Chambermaid and *Woman on the Beach*, both made in 1946, together presage many social themes that Renoir will explore further in his films of the 1950s, such as *Le Carrosse d'Or, French Cancan,* and *Elena et les Hommes*. In both films the central character is basically isolated from any social framework. Renoir's Celestine is much more of an observer of society than either Mirbeau's original or the Celestine of Luis Buñuel's 1964 film version of the novel. Buñuel's Celestine gradually becomes intertwined in the lives of those she detests, especially the violent and reactionary Joseph. But Renoir's Celestine, played by the whimsical Paulette Goddard rather than the potentially menacing Jeanne Moreau of Buñuel's film, preserves even in her troubles a sense of separation. The film begins with her in a train traveling to another job in the provinces and it ends with her traveling away, with Georges, the son who has successfully broken away from the provincial gloom with her. Yet she is still writing in her diary. Buñuel's film begins in the same way, but his ends, as does the novel, with a vision of Celestine and Joseph married, running a bar for militarists and fascists in Le Havre, while Action Française demonstrators march outside.

Renoir's Celestine is obviously visiting a kind of a dream world, and the studio sets and sound stages of the French provinces to which she travels give an image of hermetic isolation and dreamlike stupor. André Bazin in a memorable phrase has referred to the "aquarium light" of these studio films of the 1940s. But the naturalistic prejudices implicit in such a phrase is misdirected. Renoir could and did make location films in this period. The choice of the studio set is a choice of treatment and atmosphere. The world of *Diary of a Chambermaid* is as closed in its way as the occupied France of *This Land Is Mine;* but its physical tone is more integrated with its themes. After the need for opening doorways in his films of the 1930s, Renoir in the 1940s presents social worlds that are more and more internalized.

There are two possible ways to interpret this kind of isolation. When it occurs within society, it is usually self-absorbed. When it occurs outside society, it embodies a sense of potential. Outside the social framework it may renew society; within the social framework it is only another image of the sterile isolation of the society itself. Positive figures, like Keefer in *Swamp Water* or Harriet in *The River,* think they can gain some perspective from their isolation. Celestine also gains strength through her detachment from any particular social order. Says Renoir of *Diary of a Chambermaid* ". . . I made it at the beginning of the period when I conceived scenes in a more concentrated theatrical form. . . ." Unlike its role in the films of the 1930s, or the 1950s, theatricality in the films of the 1940s such as *This Land Is Mine, Diary of a Chambermaid,* and *Woman on the Beach* bodies forth a sense of social and personal claustrophobia. Only Celestine, the voyaging but separate consciousness, manages to remain free enough to act. She succeeds in provoking the forces within the provincial society to break open the home of the Lanlaires, release Georges, and punish the sinister Joseph. During the filming of *Diary of a Chambermaid* the news arrived of the liberation of Paris, and the improvised crowd scene at the end of the film, in which Joseph is killed, may be a response to that event.

Woman on the Beach Renoir considers to be the story of a woman of passion. One-third of it was cut after a particularly disastrous preview in Santa Barbara. Renoir ascribes its lack of success to the inability of the public to accept such a theme at that time. But once again the interesting figure in the film is actually someone not central to the main action, the story of the relationship between the war-fatigued Lieutenant Burnett and the passionate Peggy Butler. It is, instead, Peggy's husband, Tod Butler, an artist who has gone blind in a fight with Peggy, who seems to be the most important character. Butler has chosen to isolate himself in this lonely beach house because he believes his blindness has made him incapable of relating to society any more. Like the beach along which Lange and Florelle run in *Le Crime de Monsieur Lange,* this barren beach of *Woman on the Beach,* with its hulks of ships similar also to those in *Lange,* represents a boundary world to which the individual has been pushed in his efforts to separate himself from society. But unlike Tom Keefer in *Swamp Water* or Sam Tucker in *The Southerner,* Tod Butler finds no vitality or self-renewal in his isolation from society. The gloomy beach is a dead end of the spirit. The lonely house, like the court in *Lange,* turns out to be a precarious defense against the violent passions of nature, either outside human beings or within them. The banked passions of Peggy Butler are revived by Lieutenant

Burnett, another outcast, shellshocked by an attack on his ship, plagued by a recurrent nightmare of drowning, but unable to leave the beach and his boring job with the Shore Patrol. Water in *Woman on the Beach* achieves the malevolent potential it has always had in Renoir's films to be an image of social and personal uncertainty. Instead of the fruitful replenisher of the naturalistic dreams that Renoir's critics claim, the ocean in *Woman on the Beach* bears a closer resemblance to Conrad's "destructive medium."

In the climactic scene of the film, Tod Butler burns his house with all the paintings inside that he had been preserving from the time he could see. In *None So Blind*, the novel from which the film was taken, Butler regains his sight; in the film he is still blind. Butler does, however, finally assert his creative independence of his own infirmity. In burning his house, he signals a desire to face the blank faces of both society and nature, without the usual defenses. This image of a lonely house burning on a barren beach, while a blind man watches with glee and fulfillment, completely diverts us from the nominal romantic thread of the plot. Tod Butler's art and Celestine's detachment prefigure the theme of the artistic hero, as Renoir develops it from *The River* into the films of the 1950s, just as *Diary of a Chambermaid* prefigures his interest in the Third Republic. But both films are bleak statements of what later appears in the guise of benevolence and romance.

It is again tempting to read the change in terms of Renoir's own spiritual autobiography. The pessimism and weariness with the idea of society in *La Règle du Jeu* yields in the American films to a greater emphasis on the separateness of the individual from the (usually) corrupt society. Renoir poses the question anew: what are the virtues of aloneness? what is the best relation between the individual who must assert his will in order to be free, and the society that must bend his will in order that it survive without excessive conflict? If the films of the 1930s explore the possibilities of community and relation within society, then the films of the 1940s delve into the problem of individual freedom within society and on its fringes. From the films of the 1940s onward, the two themes of society and the individual frequently move together. In the final chapter I shall discuss the development of Renoir's idea of the individual, the hero. But before that can be done, the role of society in the films after *Woman on the Beach* will be more closely defined, so that we can later see more clearly how Renoir treats the role of the individual in relation to a social world.

After *Woman on the Beach* Renoir's remaining American projects are abortive. Hollywood itself becomes caught up in the House Un-American Activities Scare of 1947, and the vision of a society attempting to purify itself by expelling foreign elements reflects gloomily on the isolated individuals and weak societies of Renoir's American films. Why *should* Tom Keefer emerge from his swamp? A faceless crowd attacks the evil Joseph in *Diary of a Chambermaid* in a manner reminiscent of the ritual murder at the end of Olivier's *Richard III*. This crowd is more anonymous than the men who almost drowned Ben Ragan in *Swamp Water*. Even though their malevolence works positively in the plot, they seem to be too easily stung to action, like the crowds of Shakespeare's history plays, the toys of the last person who exhorts them. Doing good at one moment, they are just as liable to change quickly into the anti-Dreyfusard rioters of Mirbeau's novel. This is the American darkness of Renoir's social vision. *Diary of a Chambermaid* brings back the older world of masters and servants. But the authority of the master has turned into doctrinaire rigidity and the energy of the servants has become motiveless malevolence. Only Celestine, the wan-

La Vie Est à Nous. In a scene that presages the hunting scenes of *La Règle du Jeu,* rich French fascists shoot at a target that has been adorned with a lower-class cloth cap. Below, the spying foreman (Max Dalban) attempts to use his power to romance a worker in the plant (Madeleine Sologne).

La Vie Est à Nous. At the end of the film several surging crowds meet while singing "The Internationale." Note the variety of dress from rich to poor in the crowd.

Partie de Campagne. Jean Renoir as Père Poulain, the owner of the country inn, comments on the beauty of the Parisian mother and daughter to Henri (Georges Darnoux) (facing) and Rodolphe (Jacques Brunius). Above right, Rodolphe plays Pan, complete with syrinx, to the giggles of Mme. Dufour (Jane Marken). Below right, years later Henri rows up river to the spot where he and Henriette kissed.

Partie de Campagne. Rodolphe and Henri watch Mme. Dufour and Henriette (Sylvia Bataille) from the inn.

Les Bas-Fonds. The outside of the tenement. Kostilev (Vladimir Sokoloff) between Natacha (Junie Astor) and Pepel (Jean Gabin).

Les Bas-Fonds. The Baron (Louis Jouvet) (second on left), bankrupt through gambling, tries whimsically to recoup his losses at the tenement's cardtable. Left, beside the spouting statue of a faun, Papel tries to persuade Natacha to leave the tenement with him.

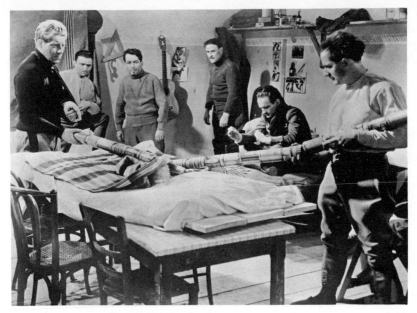

La Grande Illusion. In the first prison camp the prisoners rig up with cans a breathing system to be used in tunneling. From left to right: Maréchal (Jean Gabin), Rosenthal (Marcel Dalio), the Actor (Julien Carette), the Engineer (Gaston Modot), Boeldieu (Pierre Fresnay), the Schoolmaster (Jean Dasté). Is that a partial Star of David over Rosenthal's head? Below, another use of the central table, this time to make costumes for the amateur theatricals. The Actor, Rosenthal, Maréchal, the Engineer, and the Schoolmaster are somewhat engaged. Boeldieu looks out the window. COURTESY JANUS FILMS.

La Grande Illusion. Top, opening the trunks of clothes from Paris
to be used in the amateur theatricals, the prisoners are strangely
moved when Maisonneuve, in what starts as a joke, puts on woman's
clothes. Bottom, the theatricals. The Actor (Julien Carette) on the
tiny prison camp stage embraced by the Transvestite while the
"girls" of the chorus watch. COURTESY JANUS FILMS.

La Grande Illusion. Maréchal and Rosenthal after their escape share some food. COURTESY JANUS FILMS.

La Marseillaise. Louis XVI (Pierre Renoir) taking his breakfast while framed in the baroque elaborations of his life.

dering observer, who is basically outside the social order, retains any moral consciousness and can apply any moral sanctions, unlike the Celestine of Buñuel's version (or Mirbeau's, for that matter), who is fatally attracted to the evil. Far from being "the last real Renoir," the real vitality of *Diary of a Chambermaid* in Renoir's career is its approach toward new concerns rather than its winding down of old ones. If society is to be made whole in Renoir's films, if he wants to summon up again the optimism of his early films, then some redefinition of the individual is necessary, as well as some new idea of what constitutes the kind of heroism that can galvanize society and define it. *The River* and *Le Déjeuner sur l'Herbe* present the last faintly benevolent views of nature we see in Renoir's films, unless one would like to count the provençal section of *Le Petit Théâtre de Jean Renoir*. But nature itself plays a small role in *Le Petit Théâtre*. That film is instead an image of society in which theater and nature are truly combined. But before examining it in more detail, it is first necessary to treat the period of the 1950s.

The River, as I have discussed in an earlier chapter, brings together the house and the world around the house to affirm and accept, however partially, the processes of nature. This acceptance in fact takes place in a context in which the pressures of society are not an issue. Harriet, her parents, her sisters, and her brother live in an alien world. It may be benevolent in its strangeness and intriguing in its exoticism. But it is nevertheless alien. Satyajit Ray, the great Indian director, when he was a young film critic, interviewed Renoir on the set of *The River*. In his subsequent article, amid praise of Renoir, he allowed himself to complain that there was only one real Indian character in the entire picture. *The River*, Ray said, was not about India at all. But this sense of alienation from the "real" India is surely Renoir's point. The social context of *The River* is the family, isolated within a strange and mysterious civilization to which it never quite relates with any degree of social freedom. However kind, the family is socially embattled. It is as if Renoir has mingled the isolated house of *Woman on the Beach* with the family strength and optimism of *The Southerner*. In *The River* society and its pressures have been absorbed by the steady process of nature.

Traditionally, the river is not so much an image of nature in its variety, as it is an image of time in its inexorable flow. But Renoir begins to emphasize the possibilities of the river as an image of time only with *The River* itself. The Ganges can be such a symbol of the passage of time because, like Rauffenstein's geranium in *La Grande Illusion*, it is made into one by one of the characters, the older Harriet, who narrates the film, looking back on her youth. In one of the brief, semi-documentary sequences that describe the life of the river and its banks, Harriet remarks that the great ornate stairways that lead down into the river punctuate the river in the same way that holidays punctuate the year (and, it might be added, the festivals punctuate the film). In its inexorability the Ganges represents a powerful force of nature, linked with time, that must be yielded to, or at least understood and allowed for. Unlike the man-made fatality imaged in the railroad track of *La Bête Humaine*, the necessary rhythms of the Ganges allow some scope for human will and understanding. The "acceptance" of the rhythms of nature and the river must be more active than passive. In the beginning of the film, while the girls are still on the closer verge of childhood, Harriet says that "time slipped away unnoticed." By the end of the film Harriet and the others with her have passed from this world, in which time is unnoticed, to a world in which time exists. But this time is not the historical time of a world of politics and fame, but a personal time of human growth and understanding. After Harriet's attempt to commit suicide in the river, Captain John tells her that one of her poems might be read in A.D. 4000. The river partakes of the eternal rhythms of nature, the cycles and repetitions rather than the progress and linearity of time. Harriet's ability to detach herself from time and yet control it through her poetry parallels Sam Tucker's unremitting attempt to control nature in *The Southerner*, or Celestine's detachment from the society she serves when she writes of it in her diary. The river may be inexorable and time may bring death and loss of innocence in its wake. But art can both preserve and transcend their necessary movement. By this point in Renoir's career it has become clear that both nature and society must be absorbed into the orders and insights of art.

Because of the prominence of the artistic perspective in the recaptured innocent past of *The River,* it is fitting that Renoir's next three films, the three theater films of the 1950s, *Le Carrosse d'Or, French Cancan,* and *Elena et les Hommes,* are reconstructions of the past. Such reconstructions are not new in Renoir's work. *Nana, Le Tournoi, Madame Bovary, La Marseillaise,* and *Diary of a Chambermaid* are obvious earlier examples. But in all of these earlier films except *Diary of a Chambermaid,* the past is mainly a setting, without special meaning in itself. In these three later films, because of the theatrical method that enforces the impression of an obviously ordered and articulated world, the artistic act of reconstruction, the temporal distance between the life of the audience and the life of the film. Of the earlier films, Renoir has often remarked that one of his goals was to explode various clichés about the different historical periods, principally those clichés that might separate the life of that period from our own. The feelings of people were the same, he implies, and so he leavens the formal costume drama of *Le Tournoi* or the revolutionary

fervor of *La Marseillaise* with the realities of domestic details
and individual quirks. In *Diary of a Chambermaid* Renoir is
already closer to the attitude toward the past he will have
in the 1950s. Celestine's journey into the provincial world
of the Lanlaires is temporal as well as spatial. She seems
like an emissary from the present to the past. Their world
is theatrical and closed because they consciously erected its
limits around them through added ignorance and prejudice.
But after the possibilities of artistic order are set forth in
The River, the enclosed worlds of the theater films of
the 1950s are not images of confinement but expressions
of a vital and self-conscious artistry.

History in *French Cancan* and *Elena,* like nature in *The
River,* becomes subordinated to the demands of art. Both
films are related to *Diary of a Chambermaid* in the importance they give to the celebration of Bastille Day within
the setting of the Third Republic. Renoir in these films has
made the Third Republic into his own equivalent to Hollywood's American West, as a repository of life-giving and ener-
gizing myths for his art. Bastille Day is so important because
these films relate to the "real" history of the past in the
same way that holidays relate to the rest of the year. In
the earlier films of social reality, festivities and rituals were
the vital centers of daily human life; in these films the
entire year, the film itself, has become a festival. They
are heightenings and romanticizations of the past, not the
real thing, but a play with the real thing and therefore
more compelling. As Renoir said in 1962, "When I returned to work in France, I made films that I expressly
wished to present in a light manner. I made them for
my own pleasure, and I was tremendously amused during
their filming" (pp. 43). The films are a whimsical revival
of the past, and within the films themselves, the past is
revitalized.

The past that the films occupy is not an isolated place. Through Renoir's emphasis on their artifice, they define eternal world of art that can even absorb the parenthetical fact that Elena is actually Ingrid Bergman. Many of the actors from Renoir's films of the 1930s have roles in the films of the 1950s. They are thus cast, no doubt, because of friendship, Renoir's knowledge of their abilities, and the pleasure of bringing together something of the old *équipe*. But the symbolic effect is to make a continuity in time with Renoir's earlier work, for the film-maker to re-establish through his art a visible relation to his past career, in the same way that the films of this period attempt to make an artful continuity between Renoir's audience and a romantic yet accessible past.

The eternal perspective of art redeems the changing world of history. Renoir's emphasis in these films on the holiday is an assertion of the continuity of the unchanging amid a world of change. *La Marseillaise* and *La Vie Est à Nous* deal more seriously with history, through documents in *La Marseillaise* and documentary footage and method in *La Vie Est à Nous*, because Renoir's own interest in the reality of a society is at this point in his career more turned toward the reconstruction of its daily life. But, even when Renoir had previously contemplated great moments in history, as in *La Marseillaise*, he did not exclude the lasting values discoverable through art. This kind of interest is oddly foreshadowed in an intriguing short film he made in 1927, called *Charleston*. A black explorer in the year 2028 flies from central Africa, where civilization now has its main seat, to visit Europe, which had been thought uninhabited. In a wrecked Paris he discovers a "primitive" girl, who entrances him with her strange native dance, the Charleston. He finally hops into his spacecraft with her and goes back to Africa. Like Harriet's poems, the Charleston has outlasted the end of European civilization and all other trappings of society.

Society is expressed through theater in the 1950s because
Renoir now implies that what is worth preserving about a
society, and what he wants to express in his films, is its
sense of play rather than its sense of self-importance, its
holidays rather than its daily life. He does not raise these
values into absolute truths; they are still *divertissements* and
pochades. But they transform history rather than ignore it.

With this reconstruction of history as theater Renoir seems
finally to reject the antisocial political dimension that per-
vaded his films of the 1940s. But he turns in the direction
of a social model defined by art rather than by political
action. In consequence, the films of the 1950s are as en-
raging to socially oriented critics for their rejection of politics
as they are to naturalistically oriented critics for their rejection of nature. The whimsical way Renoir deals with the
white-horse heroism of Rollan/Boulanger in *Elena* has drawn
severe criticism. Marcel Oms, for example, has pointed to
"several ultra-fascist assertions" in *Le Déjeuner sur l'Herbe*.
This rejection of Renoir's later films may be due to the way
that certain themes, specifically those that deal with the possibility of community and a new society, take on different hues
from the nature of the times in which they are put forth.
Community, and individual renewal through community,
may remain important themes in Renoir's films. But the social
context of the times controls in great part the reaction to the
particular film. In the late 1930s Renoir could make *La
Vie Est à Nous* for the French Communist Party because
he believed that the main threat from Hitler was to the idea
of the French nation, its variety and its coherence. John
Ford, a director who shares with Renoir both the fascination
with the nature of community and the practice of working
with a stock company of actors and technicians, made *Grapes
of Wrath* in the same period. In some "objective" sense it
too is a left-wing film because it both attacks the society

for what has happened to the Joads and finds that the only solution for Tom Joad is to follow Casey the preacher and ally with the Communists. For both Ford and Renoir the primary interest rests in the possibilities of community. When that community is threatened, and left-wing solutions are the best available, they are accepted. But in the 1950s, when the community was not only threatened but seemed even totally lost, both Renoir and Ford, in their own ways, made films of the past, of the older community of relation, half nostalgic and half clearly aware of the loss. In a larger sense how much difference is there between Boudu's float down the Loing to a new life and the Provençal river of sexual liberation that carries Étienne Alexis in *Déjeuner* from his television speeches on artificial insemination to his rest beneath an olive tree near the old Renoir home at Cagnes? But in the context of the early 1930s Boudu is hailed as "anarchist," while in the late 1950s and early 1960s *Déjeuner sur l'Herbe* could be scorned for its easy pastorality, or even its "fascism." Does Renoir in the end of *Elena* really mean that the sight of love will quiet the "Rollanist" crowd? Does Ford, in *The Sun Shines Bright*, released in 1954, the year of Brown *v.* Board of Education, believe that this image of the good Judge Priest in the harmonious Southern society is an example of a social salvation that actually works? Both films are romances of history rather than history itself. In harsh times, both Renoir and Ford follow their preoccupation with community to an attempt to establish the ideal, even in the reconstructed past, rather than exploiting a more fashionable, and more acceptable, pessimism. The studio sets of *French Cancan* and *Elena* are Renoir's equivalent of the Golden World, images of possibility rather than limitation. With the loss of friends, the loss of many technicians with whom he had worked for years, and the feeling, expressed in a 1959 interview, that no one was interested in film any more, Renoir in these films could still fashion an image of coherence made by his art. Ford's communities remain in the past; when they enter time, as in *How Green Was My Valley*, they can be only corrupted. "Print the legend," says the newspaperman in *The Man Who Shot Liberty Valance*, and however Ford shows the truth behind the legend in this film, his sympathies are plainly with the affirmation of legend over truth. Renoir may also manufacture a legend. But he invites the spectator to view it as such, with all the nuances in the relation between theater and historical reality he can muster. He implies that the Third Republic does not really exist, except in impressionist painting, the cancan, and gossip about Boulanger. From his sense of artistic aloneness, he says he can make of history what he wants. Through the reconstructions and inventions of art he can affirm the possibilities of community. Renoir's perfect world of art, which absorbs the moving worlds of nature and time, accomplishes its work through the operations of the tireless and perpetually moving artistic ego. In fascinating parallel to the movement of his own career—working with the *équipe* in the 1930s, under American production pressure in the 1940s, and returning to France in the 1950s—Renoir's attitude toward the interrelation of individual creativity and social value changes from cautious idealism about community, through pessimism based on individual isolation, to the potential of a community of art created from the society of the past.

Le Testament du Docteur Cordelier (1959) and Le Déjeuner sur l'Herbe (1959) are like tragic and comic versions of the same basic situation: the assertion, in the name of society, of a scientific viewpoint that actually runs counter to the real needs of society. Le Déjeuner sur l'Herbe refers to organized society with comic allusiveness; its real subject is the pastoral retreat and reinvigoration. *Cordelier* exists within a society, the world of Paris, but it is curiously hermetic. Cordelier in his laboratory, and, more comically, Étienne Alexis on the television screen, have sealed themselves off from possible sources of vitality in relations with others. Étienne Alexis can replenish himself through love and sexuality; Cordelier's only contact with sexuality occurs when he seduces his female patients while they are under sedatives, and the room of Opale, his alter-ego, is filled with whips and other sado-masochist paraphernalia.

In *Déjeuner* the pastoral world of Provence can work a transformation on Étienne Alexis so that he can escape his world of international pomposity and television to marry Nénette. Marriage reconciles in *Déjeuner*, but the only reconciliation possible in *Cordelier* is in death. To complement its bleak world of Parisian streets, laboratories, and offices, *Cordelier* carries a heavy weight of moralism couched in semi-religious terms, which indicts man's disruption of nature in accents reminiscent of the anti-science Hollywood monster movie. The same cautionary note appears in *Déjeuner*, but there, to suit the lighter tone of the film, it is handled by the garrulous old priest who attacks Étienne's grand views of remaking society. The roof on his church is full of holes, he says. Start with that. In *Cordelier* it is Renoir himself who speaks the heavily moralistic commentary. But although these religious values are invoked, they are not really central. In *Déjeuner* the active manipulator who really effects the new society is the Pan-like wanderer Gaspard; the priest makes only a few choruslike comments. If anything, the priest and Renoir's narrator represent a kind of ineffectually severe moralism that stands apart from social structure and institutional truth. The Church takes as little care of the priest as do society and technology. The priest's real equivalent in *Cordelier* is the psychiatrist, who puts forward similar platitudes about what is most valuable, without trying at all to effect them. Gaspard and his goat Cabri, on the other hand, transform a society that communicates mainly through television into something more vital. The talk about "the international family of Europe" in the pompous rhetoric of the early sections of the film is transformed after the marriage of Étienne and Nénette into a round of handshakes with the people attending the wedding. The critique of contemporary society and technology may be as severe as it is in the gloomy *Cordelier*. But the image of renewal through romance in both the aesthetic and emotional senses relates *Le Déjeuner sur l'Herbe* to the three films of theater and history that have just preceded it, and it presages the new synthesis of art and nature Renoir will achieve in *Le Petit Théâtre de Jean Renoir*. In *Renoir, My Father*, he describes such a synthesis through Auguste Renoir's visit to an eighteenth-century ruin:

> At Sirvigny he muttered the name of Watteau to himself, and hummed one of Mozart's airs. The place had once been the property of some nobleman. The château had been razed during the Revolution. The few parts of wall which had survived were buried in a mass of vegetation. Renoir meditated with some emotion on the spectacle of a human achievement reverting to nature. He saw in it a subtle marriage, a blending of nature and art somewhat akin to what he himself was so passionately searching for in his painting. I often heard him express his regret that he had never been able to visit Angkor, to see the statues of the gods amidst the tangle of jungle growth (p. 347).

Le Caporal Épinglé (1962) has none of the fabulous atmosphere of *Cordelier* or *Le Déjeuner sur l'Herbe*. After the separations from a real society and a real history that marked most of Renoir's films after *La Règle du Jeu,* the milieu of *Le Caporal Épinglé* is totally realistic, even somberly so, with the gray mistiness of its space recalling films of the early 1930s like *La Nuit du Carrefour.* (*Le Caporal* and *Cordelier* are Renoir's only films since *Diary of a Chambermaid* not to be made in color.) In *Le Caporal* Renoir re-enters the world of history, with the adventures of a corporal and his friends during World War II, as they try to escape from a series of German prison camps. The film therefore naturally, but in fact uncomfortably, recalls *La Grande Illusion.* Any comparison between the two must take into account the distance Renoir has traveled aesthetically and personally since the earlier film. To say that *Le Caporal Épinglé* tries to do for World War II what *La Grande Illusion* did for World War I ignores differences between the two films mediated by the change in Renoir's attitude toward society. After the historical romances of *French Cancan* and *Elena,* Renoir is re-entering the world of "real" public history. To emphasize this "objective" reality he punctuates *Le Caporal Épinglé* with documentary shots—often harsh and brutal—of World War II, on the battlefield and in cities under siege. But the alternation between documentary and "story" does not try to relate the personal story of the Corporal to the larger world of the war, as a similar relation of the realistic and fictional accomplishes in *La Vie Est à Nous.* In fact the newsreel's unalloyed violence throws the complacency and unreality of the Corporal's world into greater relief. Like the news of the recapture of Douaumont in *La Grande Illusion,* the documentary footage of *Le Caporal Épinglé* shows a world of war that has little to do with the inhabitants of the prison camp. But whereas the characters in *La Grande Illusion* were trying to relate to this outside world, the self-involved characters in *Le Caporal Épinglé* totally ignore the public context. The Corporal screams in the dentist's office and his scream becomes an announcer reporting the bombing of London.

Society outside the prison is in an advanced stage of disintegration. Society within the prison does not seem at all able to renew or reinvigorate the outside society, although at first in *Le Caporal Épinglé* it appears to be the potential microcosm of a better social world that the prison camp society in *La Grande Illusion* aspired to be. The characters in the little world of *Le Caporal Épinglé* may have even greater pretensions than those in *La Grande Illusion*. They claim that the prison is a haven where no one ever speaks of class distinctions. No one there cares what you were on the outside. Paris is a place of ruts, roads, and rivers, where a man can't be free. In the prison camp there is a better kind of freedom, a new harmony worked by the situation of war and imprisonment. As the Corporal says in Renoir's traditional metaphor of sociability, "We'll all eat together in Paris when we escape."

Part of the need for escape in *La Grande Illusion* is to bring some of the evolved values of the prison camp community into the larger society outside. We do not see the possibilities realized, but they do exist as potentials. In the harsher light of *Le Caporal Épinglé* the communal and personal possibilities engendered by the prison camp are shown to be just another illusion, not a saving illusion, like the myths of the French past or the French nation, but an insubstantial and inauthentic impulse toward others that cannot bear pressure of any sort. In *Le Caporal Épinglé* the dynamics of escape run directly against the "harmony" of the prison society. After a few abortive escapes the Corporal comes to a camp where his friend Ballochet has gotten a sinecure as German-French translator, even though Ballochet knows not one word of German. But there is good food and warmth. Says Ballochet to the Corporal, "Free-

dom is not all on the other side of the barbed wire." He
sits in what he calls his tower above the battle, and
is comfortable. The Corporal at first accepts this quietness,
the freedom in isolation from the outside world. But the
image finally proves insufficient for him and he tries to
escape again. This time he succeeds, along with Pater, who
next to Ballochet has been his greatest friend in the film.
But when the Corporal and Pater reach Paris, the dream
of a new society of equals, which the prison world promised,
does not appear. At the end of *La Grande Illusion* the
meaning of the escape of Maréchal and Rosenthal may be
uncertain, but it has the potential of optimism and regenera-
tion. At the end of *Le Caporal Épinglé* the Corporal and
Pater, who have gone through so much together, separate
with a few perfunctory good-bys. Pater mumbles that he
is sure the Corporal has a few friends in Paris he will want
to see, and the Corporal does not contradict him. The social
difference implicit in the fact that the Corporal is never
given a name, only a title, has become a reality once again
in the world outside the prison camp. The lifeboat has
landed and all the camaraderie has vanished as each survivor
strikes out for his own life. Pater walks away down the
Pont de Tolbiac, while the camera, high above the roadway
of the bridge, gazes after him.

The society that the army and the prison camp has
spawned in *Le Caporal Épinglé* has no vitality to keep it
going when the threat of danger has disappeared. It has
no symbolic or mythic core like the idea of the nation in
La Marseillaise, the world made by art in *French Cancan*
and *Elena*, or even the crumbling brotherhood of the aristocracy in *La Grande Illusion*. The old German on the train,
who tells the Corporal and Pater how much he likes the
French, first tries to stop the German soldiers from arresting
them, and then is killed in an Allied bombardment (which

helps them to escape). He represents a lost internationalism that could have countered the self-centered nationalism that caused the war. As the Corporal and Pater struggle toward the border, they pass a farmer in a field, who turns out to be French and gives them food and directions. He had been a prisoner here in the last war and had returned to marry the German woman who owned the farm where he had been billeted. In a way he is Maréchal finally come back to Elsa, and to a reconciliation outside the orders of society. But the Corporal and Pater must push on to Paris and their final separation.

The distance between the social visions of *La Grande Illusion* and *Le Caporal Épinglé* might be measured, in typical Renoir terms, by the different attitudes toward food in each film. In the earlier film the food can symbolize a possible new society; in the later the symbol exists without any social reality to make it significant. The little community in *La Grande Illusion* shares Rosenthal's food. But in *Le Caporal Épinglé*, when the Corporal comes back from the dentist, full of fervor because the German dental assistant has told him she admires a man who tries to escape and does not like men who are slaves, he pushes all of Ballochet's food to the floor and punches Ballochet in the mouth, to signal his rejection of the comforts of prison life. His action is as romantic and self-deluding as was his final parting with the pretty dental assistant, who has briefly brightened his life and who has given him a copy of Ronsard when he leaves. The Corporal's rage at Ballochet's food is an attack on the symbol rather than the reality. In fact, the Corporal has no vital vision of society beyond himself and the men who continually defer to him. Étienne Alexis can marry Nénette in the pastoral fantasy of *Le Déjeuner sur l'Herbe*. Even if his tails are ripped down the back seam, or perhaps because they are, he can freely partake of a binding and har-

monizing social ritual. But in the Corporal's more realistic
world, without the solace of art or the frame of theater, he
cannot be truly free enough to relate to anyone outside himself. The Corporal's final aloneness is the tragedy of the ego
unmediated by art, the tragedy of society breaking down because no one can understand and reveal its vitality. It is
the tragedy of a desire for limits which, though freely accepted, are mistaken for a desire for freedom itself. The
Corporal uses the forms of society to escape, even to the
extent of joining a funeral procession. But he has no feeling
for the possible vitality of society. "Pinned" (*épinglé*) the
Corporal is. No matter where he goes, he carries the prison
of his ego with him.

CHAPTER FIVE

The Possibilities of Heroism

In reality, the most beautiful landscapes achieve their
true significance only when they are shown in relation
to a character . . . a human presence; therefore we
must first look for the figure of man!

—JEAN RENOIR, 1960

In the cinema what counts isn't objects but human
beings.

—JEAN RENOIR, 1961

The gloomy view of society, which permeates *Le Caporal
Épinglé*, is a direct function of the Corporal's egoism, the
realistic equivalent of the more fabulous egos of Étienne
Alexis and Dr. Cordelier. The only society that exists even
for a moment in *Le Caporal* is the society of the Corporal's
admirers. Neither Ballochet nor Pater wishes to lose face
before the Corporal. He wants to escape and they follow,
even if they don't especially want to. The Corporal is a
hero who knows it, and tries to do heroic things. He punches
Ballochet because the young girl at the dentist's office made
him think he was no longer a hero. Heroism is equated
with physical freedom and self-assertion rather than with understanding; an escape then necessarily defines the self as
heroic, even though it might be accomplished through ano-

nymity and death. In a long scene after the Corporal rejects
Ballochet's concept of the tower above the fighting and just
before Ballochet himself tries to escape, Ballochet tries to explain to the Corporal what he thinks of heroism, why he
wants to be heroic on the Corporal's model, and how his
dreams have failed. He tells all this to the Corporal, while
they are on a cistern-cleaning crew for punishment, and Ballochet himself is sitting on the toilet. The setting emphasizes
the contrast between the talk of superhuman heroism, in the
person of the World War I pilot Guynemer (whom Ballochet
calls "the Knight of the Skies") and the natural processes common to everyone. When Ballochet makes his fatal escape,
with no plan whatsoever, he reminds everyone before he goes
that he is a gas-company employee. In some sense he is
really escaping from the Corporal, who exemplifies the kind
of dead-end heroism that has led so many to needless death;
and Ballochet is also escaping from the army society itself,
no longer a place of camaraderie and equality, the possible
germ of a new society, but instead the repository of the archaic forms of the social order. As Renoir has said about
Guynemer, with whom he served in World War I, "He was
possessed by a kind of strength he really didn't understand.
He went off shooting down innumerable German planes
in a kind of frenzy, perhaps forgetting that there were
human beings inside of the planes. There's always a kind
of inhumanity about heroism. The Garden of Eden had a
population of non-heroes."

The Maréchal-like Frenchman and his German wife that
the Corporal and Pater meet as they escape may have
achieved something like a Garden of Eden without heroes.
But the world outside their farm needs some model for
human behavior, even in the post-heroic age of *Le Caporal
Épinglé*. The only kernel of heroic possibility that appears
in the film is Ballochet's metaphor of Don Quixote and

Sancho Panza: the individual will be able to realize himself when Don Quixote and Sancho Panza, the dream and the reality, can be brought together, he says. But the final image of *Le Caporal Épinglé* is, as I have said, an image of melancholic and inevitable separation. Within the social context of this world, there is no ground for the flourishing of an individuality that can be both exemplary and humanly satisfying. Because there are no authentic relationships between men or between men and women, there can be neither individuality nor society.

Ballochet's allusion to Don Quixote and Sancho Panza recalls Harriet's characterization of Nan, the children's nurse, in *The River*. She was the one, Harriet says, who brought reality back to dream and dream back to reality. The Corporal's unreflective desire for freedom leads him away from the community of others. But the possibility that lives on in Renoir's films, strengthened by the cautionary notes of *Cordelier* and *Le Caporal Épinglé,* is the bridging hero, the intermediary, who can bring together Don Quixote and Sancho Panza. *Le Caporal Épinglé* dissolves forever the belief that such a character can be found in a totally realistic social context that excludes the perspective of art. It is in fact the public historical context of *Le Caporal* that makes such a turning away so necessary. As Renoir has said,

> The 1939 war was not an epic war. It was a war of jails, a war of propaganda, a war of cruelty. It was a war for people who weren't the size of the people in the First War. The people in the First War were like knights during a crusade of the twelfth century or characters from an episode in Vergil. The 1939 period gives us characters who are petit-bourgeois. They have a greatness of their own, of course, but a different style of greatness.

In World War II men are more trapped by their social roles; they cannot see outside them and into the larger context of society. Renoir's new sense of perspective and his search for the proper hero in which to embody that perspective, arise directly from his interest in the relation of individual to society in the intensified atmosphere of war. The hero who bridges the continual antinomies of society and nature, artifice and reality, has been slowly defined in the course of Renoir's career, not by continual increment, but by Renoir's usual creative process of multiple awareness, variation, and elaboration, following first one possibility and then others.

An interest in the changing nature of the hero is often subtly influenced by a director's feeling for his actors, as he experiences them in the day-to-day business of casting, rehearsal, and actual shooting. A master of mise-en-scène like Alfred Hitchcock, who works for totally articulated effects, frequently subordinates his actors or at best treats them as technical devices equivalent in function to a camera angle or a fragment of sound. In Renoir's films, where the total effect is ironic and complex, actors become more important. The characters in Renoir's films are often in fact the vehicles of the film's complexity, their motives uncertain and their actions without straightforward significance. Repeated viewings of *La Règle du Jeu* still leave the viewer without a certain grasp of the motivations and inner nature of the main characters. What might the film had been like if Simone Simon had played Christine, Fernand Ledoux (Roubaud in *La Bête Humaine*) played La Chesnaye, and Pierre Renoir played Octave (all Renoir's first choices for the roles)? The character and physical presence of an actor could totally change a script's basic premises.

When Hitchcock talks about his films, as in the interview with François Truffaut, he often formulates each film as an experiment with a particular technical problem. When Renoir talks about the genesis of his films, he invariably leaves technique and even theme aside to discuss the actors with whom he has worked. Why did he make *La Bête Humaine?* Jean Gabin always wanted to play a railroad engineer. *This Land Is Mine?* He wanted to work with Charles Laughton. In *Diary of a Chambermaid, Woman on the Beach,* and *Le Carrosse d'Or,* Paulette Goddard, Joan Bennett, and Anna Magnani were, respectively, the main attractions.

Renoir has not always been so taken with his actors and actresses as the vital centers of his films. The films of the 1920s, in fact, tend to project a feeling, like that frequently expressed by Hitchcock, that the characters are mere puppets of the director. The puppet-show stage itself appears, as I have mentioned, in *La Chienne* (1931), carrying with it an implication of the fatality that rules the lives of the characters. The general context of Renoir's silent films is a stable society, and within it Renoir seems to consider his characters, devoid as they are of the dimension of speech, to be mere cartoons, or mechanical beings. Catherine Hessling, his first wife, who stars in *La Fille de l'Eau, Nana, Charleston,* and *La Petite Marchande d'Allumettes,* enhances the sense of mechanism by her stylized gestures and abrupt movements, which give an air of comic geometricity to even the most serious scenes.

Far from allowing this kind of mechanical style to be an overwhelming limitation, Renoir plays with its implications, just as he exploits and expands all the givens of film. Hessling's comic bustle in *Nana* enhances the presentation of Nana's self-enclosure and theatricality. Renoir himself in this period is preoccupied with technical problems and experiments, even as he brings his cameras outside to explore nature, piling Méliès on Lumière. His fondest and clearest memory of the lost film *Marquita* (1927) is the miniature reconstruction of the Barbès-Rochechouart Métro station, enlarged by mirrors, with holes especially cut out to fit the shapes of the actors. For the production of *La Petite Marchande d'Allumettes* the next year, Renoir and his associates set up an atelier in the garret of Le Vieux Colombier, appropriately enough a theater that had adhered to the older theatrical illusions in the face of the growing popularity of "naturalist" theaters like André Antoine's Théâtre Libre. There the group invented many new technical devices and brought the film from first day to completion by their own aesthetic and artisanal efforts. As Renoir has said,

I began to make movies because I loved trick shots (*trucage*). At the beginning I had no intention of writing or becoming an author and inventing stories. My ambition was to create trick shots, and I haven't done so badly since then.

Renoir in these films is therefore as much *menteur* as *meneur*, to adapt a pun from the *Phaedrus*. And this "love of faking," this fascination with special effects, permeates *La Petite Marchande d'Allumettes*. The Little Match Girl walks through a world of double exposures, matte shots, stop-motion, and innumerable other bits of cinematic fantasy and surrealism. Three years before Cocteau's *Le Sang d'un Poète*, Renoir in *La Petite Marchande* encyclopedizes and half-invents all the devices of the avant-garde cinema. The story furnishes only a pretext, or at best a liberation, for his technical imagination. When the Little Match Girl arrives in the world of her dreams, the human figure she first sees is a ballerina forever impaled on her turning bar, endlessly spinning when someone winds her box.

To complement this interest in the mechanical and the technical, few of the characters in Renoir's films of the 1920s are as problematic as they are to become in the films of the 1930s. Whether the Little Match Girl of fantasy or the Pierre Hoffer of reality (in *Le Bled*), these heroes fill forms rather than define complex personalities. Stylization and social acceptance are the keys to the way these films express character; they amalgamate Renoir's personal interests with the silent film canons of expressionist characterization, broad gesture, and frequent mugging. Even in the more elaborate productions like *Le Tournoi* and *Le Bled* the characters are caught up in a world and a society that they can only join; and they are rarely recalcitrant.

Such mechanical and socially conservative heroes disappear from the films of the 1930s because Renoir can no longer manipulate them as easily as he had before. With speech, they have become more complex. They imply a richness beyond the lines they speak and the actions they make, and that extra dimension must be understood and utilized. One reason Renoir is considered the father of neo-realism is his use of non-professionals in *Toni*. In fact, there are also non-professionals in important roles in *La Nuit du Carrefour*, to name only one earlier film. The Russian directors are great theorists of the non-professional actor. But such theories are obviously unsuited for the sound film, or at least they were solely created for the silent film, in which personality makes little difference, because the goal of the director is so often related to texture and atmosphere. Renoir uses non-professional actors in *Toni* to image their confinement through their inability to see beyond the surfaces of their role, a typically non-professional attitude. During the making of *Le Caporal Épinglé* he said that he liked non-professionals in everything but acting. When I later reminded him of this statement and the use of non-professionals in *Toni* and films as late as *The River*, he elaborated by saying that it was the play between the professionals and the non-professionals that he was after there. No canon of art should be absolute, and contrast and enrichment is more to be desired than any simple equation. The professional learns spontaneity from the non-professional, and the non-professional learns order and shape from the professional. Like the distinguishable but separate world of the natural and the stylized, or the different make-up of the main characters in *Nana,* both work together to enrich the final picture.

The concentration on the hero and the society against or within which he defines himself is, then, basically a development of Renoir's sound films. Renoir has said that the one thing that the sound era accomplished was to take the focus away from the stars, because with the heavy sound camera directors could no longer easily concentrate on a face and its nuances. As if to compensate for that technical separation of the camera from the character, Renoir's sound films focus more and more on the dynamics of the relation of a character to his milieu. As our apprehension of cinematic character moves from the external to the internal, so the character itself is placed within a social milieu, and defined by its own circumstances and the many connections it has with the world around it. In a play the character will often step outside the proscenium frame in order to approach the audience and explain his particular perspective, like Thersites in Shakespeare's *Troilus and Cressida.* But in Renoir's films, the pressure of society always must have an effect on the main character. The theme of his films through the 1930s and 1940s gradually becomes the character's effort to define himself against rather than within the social framework. The silent films accept a hierarchic but benevolent society. In the early sound films the society is more inimical, its taboos more ridiculous and venal, as in *La Chienne* or *Boudu,* and the possibilities of communities created by persons of good will are more precarious, as in *Lange,* or farcical and dreamlike, as in *Chotard.* Gradually through these films the shape of Renoir's typical hero takes form, varying as Renoir's own views of the different forces creating his character vary. The

individual in many of these films tries to bring his natural
energy into the structures of society. Theater may order and
protect this energy against society's potential violence, but by
the end of the 1930s such protection is futile, and society
becomes a crowded monster swallowing up a fragile and
crumbling inner world. What refuge there is from such pessimism about society centers on the hero. Robert de la Chesnaye's theatricals in *La Règle de Jeu,* however ineffectual, are
a momentary attempt to absorb and possibly to transcend
the malevolent forces of society and politics. The guests even
sing on the stage a boulangist song, "En revenant d'la revue,"
a presaging of the romanticization of the boulangist era
that Renoir is to accomplish in *Elena et les Hommes.* But
La Règle du Jeu tries to leave politics out. One firm mark of
the change in Renoir's idea of character in these films is the
movement from Boudu in 1931 to La Chesnaye in 1939.

Two possibilities for heroism present themselves in the
films of the 1930s: heroics to help society, and heroics that
exist in spite of society. Renoir's central characters in these
films have a sense of their own separateness that none of
the characters of his silent films possess. René Fauchois'
play focuses on Lestingois, not Boudu, and it ends with
marriage. Renoir's film ends with Boudu's return to a life
outside society. He has tasted the world of Paris and he
doesn't like it. But the tragic figure of the film, if such farce
can be tragic, is Lestingois, decked out in leaves and tunic
with all the women around him, in weary contrast to the
leaping faun of the stage prologue. Boudu can be free, but
such a choice is not open to Lestingois. Through artifice he
flirts with freedom. Boudu and Lestingois are a fated pair,
with the socialized man forever mesmerized by the boorish
man of nature. But the true process of Renoir's films explores
the possibilities open for Lestingois much more than it does
the freedoms of Boudu. The only figure in all the films of

La Marseillaise. A dinner given by the Jacobins for the Marseillais in a
Champs-Elysées restaurant is interrupted by a group of Royalists. On the
right side of the table are Arnaud (Andrex), Bomier (Charles Blavette),
and the painter Javel (Paul Dullac). The role of Bomier in the finished film
is played by Edmond Ardisson. Charles Blavette, who had played Toni,
began the role but became ill at ease in it and was replaced. He remains in
scenes like this one, which had been taken before his departure and were
perhaps too expensive to reshoot. Below, two little girls sit under an arch
of the fallen Bastille, while around them Paris is draped in celebration.

La Marseillaise. The Parisians welcome the
Marseillais to Paris. One of Renoir's rare crowd scenes.

La Bête Humaine. Grandmorin (Jacques Berlioz) is discovered
murdered in his train compartment. In the novel Jacques Lantier had
seen the murder through the train window while he had been
walking in the woods. In the film he is on the train itself, but the
audience sees it through the window.

La Bête Humaine. Renoir as Cabuche, the poacher falsely accused of the murder. Below, Séverine (Simone Simon) is embraced by her husband Roubaud (Fernand Ledoux) before a mirror that reveals her growing disdain for him.

La Bête Humaine. Jacques Lantier (Jean Gabin) peers at himself in the mirror, doubling his nature, human and bestial, as he picks up the knife with which he will murder Séverine. Below, the murder of Séverine, on the bed, like the murder in *La Chienne,* and, like that murder and the earlier murder of Grandmorin, observed from a distance, in those through a window, here through a doorway.

La Règle du Jeu. "Oh well, what is natural these days?"
asks Christine (Nora Grégor) as she sits before her make-up
mirror, while Lisette (Paulette Dubost), her maid, looks on.
Below, Robert de la Chesnaye (Marcel Dalio) unveils on the
small stage of his home the latest addition to his collection
of odd mechanical objects—an elaborate calliope. COURTESY
JANUS FILMS.

La Règle du Jeu. In a scene reminiscent of his party-wrecking role in
Buñuel's *L'Age d'Or,* Gaston Modot as Schumacher the gamekeeper
fires at Marceau the poacher (Julien Carette), crouching behind the
chair at right. Lisette, the wife Schumacher fears is being poached,
tries to pull his arm away. Above right, Christine and Octave
(Jean Renoir) outside the La Chesnaye chateau. Below right, a
production shot showing the camera setup for the previous shot.
COURTESY JANUS FILMS.

Swamp Water. The search for Tom Keefer (Walter Brennan). In t' center pirogue from left are Thursday Ragan (Walter Huston) the Sheriff (Eugene Palette), and Julie Keefer (Anne Baxter)

This Land Is Mine. Polite banter by the Nazi Major von Keller (Walter Slezak) (second on right) answers the sharp remarks of Louise Martin (Maureen O'Hara), while collaborationist Georges Lambert (George Sanders) looks on. Below, Albert Mory (Charles Laughton) is arrested before his class, while Louise Martin (at left) stands ready to take the class for him.

The Southerner. Left, Sam Tucker (Zachary Scott) catches a fish barehanded to show the plenty of his new land. Below left, Devers (J. Carroll Naish) (at right) refuses help to Sam Tucker, even though they are neighbors. Below, on their return from the festivities in town, Sam and Nona, his wife (Betty Field), look at their storm-wrecked home. Sam's grandmother (Beulah Bondi) is in the center.

Diary of a Chambermaid.
Joseph (Francis Lederer)
confides to Célestine
(Paulette Goddard) his
plan for stealing the Lanlaire
silver. Below, another
production shot. Renoir (at
right) directs the final fight
between Georges Lanlaire
(Hurd Hatfield) and Joseph.
Paulette Goddard is between
them.

the 1930s who achieves some kind of perspective on both his own nature and the nature of the society of which he is a part is Pierre Renoir's Maigret in *La Nuit du Carrefour*. I have described its gloomy atmosphere above, in Chapter 1. Maigret represents in the context of Renoir's other films of the 1930s, a detachment from nature and society that can view them both fully, and at the same time present some kind of rational solution for their contradictions. He is a touchstone, a kind of ideal of understanding that stands in the background, while more central figures like Maurice Legrand of *La Chienne* and Boudu choose the way of the declassed clochard.

The lack of sympathy for the Boudu figure as a hero is supported by the way in which only the nasty characters in many of the films of the 1930s—Rodolphe in *Bovary*, Gaby in *Toni*, Rodolphe in *Partie de Campagne*—have any real freedom; all toy with the more serious characters and come out ahead. Boudu as hero embodies a kind of spontaneous behavior that exists without any understanding of society. In the context of a search for heroism within society, he is a dead-end. If he stays in society, Boudu is in danger of turning into Batala, the scheming publisher in *Le Crime de Monsieur Lange*, with his whimsical violence and rapacious sexuality. But in *Lange* society is not made up of fusty liberal Lestingoises, and Batala is opposed by an overpowering sense that values beyond the individual must also be served. In self-seekers like Batala, the natural morality of the oblivious Boudu has soured into sexual and economic opportunism. Boudu's seduction of Madame Lestingois and his winning of the raffle can be equated with Batala's rape of Edith and his attempt to take back the flourishing commune.

Renoir's paradigm for heroism in the 1930s derives more from the social problems of Lestingois than from the natural solutions of Boudu. The example of Maigret is not developed further because at this point in Renoir's career it may be too cynical, too separated from society, to suit Renoir's other themes. Maigret serves his society by finding criminals. But in order to do this he must subordinate all parts of his own nature but his eyes and brain. Renoir has pruned away Mrs. Maigret from the Simenon novel and emphasized the attraction of Else Andersen for Maigret, in order to underline Maigret's coldness and personal detachment. The society he deals in is a primitive one of basic needs and natural barrenness. In this simplified crossroads world Renoir can explore the hard-eyed detachment of Maigret. But the pressure to deal with a more complex society yields different conceptions of the hero in the other films of the 1930s.

After *Lange* the most important hero in Renoir's films up to *La Règle du Jeu* is the displaced aristocrat, the man who reaches out to define himself individually in the face of a crumbling order to which he can no longer relate. Some of the values Renoir expresses through this figure draw on a combination of Maigret, the man who can move easily into intimacy with all classes (including the criminal) and Boudu, the clochard from outside the normal class structure, who disrupts everyone within it. But, unlike the two earlier figures, the aristocrat has the virtues of both detachment from the social order and involvement with his individual fate. The Baron in *Les Bas-Fonds*, Boeldieu in *La Grande Illusion*, Louis XVI and Saint-Laurent in *La Marseillaise*, and La Chesnaye in *La Règle du Jeu*, become heroes of perception who are set against the more obvious heroes of action. Lange can be both, his perception directly transformed into action for the good of the co-operative. But the aristocrat is a man who is politically and socially isolated, because his own class or group is vanishing, even while he sympathizes with the classes that are on the march. The Baron accepts the financial loss that declasses him and enters fervently into the life of the tenement. Boeldieu approves the new world, but he accepts his personal doom and dies quixotically. Saint-Laurent can stand neither his own class nor the revolutionaries, but admires the latter, while Louis XVI views the Revolution as a play he would rather be watching than acting in. La Chesnaye preserves order in *La Règle du Jeu* because he knows full well that he is standing on the verge of chaos. In the films without such figures, some balance is lost. The rhetoric aimed at workers and farmers in *La Vie Est à Nous* threatens to overpower Renoir's larger vision, of a society made up of all classes and peoples in France. Toni and Jacques Lantier (in *La Bête Humaine*) can act and have authentic emotions; but they cannot in fact get enough outside themselves to achieve anything more permanent. Each in effect commits suicide. Both "deaths" proclaim the bankruptcy of the heroic pretensions of the natural man in Renoir, of the Boudu conception of what is freedom in human nature. Without limits man cannot define himself and his will; and he becomes a slave to the demands of the nature within or the nature without.

The puppet-show frame of *La Chienne* and the cold eye of Inspector Maigret hold the events of the world at a distance in order to control them, in much the same way that the director can control his actors and the created world in which they live. In the films without such control, such as *Toni* and *La Bête Humaine,* the inexorable forces of nature dominate the characters. Between these poles of fate and will Renoir constructs his films as forever interplaying relationships between himself and his actors. Even when there is a prepared script, he emphasizes improvisation.

During the filming of *Boudu,* Renoir developed what he refers to as his invariable rehearsal method. The lines are spoken the first few times without any expression at all. Only gradually do the actors work their ways into the parts. The movement is from the inside; the characters must have an inner authenticity apart from his costume. In an example Renoir cites frequently, he tells of a director assigning the part of a sailor. "A normal bad actor would work hard in order to have the real costume, the real walk, the real language of a sailor. Perhaps he will even take a trip on a boat to be burned by the real wind of the sea. Perhaps he will buy a real sailor coat from a real sailor. As a result, when he appears on the set, he will look like a real ham. Now let's try Chaplin as a sailor. He will arrive with derby, little cane, big shoes. But inside he'll be so much a real sailor that he'll be convincing despite the fact that his costume isn't right." Such a method of displaying character is developed by Renoir only with the advent of sound films; the more stylized and stereotyped characters of the silent films, with their unexamined societies, urged no interplay between personality and role. But the sound film and the 1930s themselves, as a cultural context, work on Renoir's method and ideas to yield a new interest in both society and the perspective from which society is viewed and defined. In the two films made within a six-month period, *Les Bas-Fonds* and *La Grande Illusion,* Renoir ends with a long shot of two people, in the first surrounded by the black of an inset, in the second by the white Swiss snow. I have already discussed our interest in the individuals: where are they in their frailty? But we are also interested in the perspective from which we view them: why has the director chosen this detached point of view? I have argued above that the ends of these films are inconclusive statements about the nature of society, because there is no clear future indicated for the characters. They are also inconclusive because Renoir's own perspective—the choice of position for the camera eye—has not itself been resolved, poised as it is between detachment and involvement.

The figure of the detached aristocrat who sympathizes with

the world to come offers a preliminary resolution of the problem of social involvement and aesthetic detachment. Our sympathies are attracted to these figures from almost the first moment. In *Les Bas-Fonds* we are with the Baron for the first few scenes and in many later scenes we adopt his perspective. Boeldieu's desire for clarity dominates the first scene of *La Grande Illusion,* and the moving camera of the first scene of *La Marseillaise* ends down many hallways and opening doors with Louis XVI in his canopied bed. But all these figures must be left behind in one way or another by the end of their respective films, as Renoir himself leaves behind this kind of character to search for new possibilities. From the Baron we move our center of interest to Pepel and Natacha; from Boeldieu to Maréchal and Rosenthal; from Louis XVI to Arnaud and Bomier. In *La Règle du Jeu* the movement from La Chesnaye to Octave and Marceau seems to repeat this pattern. But the effect is in fact more complicated, first because of the presence of André Jurieu, the aviator and hero in the eyes of the world, and second, because of Octave himself, played by Renoir, who in his intermediary status partakes of the role of the aristocrat and in his personal artistic classlessness looks forward to the kind of heroes who will preoccupy Renoir in the 1950s.

One possible clue to Renoir's sympathies for particular characters is the roles he plays himself: the relatively minor. part of Poulain, the innkeeper in *Partie de Campagne,* the larger part of Cabuche, the falsely accused poacher in *La Bête Humaine,* and the major role of Octave in *La Règle du Jeu.* Poulain can express Renoir's ambivalence in the role of director, the front man for the *équipe,* for he is a kind of go-between, who furnishes house and food for both the local young men and the visiting Parisian family. He opens the window of his inn to the young men so that they can see Henriette swinging on the swing, and then he disappears, along with his servant, played by Marguerite Renoir, the film's editor. Thus the two constructers of the film have in effect set up the situation and allowed the characters to work it out for themselves. Their actions may constitute an image of the process of improvisation, the amalgam of order and spontaneity through which Renoir defines a film. But in terms of political involvement and the pressure on the individual to decide what society he wishes to belong to, such a disappearance constitutes a kind of aesthetic evasion, similar in its way to the mock-idyll of *Partie de Campagne* itself.

The figure of Cabuche explores further this kind of evasion. In many ways he is a counterpart to Jacques Lantier. But instead of being dominated by nature as Lantier is, Cabuche is a natural, a man who can fly into rages, but who is basically gentle, only to be imposed upon by the officiousness of the society that has decided in its analytic wisdom that he has murdered Grandmorin the railroad magnate. Cabuche represents the freedom within nature of the poacher, with a kind of natural wisdom and directness. Unlike the demonic Pans of Boudu, and Rodolphe in *Partie de Campagne*, Cabuche softens the vision of man in nature, otherwise so harshly presented in *La Bête Humaine*. He is almost a redemptive natural figure, who does not try to impose his nature on the city bourgeois, but goes his own way. The warmth of Cabuche and the Panic spirit of Rodolphe together prefigure a later character like Gaspard in *Le Déjeuner sur l'Herbe*, who with his goat Cabri sets off the magical winds that destroy the scientific and rational orders of Étienne Alexis and his party. But this magical resolution is as yet far off in the films of the late 1930s. Cabri, the poacher of *La Marseillaise*, declines to join the Revolution; Cabuche is falsely accused; and Marceau, the poacher in *La Règle du*

Jeu, wants to become a house servant because of the greater status.

Since the real poacher, Marceau, no longer has the true "poacher sensibility," his kind of perspective is reserved instead for the socialized poacher, Octave, forever arriving just in time for dinner, the weak observer who can see and understand what's going on, but can do nothing about it, and who only accidentally saves himself from some final absurd destruction. Octave and La Chesnaye parallel each other as self-described cowards and agents of reconciliation who do not want any conflict and do their best to smooth things out. But Octave can potentially accomplish more than La Chesnaye, because his artistic background makes him more socially fluid. La Chesnaye follows the line of the Baron, Boeldieu, Louis XVI, and Saint-Laurent. But Octave comes from the perspective of the camera itself: *"l'oeil cynique"* (as one subtitle has it) of Bordenave, the theater manager in *Nana;* the poets in what is at first joyful ribbing of society in *Tire-au-flanc* and *Chotard;* and the painter Javel of *La Marseillaise,* whose personal vision of the Revolution includes a painting of Brutus killing Caesar for a local Revolutionary Committee, "with 1500 recognizable faces." That Octave is a failed artist who never dared to use his musical training adds to the poignancy of his efforts to be a bridge for others. Renoir tells us that André Jurieu was an orchestra conductor in one of the earlier drafts of the script. But by the final film he has become the romantic hero of action, while Octave is the failed artist; and Jurieu asserts his own emotional needs without apology, while Octave must subordinate his own feelings and smooth Jurieu's way. Jurieu is the nominal hero of *La Règle du Jeu,* or so he is defined by the public world of the film; when he and Octave argue on the hillside early in the film, after Jurieu has tried to commit suicide by crashing his car (with Octave in it), the camera makes

the quietly authoritative Jurieu dominate the wildly gesturing
Octave. But in fact Jurieu has as little idea of his real goals
as Octave. Marceau and Schumacher have definite ideas
about their desires, but neither has any social sense. Renoir's
real heroes may be La Chesnaye and Christine, both of
whom make some commitment to order that involves a loss
of personal happiness.

By *La Règle du Jeu*, the definition of heroism has become
almost overwhelmingly complex. Who is the real hero? As in
La Grande Illusion there remains a nostalgia for the outmoded. Jurieu is the old-fashioned man of action, "the modern
hero," forever soaring, never having his feet on the ground.
La Chesnaye, meanwhile, preserves the old cultural and social
values. The weaker characters, Octave and Marceau, each
secretly desires the virtues of his counterpart: Octave admires
the aggressiveness of Jurieu's love for Christine; Marceau, the
order of La Chesnaye's household. But at the end of the
film only the weaker have really survived. Jurieu is dead and
La Chesnaye has chosen the closed world of the château.
The hunt had brought everyone outside into nature, but its
co-ordinated activity denied exuberance and feeling. Octave
at the masquerade cannot take off his bear costume without
special help; this is the bumptious, cuddly personality he has
projected all his life. Without these defenses, he is as lost as
La Chesnaye without his society, Jurieu without his airplane,
or Marceau without his poaching traps. When Octave and
Marceau stand in the gloom of the garden of La Colinière at
the end of the film, neither knows where to go or what to do.
Octave thinks he will go to Paris and Marceau back to his
cabin in the woods. Neither Octave's social orchestration nor
Marceau's natural energy has accomplished anything but
failure and death. The characters in *La Règle du Jeu* have
doomed themselves to their social roles, with little chance of
self-realization. Only Octave has the potential to stand out-

side society and see it whole. But he too sacrifices his own
nature to the intangible rules.

Renoir's five American films present various versions of
these two kinds of heroes. The first three films tend to focus
on the heroes of action, and the next two on the heroes of
perception and understanding. But in fact the heroes of
action really don't do very much. Tom Keefer would rather
stay in his isolated swamp; Sam Tucker wants to achieve
independence away from the orderly upcountry farm. Albert
Mory does make a heroic gesture by taking on blame for
what he could not in actuality do. But his heroism is basically an accident, accomplished in the bare streets and expressionist sets of a world that exists only in films. *Diary of
a Chambermaid* is a more authentic film of detachment because the central character, Celestine, is specifically presented as an observer. The characters who are more conscious
actors, like Joseph, the valet, are evil, and Celestine chooses
to marry the weak Georges (in contrast to Mirbeau's novel).
Her character shifts the balance in Renoir's idea of the
hero away from action to perception. Lange could both create
and perceive. But the pressure of social action forces a separation between action and understanding in Renoir's conception of the hero. Paul Martin in *This Land Is Mine*
throws bombs as a resistance fighter; but we know little of his
motivations and beliefs. Albert Mory comes to his own
heroic gesture not through action but through a sense of his
own cowardice. He becomes a hero mainly because the young
must have heroes (a sentiment frequently expressed in the
film). There is no clear observer in *This Land Is Mine*.
In *The Southerner* Renoir gives us the detached Tim so that
we may better understand the acting Sam. Celestine's character then embodies the perceptiveness of figures like Albert
Mory and the detachment of Tim, without having to endure
the reproach of cowardice in inaction.

Woman on the Beach enlarges the themes of these films, from *La Règle du Jeu* to *Diary of a Chambermaid*, by defining the hero specifically as a failed intellectual and—most important—a failed artist. Renoir enhances the focus on Tod Butler, the blind artist, by stripping Lieutenant Burnett, in the novel a former Assistant Professor of English, of any cultural pretensions at all. The theme of the artist-hero is a thread in Renoir's work that goes as far back as *Lange,* in which the creator of an artistic dream world must finally be pushed to the point of social action. But by *Woman on the Beach* the plot no longer has a social dimension. It is purely internalized, either in the passions of Lieutenant Burnett and Peggy Butler, or in the wrestling of Tod Butler with the fact that he is a painter who has lost his eyesight. Blindness represents the very depths of isolation for this artist-hero; not only can he no longer act, he can hardly even perceive. Tod Butler is cut off aesthetically and physically from the world that he is trying to understand. Tom Keefer is brought out of the swamp; but Tod Butler must burn his paintings and start again, burn his house on the isolated beach, and go back to the city, to New York, in fact, to work again.

Woman on the Beach is of course Renoir's last film in America and we could indulge here in neat biographical-critical allegories. But the sense of isolation is certainly very strong in all his American films and the kind of heroes he portrays in them. Isolation can be a strength (*Swamp Water* or *The Southerner*); a thing of ambivalent value (*Diary of a Chambermaid*); or a weakness (*Woman on the Beach*). What makes the otherwise isolated individual strong is frequently the presence of a real family, as in *The Southerner* or *The River,* to come. Albert Mory, in *This Land Is Mine,* can live out at least the fantasy of a revitalized society because he has replaced his overbearing mother with the new family of Paul and Louise Martin. In fact, Albert's acceptance of

Paul and Louise as his new family for himself (and his acceptance of his complicity with Paul's Resistance activities over the dinner table) goes a long way to explain why any sexual feeling between Albert and Louise is never expressed.

This sense of security in the family may reflect in part Renoir's incipient use of an American-based *équipe* for his films, especially the later ones, when he had to a certain extent established himself in his new home, remarried, brought his son Alain over from France, and made many new friends. In the light of his many other affinities with John Ford, including the idea of the *équipe*, it was appropriately coincidental that *Swamp Water*, the script that Renoir decided to do first, after turning down innumerable scripts set in Hollywood-Europe, was written by Dudley Nichols, who had been Ford's top script writer in the 1930s and 1940s. Nichols worked with Ford on such films as *The Informer* (1935), *Stagecoach* (1939), and *The Long Voyage Home* (1940). Nichols also worked with Renoir on *This Land Is Mine*. Another friend was Burgess Meredith, who collaborated with Renoir on the Office of War Information short *Salute to France*, and who helped produce, write, and acted in *Diary of a Chambermaid*. Set designer Eugène Lourié also worked with Renoir on his American films, as he had on many films of the 1930s, including *Madame Bovary*, *Les Bas-Fonds*, *La Grande Illusion*, *La Bête Humaine*, and *La Règle du Jeu*.

But aside from the biographical reverberations of Renoir's thematic concerns, within the films themselves Renoir's exploration of the problem of heroism reaches a point in *Woman on the Beach* that it had not reached in *La Règle du Jeu*. The move to America resulted in *Swamp Water*, a film that plunged into nature in an effort to leave the problems of society behind. The film with which Renoir left America enforced a similar kind of asocial conclusion. With *The River*

Renoir subordinates active heroism to a combination of natural rhythms and aesthetic understanding. Captain John, the amputee hero of World War II, is an answer to the Jurieu of *La Règle du Jeu*. His heroism is only to be forgotten. After World War II that kind of heroism is no longer a real possibility. In *La Grande Illusion* there could still be a nostalgia for some of the lost heroic figures of World War I. But, as Captain John says, "when the war is ended, yesterday's hero is only a man with one leg." Captain John is a stranger wherever he goes, even a wooden actor to match his leg, because he cannot free himself from the heroic definition of self created by the context of war. In the movement of the film, as Harriet is freed from her childhood, so Captain John is freed from the war, by love, and by the bond of family. Renoir says that Guynemer, the World War I pilot, was someone intoxicated by heroism. That characteristic may be fascinating to Renoir, but it is completely unfruitful, caged hermetically in a past, recapturable only through romantic nostalgia.

In the films of the 1950s Renoir explores with great richness a kind of heroism hinted at only fleetingly in the films of the 1930s and 1940s. This is the heroism of perception, understood specifically as an aesthetic perception and creativity that can restore a society as well as understand it. *Le Carrosse d'Or* resembles *The River* in its basically apolitical view of society. The true co-ordinator is Camila, the *commedia dell'arte* traveling heroine, and in Renoir's world of popular art the lineal descendant of the pulp-novel writer Monsieur Lange. *La Grande Illusion* hinted that the international fellowship of art could substitute for the old aristocratic internationalism. Such hints are realized in *Le Carrosse d'Or*. Camilla is a hero of aesthetic understanding. Her three lovers represent not only forces in the world that she absorbs into her newly made world of the

theater, but also, in a whimsical way, a new kind of international integration in Europe. Each of the three male stars
speaks a different language: French, English, Italian; and
three versions of the film were made: French, English, and
Italian. Thus the technical problems of co-production become
transmuted into one of the film's main themes, in the same
way that Renoir absorbs so much of the mechanics of filming
into the total meaning of a particular film. As the *équipe*
behind the camera influences the vision of society before
the camera, so the polyglot of languages must be integrated
into Camilla's all-embracing aesthetic. The alliance between
Camilla and the Archbishop at the end of the film is an
alliance between two world orders that must respect each
other. Religion appears fleetingly in the later films of Renoir,
but enough to convince some sympathetic and unsympathetic young French critics that Renoir has found a new piety.
Yet religion represents merely a more traditional order that
purports to reconcile nature and society in much the same
way that the theatrical and aesthetic vision of life does.
Both priests and actors wear costumes, and both bear allegiance to some invisible force, in the sky or behind the
camera. But despite the possibility that is never far from
any art form, Renoir does not assert that the Director is
God. It is God's order rather than God's authority or
judgment that he seeks. And his idea of the artistic vision
asserts pervasive harmony and understanding rather than
hierarchy or control. Camilla steps out on the stage at the
end of *Le Carrosse d'Or* and remarks that she misses her
lovers "a little." But her real life is to perform, and to please,
and to subordinate herself to the pleasure of the audience.
While the puppet-show frame in *La Chienne* is satiric
and detaching, in *Le Carrosse d'Or* it realizes and makes
eternal what occurs within it. The coach itself is perhaps
one of the most elaborate symbols in any Renoir film. Most

symbols ask to be explicated, but the coach, bulking so grandly in the foreground of many scenes, refuses to be reduced to any simple significance. Instead of being an object charged with some abstract meaning, it is a symbolization of the aggressive and inclusive forces of imagination itself, and the way the imagination supersedes the forces of politics, the heroism of action, and, after a brief moment of equality, the universal pretensions of religion as well.

The typical hero of these films is more often a woman than a man, Magnani in *Le Carrosse d'Or* and Ingrid Bergman in *Elena et les Hommes*. They harken back to Catherine Hessling in *La Fille de l'Eau, Nana,* and *La Petite Marchande d'Allumettes*. Her world of dream and artifice was always threatened by the forces of evil and death. But the female heroes of the 1950s have few such fears. A transitional figure between the heroines of the 1920s and those of the 1950s, Christine in *La Règle du Jeu,* is suffocated by the social world for which she has given up the artistic life with her father, a Viennese orchestra conductor. Octave, her father's former student, is the last fragment of that world that she holds onto, and his own displacement in French society shows the gaps between the two worlds. In contrast to Christine's isolation and the detachment of Celestine, Camilla's heroism becomes the coordination of all her worlds and the final subordination of them to the proscenium frame of art.

Danglard in *French Cancan* is the male hero to complement these female heroes. He is the showman, the entrepreneur, who causes the Moulin Rouge to be built and revives the cancan as its show piece. When the great dance finale comes on opening night, he sits backstage in a large chair, swinging his foot to the music. Since he has arranged it all, there is no need for him to be onstage. Instead of the star, Camilla, the hero has become the impresario Danglard. *French Cancan* tells the story of the genesis of the café, an enclosure for art and for nostalgia that subordinates everything in the artist's personal life to art. Just before the finale Danglard has an argument with his mistress Nini. She is upset because she has seen him making up to another girl in the show, and now she refuses to perform her own role. From one point of view Danglard's argument seems self-centered, for he says that Nini cannot expect to have him all for herself. But his larger point is that both of them must serve the audience and if necessary subordinate their private lives to that service. Jean Gabin plays Danglard and, as so often in Renoir, the sense of changing perspective through the refocusing on a past image strengthens the new ideas. Here is the face of Maréchal and Jacques Lantier, now grown older, no longer out of touch with society or dominated by nature, but in control and dominating through his creativity and artifice. Gaston Modot is in *French Cancan* too, and Max Dalban, and Valentine Tessier, all plucked from the films of the thirties and placed here in a reconstructed past. Since Danglard both subordinates and realizes his own life in the theater, it should be more important to Nini that she be the star of the show more than his mistress. Indeed, Renoir himself has made of his own childhood in Montmartre a world both imaginatively more and realistically less than what it actually was.

Danglard not only orders the aesthetic world of the Moulin Rouge, as Renoir does the romantic Montmartre of *French Cancan*, but he also brings the world outside into his creation to be entertained. The potentiality of the theatrical illusion to draw its spectators into its world and there transform them becomes realized with more complexity in *Elena et les Hommes*, where the entire political world becomes a farce manipulated by love. *Elena* romantically evokes a historical period actually marked by intense left- and right-wing wrangling, and the constant political and military pressure of Germany. But the true heroes of *Elena* are the heroes of love and feeling and style; the political characters are weaklings and fools, and political action is a meaningless, although often impassioned, ritual. *Elena* attempts to portray a kind of political Eden before the fall into history that occurred with World War I. Politics is unconscious theater in this world, but love is self-conscious theater, and therefore superior. "Elena is a real hero," says Renoir. Although her actions are seemingly dictated by what she believes to be the "good" of France, she, like Camilla, is actually making an order amid the men around her more through her own nature and control than by some dim adherence to political principle. The political world is a vaudevillian panoply of costumes and absurdities. In *French Cancan* and *Elena* the potentially destructive crowd of the films of the 1940s becomes a crowd of romance, surging into the Moulin Rouge in *French Cancan* or singing in the street while they watch the silhouettes of Elena and Henri embrace in the window above. A group of separate individuals have been brought together like a theater audience and transformed by the magic of the illusion to which they give their assent.

But even as Renoir in *Elena* has resolved some part of his thematic preoccupation with the relative value of action and understanding, new complexities appear. General Rollan remains a toy in Elena's hands until Henri arranges for his wife to spirit him away to Russia. He has been vindicated by an election and he could assume absolute power. But he does not, and behind his refusal to take responsibility of any sort is the weak Boulanger who, luckily, refused the role of military savior thrust upon him and died a suicide on the grave of his mistress. Elena too shares some

of Rollan's imperceptiveness, if only because she believes she
is acting for some dutiful political end in wooing him. It
is the uninvolved characters, rather than the involved Rollan and Elena, who can perceive most clearly. If Elena is
like Camilla, the star and center of attention, Henri resembles Danglard, the impresario of order. Henri has few
visible political connections, and Elena berates him for being
a man unlike her other men, without ideals or ambitions.
But Henri helps to arrange the final resolution. Love, he
says, makes people forget politics; it is France's greatest
gift to civilization. But Henri does not realize that there is
a gift and a harmony even beyond love. He has engineered
the final scenes, but their energy and their magic has been
supplied by Miarka, the gypsy girl who enters the film with
her caravan from someplace outside the momentary Eden
of the studio set. With her troupe she moves forward into
the street and the house, singing and inspiring the crowd
to sing with her. While Henri and Elena sit on one window
sill and embrace, she sits on the other and sings alone.
Finally they are gone and the crowd outside is gone too.
Like Camilla at the end of *Le Carrosse d'Or,* or Danglard
backstage in *French Cancan,* Miarka, the true artist and
reconciler, must be left to stand alone. For her, as for Renoir, the satisfaction must be found in the order created,
with nothing gained from it for herself.

Renoir's acceptance of artistic separation from his creation, defined by a figure like Miarka, announces a fascination
with the nature of creation that exhibits itself strongly in
all his work beginning in the middle 1950s. In this period
he also branches out artistically beyond the film to embrace
areas in which he had begun work before, but never so
concertedly. In 1955 Renoir writes and directs the play
Orvet, the story of a writer who has gone back to his
childhood home in the country to write a play based on

Hans Christian Andersen's *Little Mermaid*. There he meets Orvet, the child of poachers, a young girl of the woods, not unlike Miarka. Around her the writer Georges spins a world of fantasy, transplanting her to Paris, where she becomes a sophisticate and loses all that made her attractive. Finally Georges returns to reality and discovers once again the real girl. The play is a fascinating footnote to Renoir's films, reflecting the tone of gently mocking romance common to *Partie de Campagne* and *Le Déjeuner sur l'Herbe*. But it is as an effort to experiment beyond the film with methods new to Renoir that *Orvet* achieves its greatest importance. In 1954 Renoir remarks ". . . I can truly find my individual way of expressing things only thanks to my contact with other people." Renoir's artistic nature is challenged in the 1950s by the problems of artistic coordination that arise from the end of the *équipe*, not only as a group of kindred creators, but even as a technological possibility. Stage direction and writing in the middle 1950s remain a collective art, even while the sense of collective enterprise has vanished from the super productions of films. Renoir's experimentation with television also helps to recapture the kind of intimacy of production that was possible in his earlier films. Also during this period Renoir directs for the stage Clifford Odets' *The Big Knife* and Shakespeare's *Julius Caesar*, the first a farewell to the Hollywood of the blacklist and the second a delving into the problems of theatrical spectacle and the political hero. *Julius Caesar* was staged by Renoir in the Roman arena at Arles with a huge cast, and Renoir tells of his efforts to make the act of direction an intimate one in this grandiose setting, by arranging an elaborate system of microphones with which he could be in close contact with all aspects of the production at once. The isolation of Miarka is truly realized by Renoir's literary work of the 1960s, the biographical

Renoir My Father and the fictional autobiography of *The Notebooks of Captain Georges.*

The turning away from "realistic" political and social goals could invite the presence of the rampant individual, the hero who ignores society in his self-assertion. But Renoir does not lapse unconsciously into the solipsism of art in these films, for as always he is aware of the dangers of any absolute position. In his own later films John Ford seems to rest with the heroic individual and the social myth he creates. He never takes the final step that Renoir takes toward the distinction between heroic ego and artistic ego. He never has Renoir's awareness of the dangers of heroic self-assertion, nurtured in films like *La Règle du Jeu,* that reappears in the two television films of 1959, *Le Testament du Docteur Cordelier* and *Le Déjeuner sur l'Herbe.*

In the same way that *Cordelier* and *Le Déjeuner sur l'Herbe* complement each other in their views of nature, they also present contrasting critiques of the kind of hero already established in the films of the 1950s. Both attack the abuses of the intellect wrought by science and technology; both seem to seek an animating nature that will rehumanize and revitalize the humorless scientists. After the exuberance of the theater films and Renoir's own work in the theater in the middle 1950s, *Cordelier* is preoccupied with the darker side of creativity, the split between intellect and energy. Dr. Cordelier is a scientific genius whose experiments have transformed him into a figure of evil. In his severity he is a kind of highbrow artist, to contrast to the popular artists of Renoir's previous films. Cordelier's work in his laboratory is an image of the intellect in isolation, and the bareness of the Parisian streets in the film contribute to this sense of aloneness. Cordelier is the artist finally face-to-face with himself, and disliking what he sees because, he thinks, it is an image of inhumanity and evil. He cannot come to terms with these impulses in his basic nature. And ironically enough, Opale, Cordelier's alter-ego (both parts are played by Jean-Louis Barrault), the Hyde to his Jekyll, is the most attractive character in the film, projecting an ambivalent nature reminiscent of the problematic villainy of the Nazi Major von Keller in *This Land Is Mine*. Opale relieves the general gloom of *Cordelier* by manic energy alone, as he prances down the dim streets of nighttime Paris, gleefully kicking the crutches out from under cripples, attacking little girls, and beating passers-by into insensibility. Despite his threat to society, he is much preferable as a character to the dried-up Cordelier, with his white-shoe-polished hair and his puritanical manners.

Opale is in fact the natural self that Cordelier should have tried to understand and instead has repressed. When Cordelier was young, he was called *"le docteur de la vertu,"* because he demanded such discipline and restraint from himself. He had contempt for doctors who took sexual advantage of their patients until one day his contempt turned to fascination. He administered a sleeping drug to a young woman, and all that he had been disciplining was let out into the open. Étienne Alexis in *Le Déjeuner sur l'Herbe* needs only a strong dose of the natural in geography and human beings to cure him of his desires to be President of Europe and legally enforce artificial insemination. The provençal countryside is enough to revive the natural self that had been disguised by his scientific and political pronouncements. Cordelier is Étienne Alexis without humor or imagination, with only the cold light of creativity.

To suit these two complementary films, there are also two Renoirs. In *Cordelier* his voiceover narration enforces a rigidly moralistic view of the relation between Cordelier and Opale, even while the film itself invites us to see the flaws in

Cordelier's moralism and the virtues in Opale's violence. On the other hand, Gaspard, the wandering goatherd of *Le Déjeuner sur l'Herbe,* who reshuffles the characters with his magic wind, continues the tradition of the benevolent creative outsider, without moral schemes or personal grievances to confuse his perspective. *Déjeuner* is made a few months after *Cordelier.* Does this chronology tell us anything about Renoir's ideas at this point in his career? In fact the two films must be viewed as a diptych: the one set in the city in black and white, the other set in the country in color; the one about the destruction of the self by science and bestial nature, the other about release from science by exuberant nature; the one heavily moralistic and the other poking fun at conventional morality. Pan and the moralist are not alternatives, but two possibilities in the continuity of Renoir's perspective. *Le Testament du Docteur Cordelier* and *Le Déjeuner sur l'Herbe* are Renoir's inspired play with the themes of character, society, and nature that have preoccupied him for many years, and it is the partial resolution of some of these themes that allows him the freedom to indulge himself in the creation of these fables.

Le *Caporal Épinglé* (1962) casts a final jaundiced eye on the concept of heroism among members of the public world of war and politics. Like *Cordelier* and *Le Déjeuner sur l'Herbe,* it firmly walls out, this time in a context of historical realism, the possibilities of any heroic action without artistic perspective and detachment. The Corporal spins out his dreams of heroic self-assertion to the fascination of Pater and Ballochet. But his actual escapes are constantly thwarted, and he is ritualistically led back to the prison camp to march on his knees or duck walk around the punishment circle. The Corporal invariably catches himself in circle after circle of self-involved motion because he is not free enough inside. Neither society nor individuals, neither nature nor art, are redeemed, transformed, or understood by the Corporal's heroic ego. Nor is his detachment from the personal lives of those who admire him in any way equivalent to the vital perspective allowed by the detachment of art. Jean-Pierre Cassel's resemblance to Georges Pomiès only underlines Renoir's view that such gymnastics and personal flamboyance now exude only stale self-absorption. As Renoir will affirm more elaborately in *Le Petit Théâtre de Jean Renoir*, artistic detachment makes connections, while the heroic ego of action invariably separates, isolates, and, in *Cordelier* and *Le Caporal Épinglé*, even destroys.

Le Petit Théâtre de Jean Renoir (1969) grandly recapitulates many of the themes and methods I have discussed above, subtly blending one with another, as if in this last film Renoir were writing a coda to his film career. Stylized theater is the manner of *Le Dernier Réveillon* (made last although first in the order of the four vignettes—three stories and a song—that make up the film); in *Le Roi d'Yvetot*, the final section, the artifice of *Le Dernier Réveillon* has been transformed into the natural beauty of Provence. Between the two is something new for Renoir, but perfectly suited to its middle position, *La Cireuse Électrique*, a comic opera set in the new apartment houses that ring Paris and authentically shot in these apartments rather than in studio sets. This section is a gentle mocking of both Jacques Demy and Jean-Luc Godard, Renoir being surely the only critic or film-maker who could see the common point of their vulnerability. Each sketch in *Le Petit Théâtre* summons up a particular kind of world and a special cinematic vision. Even the painful in-and-out tracking shot on Jeanne Moreau, who sings a horrendously wooden and sentimental song from *La Belle Époque*, mocks the veneration and nostalgia for the last years of the nineteenth century that moved Renoir himself in *French*

Cancan and *Elena.* As Renoir has said, "As soon as people are dispossessed from the past, they like to coat it with a nice layer of sugar," a fault that he himself may indulge in. The coherence of *Le Petit Théâtre* draws its strength from Renoir's continuing fascination with the themes that have interested him since the beginning of his career, and his ability to mark the limits of his interest through self-parody.

Renoir brings together in this "anthology" film some of the variety of what he believes films to be capable of. But even more important is his intriguing decision to present himself for the first time as the maker of this world—not a surrogate Camilla, Danglard, or Miarka, but Jean Renoir himself, now seventy-five years old, posed stiffly and stooped beside a little model of a stage, furnished in red and gold, like the theater that framed *La Chienne* and *Le Carrosse d'Or,* or the theater within whose compass he saw the puppet shows of his youth. And the most striking thing about *Le Petit Théâtre de Jean Renoir* is the interplay between the separate worlds of the film and the figure of Jean Renoir. As each section ends, we return to that slightly bowed old man, dressed in unobtrusive black with a thin black tie who, with an odd mixture of warmth and formality, introduces the next section. Each time we see him we are forced to connect what we have seen, the world created, with this now old man, and connect it too with his past works, *Le Dernier Réveillon* with *La Petite Marchande d'Allumettes, Le Roi d'Yvetot* with *Le Déjeuner sur l'Herbe.* The public hero of strut and stature is forever gone for Renoir. The only hero who can really achieve is the hero of art, who mingles Don Quixote and Sancho Panza, seeing all worlds, real and dream, with full sympathy and understanding. In 1960 Renoir directed his play *Carola ou les Cabotins* at Berkeley. *Carola* is the story of a girl who tries to forget the world of the German Occupation and the French Resistance by living only for her art as an actress. Such isolation is never a total virtue for Renoir, although he acknowledges its appeal. In a remark made during the production of *Carola,* recorded in an article by Virginia Maynard, he parallels this attitude with his method of direction: ". . . I am never able to forget that there is a world around me—that around this plot, this play, life is going on. Stanislavsky played in a world limited by his play—outside of this world there was nothing. I believe this is why Stanislavsky's direction was so magnificent: his actors were entirely involved in the life of the play, no longer in lives of their own."

Carola's inability to lose herself in art is Renoir's answer to Stanislavsky's method. That line of artistic observers that so surprisingly and appropriately ends in himself must similarly be brought out of their detachment. To introduce *Le Roi d'Yvetot,* which is the most realistically presented of the four sections of *Le Petit Théâtre de Jean Renoir,* Renoir picks up a tiny marble and rolls it onto the stage of his little theater. The marble rattles across the boards and then onto some inner space of hard-packed provençal earth, becoming a bocce ball within the film within the film. The typically whimsical device of this metamorphosis emphasizes at once the artifice of the real provençal world of *Le Roi d'Yvetot* and Renoir's own creation of the interplay between the two. So also at the end of the sketch, which will be the end of the entire film, Renoir does not preserve the illusion of a realistic film. The actors first break out into infectious communal laughter to resolve the embarrassment of the now complaisant cuckolded husband. Then they all turn toward the camera and arrange themselves as if for a traveling photographer, while the camera pulls back the appropriate distance. And then, like some smiling society that could be, they bow to us, the audience. We do not return to Renoir's own figure. We remain instead within this world, not broken by this gesture of artifice but strengthened, vitally engaged yet perceptively detached, alone in our seats yet bound with a sense of new community to the moving vision of Jean Renoir.

CHAPTER SIX

Biographical Sketch

Jean Renoir was born on September 15, 1894, in the Montmartre district of Paris in an apartment house called the "Château des Brouillards," which appears distantly in his 1955 film *French Cancan*. Renoir was the second son of Auguste Renoir, the great Impressionist painter. His elder brother Pierre, born March 21, 1885, later became a stage and film actor, appearing in several of his brother's films, principally *Madame Bovary* (Charles Bovary), *La Nuit du Carrefour* (Inspector Maigret), and *La Marseillaise* (Louis XVI), as well as in other films, including Marcel Carné's *Les Enfants du Paradis*. In the late 1940s Pierre succeeded Louis Jouvet as artistic director of the Athénée Theatre in Paris. He died in 1952. Claude Renoir, the cameraman and cinematographer, is Pierre's eldest son. Jean Renoir's younger brother Claude (Coco) was born August 4, 1901. He now works in television production and earlier had been director of production for some of his brother's films.

Renoir was raised in Paris and at the family farm in Provence, "Les Collettes" at Cagnes, which figures as the setting of *Le Déjeuner sur l'Herbe* (1959). He was cared for by Gabrielle, the family serving girl, who figures in so many paintings by Auguste Renoir, including the first with Jean as the subject, "Jean Renoir jouant avec Gabrielle et une fillette" (1895). Other paintings in which Jean Renoir figures are "La Famille de l'artiste" (1896), "Le Déjeuner à Berneval, Jean Renoir tenant un cerceau" (1898), and the large "Le Chasseur" (1910), which hangs in his home in Beverly Hills, and appears in the background on the dust-jacket of this book. When Renoir emigrated to the United States in the early 1940s, he arranged that Gabrielle and her husband, the American painter Conrad Slade, live near by.

Like his brother Pierre, Renoir attended the preparatory Collège Sainte-Croix at Neuilly. It was at Sainte-Croix that he saw his first films, some documentaries and a comic film about a driving fanatic called *Les Aventures d'Auto-Maboul*. Renoir received his degree from the Nice extension of the University of Aix-en-Provence in 1913.

After graduation Renoir became a sergeant in the First Dragoons at Vincennes until he was kicked by a horse and was hospitalized. At the outbreak of World War I in 1915 he went to the front as a second lieutenant in the 6th Battalion of The Alpine Cavalry. Once again he was wounded, this time with a fractured femur. His mother successfully pleaded with the authorities that his leg not be amputated. While he was recovering in a military hospital, she died of diabetes.

Except for a brief infatuation with Elaine Dodge in *Mysteries of New York,* Renoir's first strenuous immersion in films came during the period of recovery from his wounds, when he was seeing what he has estimated as twenty-five films a week, including innumerable American serials and Charlie Chaplin shorts. He talked about films to his father, who even got hold of a projector to screen a few.

At the beginning of 1916, Renoir changed his branch of service, gained a pilot's license, and became an aerial reconnaissance pilot. Shortly after his father's death in 1919, Renoir married Catherine Hessling, who had become acquainted with the Renoir household in 1917, when the pregnancy of Madeleine Bruno, one of Auguste Renoir's favorite models, made her unable to pose. Catherine Hessling, or Andrée Heuschling, as she was then named, was recommended and approved. She appears in such paintings as "La Femme en robe de mousseline" (1917), and "Les Grands Baigneuses" (1919), much rounder and more languid than the mugging sensualist of Renoir's films. She and Jean Renoir were married January 24, 1920, and shortly after, they left Provence to live in Paris.

For four years Renoir worked as a ceramicist and started a modest ceramics works at "la Nicotière," the home of Jacques Nicot, the popularizer of tobacco, on the borders of the forest of Fontainebleau near Marlotte. The works was on property owned by Paul Cézanne, *fils*. While Renoir was working with ceramics, he was also going to the movies, frequently three times a day. At this time he was so impressed by American films that he could not see the possibility of films apart from American methods and subjects. But the experience of two films, Erich von Stroheim's *Foolish Wives*, which Renoir saw at least ten times, and the Russian actor Mosjoukine's French-based *Le Brasier Argent* (directed by Alexander Volkov, and produced by Alexander Kamenka, who would later produce *Les Bas-Fonds* for Renoir), convinced him both that a national cinema, based on French rather than American life, could exist, and that he himself could find a place in this new artistic world.

Renoir wrote the script for a film called *Une Vie Sans Joie*, which starred Catherine Hessling and was directed by Albert Dieudonné, an actor and scenarist who in 1926 was to play Napoleon in Abel Gance's classic. Renoir did not like the way Dieudonné handled the film and resolved in the future to direct himself. After this falling out, Dieudonné added several shots and released the film in 1927 with the new title of *Catherine*.

La Fille de l'Eau (1924), Renoir's first film, was made at "La Nicotière." Pierre Renoir appears in a small part armed with a pitchfork in the "lynching" scene. Exteriors were filmed along the Loing River and the nearby canal, and in a local bar called Au Bon Coin. The role of Jeff, the wicked uncle, is played by the scenarist Pierre Lestringuez, under the pseudonym of "Pierre Philippe." His father had been a close friend of Auguste Renoir's.

Nana (1926) cost one million francs, a big budget for the times. It had some success but failed to recoup the large investment, and Renoir has described it as a commercial failure. Organized by Pierre Braunberger, who was to be associated with Renoir on many later films, *Nana* was the first French-German co-production. At the Moulin Rouge premiere the orchestra accompanied it with Offenbach music, and one outraged French film professional stood up and denounced it as a "German film." Renoir began his technical fascination with film by devising an old Ford chassis with deflated tires to make the long backstage traveling shots. He worked on the intertitles with Zola's daughter, Denise Leblond-Zola, for greater fidelity to the novel. Zola himself, of course, had been part of Auguste Renoir's circle of friends, although the painter never quite forgave him for the picture of Cézanne in Zola's novel *L'Oeuvre*. Renoir's costume designer and set decorator for *Nana* was Claude Autant-Lara, who later became a director in his own right.

Although Renoir has been quoted to say that the failure of *Nana* ruined him financially, *Charleston* (1927) appeared the following autumn. It was made in three days and boasts only two main actors, Catherine Hessling, sensuously dancing the Charleston amid a wrecked Paris, and Johnny Higgins, the tap dancer at the Champs-Élysées *Revue Nègre*, who plays a black astronaut. One very elaborate, and seemingly expensive, set is used to depict post-civilized Paris. Renoir's interest in jazz and contemporary music had been whetted by Jacques Becker, who sent him records from New York.

Marquita (1927) is a lost film; no known copies exist. It was commissioned by Marie-Louise Iribe, the second wife of Renoir's brother Pierre, and the sister-in-law of Pierre Lestringuez. For it Renoir constructed an elaborate miniature of the Barbés-Rochechoart subway station which was reflected on mirrors before which the actors performed. It opened on the same bill with *Charleston*.

At the end of May 1927, Renoir was involved in a serious automobile accident in which the driver, his friend Pierre Champagne, the scenarist and actor, was killed. Renoir was taken to the hospital by some poachers whose characters had interested him in *La Fille de l'Eau* and continued to fascinate him in such later works as *La Règle du Jeu*, *Le Déjeuner sur l'Herbe*, and the play *Orvet*. François Truffaut has said that the scene of André Jurieu's attempted suicide in *La Règle du Jeu*, with Renoir as Octave in the car, takes place at the site of the real-life accident.

La Petite Marchande d'Allumettes was begun in 1928 as a project of a film "atelier" set up by Renoir and his partner Jean Tedesco in the attic of a theater called the Vieux-Colombier. It was an effort to liberate themselves from the technical tyranny of the commercial studios. They made their own sets and took the film through all its stages from shooting to final print with their own equipment. This kind of freedom allowed them to experiment with many technical tricks. With the aid of Philips Company, Renoir and the cameraman Jean Bachelet designed lighting that was the forerunner of floodlights. They needed the new lighting because they had decided to use a panchromatic negative instead of the usual orthochromatic; until that time panchromatic, which was more sensitive to reds, had been used only on outdoor shots. After Renoir's use, it became standard for indoor work also. Five cameras were used at once in some scenes, presaging Renoir's adoption of multi-camera television shooting methods in *Le Déjeuner sur l'Herbe,* thirty years later.

Although the film was ultimately successful, it was delayed more than two years in release. First Renoir was sued for plagiarism by Maurice Rostand and Rosemonde Gérard, the authors of a comic opera based on the same Hans Christian Andersen story. An organ grinder appears for a few moments in Renoir's film; the same organ grinder plays a central role in the Rostand-Gérard opera. After two years the suit was decided in Renoir's favor, but by that time sound was in and the producers wanted the addition of postsynchronized sound. Over Renoir's objections both music and intertitles were added.

Renoir traces his interest in Andersen back to his periods as a model for his father, when Gabrielle used to read the stories to keep him still. In his 1955 play *Orvet,* the main character, a playwright named Georges, is trying to write a stage adaptation of Andersen's "Little Mermaid."

Tire-au-flanc (1928) interested Renoir because he wanted to work with Georges Pomiès, the dancer who here made his acting debut. *Tire-au-flanc* also marks the first substantial role for Michel Simon. François Truffaut has remarked about its strong influence on Jean Vigo's *Zéro de Conduite,* and in 1962 co-directed and wrote the script for a remake, *Tire-au-Flanc 62,* that concentrated on portraying the soldiers-in-training as slightly taller versions of Vigo's schoolchildren.

Le Tournoi dans la Cité (1929), together with *Le Bled* (1929) were the two most financially successful of Renoir's silent films. *Le Tournoi* is an elaborate period film that cost much but made a great return. The film was shot on location at Carcassonne and used the members of the Saumur Cavalry School, who had been perfecting their technique for the two thousandth anniversary of Carcassonne. Renoir experimented with directing groups and invented a special camera for use at the banquet table to get plate- and candle-eye view shots. Only about ten minutes of the film now exist, together with a few stills from the otherwise lost sections, the rest having been burned up in the Cinémathèque fire of 1959.

Le Bled (1929), like *Le Tournoi*, was expensive, was financed by the Société des films Historiques under the direction of Henry Dupuy-Mazuel, and was very successful. It took a long time to make because of the need to construct special tracks for the many desert shots.

In late 1929 Renoir made two films as an actor with a communal group of film people that included Catherine Hessling, André Cerf, William Aguet, Pierre Prévert, and Alberto Cavalcanti. The first was *La P'tite Lili*, a filmed song, perhaps a forerunner of the brief Jeanne Moreau song sequence in *Le Petit Théâtre de Jean Renoir* (1970). The next was *Le Petit Chaperon Rouge*, in which Renoir played the wolf and shared directorial credits with Cavalcanti. During the same time Renoir also made a brief acting appearance in Lotte Reiniger's and Rochus Gliese's *Die Jagd nach dem Glück* (*The Pursuit of Happiness*). In 1930 he and Catherine Hessling separated.

Renoir's friend Pierre Braunberger had with Roger Richebé renovated the Billancourt Studios and equipped them for sound. *On Purge Bébé* (1931) was made there in order to prove to producers that Renoir could make a successful, quick, and cheap sound film, since his silent film reputation for extravagance had made it difficult for him to find work. *On Purge Bébé* fulfilled all expectations. The film cost 200,000 francs and made more than a million. Renoir wrote the script in a week, shot it in a week, and cut it the next week. It opened a week later at a Champs Élysées theater and by the following week had broken even. Many of its uses of sound seem to satirize the contemporary rush to get odd sounds on film. Renoir, for example, became the first to record the sound of a toilet flushing, which required two synchronized microphones, since there was as yet no possibility of sound mixing.

On the money and prestige Renoir made on *On Purge Bébé*, he made his first serious sound film, *La Chienne* (1931), perhaps the least known of his great films, in part paradoxically because Fritz Lang's remake, *Scarlet Street* (1945), makes it difficult to show the Renoir film commercially in the United States. Renoir demanded and got total freedom in making the film; he showed neither rushes nor dialogue to the producer until the film was over. When the producer, Roger Richebé, finally saw the film, he chased Renoir out of the studio. He had expected a farce, not the black comedy that emerged. Richebé gave the film to Paul Féjos to cut, but Féjos couldn't and had to turn it back to Renoir, with a reel of the sound, including all the street noise, lost. The first showing, at Nancy, to an audience also expecting a comedy, was a disaster. Then Leon Siritzky, a friend of Renoir's, showed it at his theater in Biarritz with advertisements telling the audience to stay away. The film became a great success, but Renoir had once again gotten the reputation of being a difficult man for producers to deal with. Janie Marèze, the female lead, died in an auto accident two weeks after the completion of the film. *La Chienne* was Georges Flament's first film and launched a career of playing the kind of world-weary sardonic role he does so well here.

The exteriors for *La Nuit du Carrefour* (1932) were shot in three weeks near Bouffemont, about twenty miles north of Paris, although the Simenon novel is set to the south. It was the first Simenon film, and the only one that Simenon himself had any connection with. (In the same year, Julien Duvivier made Simenon's *La Tête d'un Homme* and Jean Taride made *Un Chien Jaune.*) Simenon has said that Pierre Renoir is the best Maigret he has seen; while Pierre worked in the film during the day, he was stage-acting in the play *Domino* at night. It was Jacques Becker and Claude Renoir's first film. Renoir used as actors two non-professionals in important roles: Dignimont, who was a painter, and Michel Duran, a journalist—amateur actors several years before the "neo-realism" of *Toni*.

Michel Simon, by now a very successful actor, gave Renoir major help in financing *Boudu Sauvé des Eaux* (1932). René Fauchois, from whose play the film was adapted, was annoyed at the film version. In the play Lestingois, the bookstore owner and bourgeois, is the center of the action; Fauchois in fact took his part in the stage production. Boudu in the play is much more unsympathetic than in the film, and he is much more a peripheral character. *Boudu* has been described by Renoir as "a kind of free exercise around an actor."

Chotard & Compagnie (1933) is a light farce that deserves better than it has gotten from the critics, if only for its further glimpse of the manic exuberance of Georges Pomiès, who also played the hero in *Tire-au-flanc*. Originally, *Chotard* was a play written by Roger Ferdinand who, perhaps following the example of Marcel Pagnol, decided to produce movie versions of his works. He worked on the script with Renoir two months, and the shooting took twenty-three days. Fernand Charpin recreated the role of Chotard that he played in the stage version.

In a return to authentic locales, Renoir shot *Madame Bovary* (1934) in the original Normandy setting. It was not a great success, and the distributors cut its originally almost three-and-a-half hour length down drastically, inserting time and scene titles to patch the transitions. The version released in the United States was less than two hours long. The full version has disappeared because the cuts were made on both copy and negative, and the offending footage thrown away. *Bovary* may have been a commercial failure, but it was the first Renoir film to receive elaborate coverage in the New York newspapers. It opened at the Acme Theatre in Union Square, which had previously been noted for showing Russian films. The Acme's program for the occasion includes an advertisement for a restaurant "with comradely atmosphere and proletarian prices."

Toni (1935) was financed with the aid of Marcel Pagnol, who was in the process of making his own films about Marseilles and provincial life. The story is based on a dossier assembled by Jacques Mortier, then police commissioner at Martigues, near Marseilles. Mortier had been a school friend of Renoir's at Sainte-Croix and the École Massena in Nice. The crime had occurred twelve years before Renoir made the film, and the events of the film had actually taken about ten years. One scene was cut from the released version, in which Toni and Josefa wheel Albert's corpse to the woods in a washing cart, followed by three singing charcoal men, because, said Renoir, it was thought too macabre.

Le Crime de Monsieur Lange (1936) began as an idea by Jean Castanier that Jacques Becker brought to the producer Halley des Fontaines in 1935. Des Fontaines was afraid to give the film to Becker, who until then had made only two shorts. Becker was angry at everyone, especially Renoir, and left the project after arguments about the way the film was going. The breach did not last long and Becker was working again with Renoir on *La Vie Est à Nous*. He did not make a feature of his own for seven years.

Although Renoir signed the film and is its director, the

artistic management is a more complex question. After the atelier experience of *La Petite Marchande d'Allumettes*, Renoir attempted again and again to form a kind of film group or *équipe* that would work with him on many pictures and be a kind of stay against the usual directorial rootlessness caused by having almost all technicians attached to the commercial studios. In *Le Crime de Monsieur Lange*, then, the Groupe Octobre behind the scenes mirrored the co-operative before the cameras. The Groupe Octobre was a radical culture group that included among others, Jean Castanier, Pierre Prévert, Jacques Prévert, Joseph Kosma, Maurice Baquet, Marcel Duhamel, Sylvia Bataille, J.-B. Brunius, Fabien Loris, Guy Decomble, and Jean Brémaud. Renoir had entered the group through Jacques Prévert in 1932. From 1933 to 1936 it had done mainly theater work. *Lange* was its first film. The shooting of *Lange* took twenty-eight days. Much of it was improvised, especially the dialogue involving Jules Berry as Batala, the villainous publisher. In an odd sidelight on the "360° shot" discussed above, Nadia Sibirskaïa (Estelle in the film) reminisced in an interview that Renoir had forgotten to shoot the scene of the dead Batala, and her husband was enlisted to play the body so that the expensive Jules Berry didn't have to be brought in again.

La Vie Est à Nous (1936) was a similarly collective enterprise that Renoir made for the French Communist Party. Based primarily on the 1936 party program, it was never released commercially in France and was shown only at private and political meetings. Until the late 1960s it had been described in film histories as a short, although it has been argued that "short" (*court metrage* in French) was also a derisive term for a documentary film. But then a full-length print was discovered by *L'Avant-Scène* magazine. Neither Renoir nor most members of his company were Communists, but *compagnons de route*. As Renoir has said recently, "The

Communists were the ones most strong in the fight against Hitler at this time, and I believe I should give my little bit to support them." The American subtitles were done by the poet Muriel Rukeyser.

Une Partie de Campagne (1936) was originally planned as a feature of about fifty to sixty minutes. Renoir began shooting on July 15 and expected to finish quickly, but excessive rain in July and August prevented completion until early September. By that time Renoir had already signed to direct *Les Bas-Fonds*, and could not finish the Parisian portions of the film that had been planned. Sylvia Bataille remembers an atmosphere of tension and despair, but Renoir now says that the only problem was the rain. "I had written a script for sun and it rained. But that made me think of new things." Among the many people who worked on the film were Yves Allègret, Claude Heymann, and Luchino Visconti (third assistant and costume-maker), who had been introduced to Renoir by Coco Chanel. Pierre Braunberger later asked Jacques Prévert to write a scenario that would extend what had already been done. But by the time Renoir was free to film, the actors had changed physically too much for new scenes to be effective. Braunberger then added the explanatory titles to cover the projected Paris scenes. The edited copy was destroyed when the Germans occupied Paris, but Henri Langlois had saved and hidden a copy of the uncut negative. After the war it was recut by Marguerite Renoir and Pierre Lestringuez, and was finally released in 1946. The little boy fishing at the beginning of the film is Renoir's son, Alain.

The scenario of *Les Bas-Fonds* (1936) was written by Eugene Zamiatin, the author of *We*, and then an émigré in Paris. Renoir agreed to the project with only one stipulation: that he need not try for a Russian authenticity or atmosphere. Zamiatin sent the script to Gorki for his approval, and Gorki sent back a long letter dealing mainly with the reasons why the name of one character was "Louka," not "Luka." Gorki died before the film was finished. It received the first Prix Louis Delluc, which had been founded by younger critics in opposition to the Grand Prix du Cinéma, the film establishment prize. Renoir was made a Knight of the Legion of Honor by the Blum government for his direction.

Renoir says that *La Grande Illusion* (1937) might never have been made without Jean Gabin's help in persuading producers to back it. Renoir had spent three years trying to sell the story to people who complained that the only female role was a peasant and the love interest in general was too small. The script originated in stories told to Renoir by a friend of his, Pinsard, who had been in Renoir's fighter escort and had himself made seven escapes from prison camps during the war. It was originally called "Les Evasions du Capitaine Maréchal." Producers were finally found to invest two million francs in the film on the basis of Gabin's popularity. The role of Boeldieu was first proposed to Louis Jouvet, who wasn't free, and then to Pierre-Richard Willm, who refused, before it was finally accepted by Pierre Fresnay.

Raymond Blondy, the production director, first proposed Stroheim for the Rauffenstein role, which at that point was comparatively small. Renoir's respect for Stroheim, combined with his practice of rethinking the script in terms of the actors, enlarged the Rauffenstein role. Stroheim suggested the extra props of Rauffenstein's iron corset and chinstrap.

Censorship in 1937 altered the film considerably. Goebbels liked it personally, but banned it in Germany. It was also banned in Italy, and, it is said, also in Belgium, ironically enough by Paul-Henri Spaak, the brother of Charles Spaak, the scenarist of the film. Louis-Ferdinand Céline devoted a full chapter of his 1937 anti-semitic polemic, *Bagatelles pour un Massacre,* to an attack on the character of Rosenthal. *La Grande Illusion* was, however, enthusiastically received in the United States. The National Board of Review voted it the best picture of the year from any country, and in its first New York showing it ran twenty-six weeks.

The original negative of *La Grande Illusion* was destroyed in the bombing of the Maurice Laboratories in Paris. After the war a negative was recovered in Munich by Captain Wiederer of the American Army Cinematographic Services. The production company re-released it, but it was too soon after the war for it to be appreciated. After the production company went bankrupt, Renoir and Spaak bought the film back and recut it with the aid of Renée Lichtig, the editor, using the Munich negative and a print Renoir had discovered in America in 1957. It was shown at the Brussels World's Fair in 1958 and the assembled critics voted it one of the ten best films ever made.

La Marseillaise (1938) took the *équipe* method one step further by becoming one of the only commercial films that was financed by "the people." Nominally it was financed by the French trade union group, the Confédération Générale du Travail (C.G.T.). Union members were circularized by pamphlets, headed "Le film de l'union de la Nation française, le film des Droits de l'Homme et du Citoyen," that asked for a two-franc donation that would be reimbursed with the release of the film. One and a half million shares were projected, with a fifty-thousand-franc loan from the government to meet immediate needs. On October 15, 1937, *Variety* reported that a benefit was planned to raise extra funds, and on November 5, the New York *Times* announced that ten million francs had been accumulated. (During the planning for the film, the *Times* had reported on March 14, 1937, that Maurice Chevalier would play a Parisian workman and sing the title song; but none of this materialized.)

In addition to money, the C.G.T. also furnished extras for battle scenes and other group scenes, like the entrance of the Marseillais into Paris. Shooting took nine weeks, three at Fontainebleau, three in Provence, and three in Alsace. An article in *Le Canard Enchaîné*, the French satiric magazine, reported that Daladier had given Renoir trouble when he had requested army help in making the film, although Daladier had turned the entire Navy over to Marcel l'Herbier for a film with more right-wing goals. *La Marseillaise* was later banned by the Pétain government. For its re-release in the 1950s, a soundtrack recovered in Russia was used to establish continuity.

La Bête Humaine (1938) was first begun because Jean Gabin had always wanted to drive a train in a film. He had signed to do *Train d'Enfer* with Jean Grémillon, but the project dissolved. Gabin then thought of Zola's novel and with Raymond Hakim proposed the subject to Renoir. Renoir agreed and wrote in two weeks a scenario that he now considers very bad. But in the process of making the film and after discussions with Mme. Leblond-Zola (with whom he had worked on *Nana*), he completely redid the script, bringing it closer to Zola's own language. Since Jacques Becker ceased working with Renoir after *La Marseillaise*, Renoir's brother Claude was called in as assistant director. *La Bête Humaine* has also suffered from censorship. It was thought immoral when first shown after the war, and was banned at Bruay-en-Artois, Cherbourg, and Soissons. Renoir wrote to Hakim about cuts in one sequence particularly, Lantier's attempts to murder his cousin; shots of Simone Simon's body have also been cut from the original. Like *La Chienne*, *La Bête Humaine* was remade by Fritz Lang: *Human Desire* (1954), starring Glenn Ford, Broderick Crawford, and Gloria Grahame. *Variety* reported that because Robert and Raymond Hakim were contemplating yet another remake it was not allowed to be shown at the 1969 Lincoln Center Renoir retrospective. This new remake has not yet appeared.

For *La Règle du Jeu* (1939) Renoir once again founded his own production company, this time with Claude Renoir, Camille François, and Olivier Billioux. His son, Alain Renoir, was an assistant cameraman. The company originally planned to do two films a year, but the war intervened. The Technicolor company had expressed an interest in having Renoir shoot *La Règle du Jeu* in color. Renoir thought that the Sologne countryside, where the film is set, would be perfect for color, and was willing to make a deal if Technicolor would pay for all expenses beyond those normal for a black-and-white film. But he needed the agreement in a week, since the shooting schedule was already arranged. He thought the time would be too short. Technicolor couldn't respond in time, and Renoir was not to make his first color film until *The River* (1950).

After Simone Simon had asked for more money than the producer was willing to give for the part of Christine, Renoir, according to André Zwoboda, spotted Nora Gregor, Princess Starhemberg, at a play (in the audience, not on the stage) and hired her: she had recently come to France in the aftermath of the *Anschluss*. Unfortunately, she turned out to be a bad actress (she had never acted before) and Renoir was forced to eliminate her from many scenes and introduce more improvisation into the script, expanding the parts of Paulette Dubost (Lisette) and Mila Parély (Geneviève)—a fascinating example of the way casting and the dynamics of production influence the final shape of a film.

The production schedule was aimed toward a showing at the New York World's Fair later that year, but the violent reactions of the first audiences and the onset of war prevented the showing. The Union Sacrée, a French clerical fascist group, organized noisy demonstrations wherever *La*

Règle du Jeu was shown. Matters had not been helped by preceding the film by a 40-minute short extolling the French empire. Renoir himself was horrified at the audience response. "I thought that I was gentle with them, and they thought I was laughing at them." He cut one scene after another, until the film was shortened from 113 to 85 minutes, but still the audiences rioted, and the film was a complete commercial failure. It was banned by the government shortly after the start of the war and then re-banned by the occupying German forces. The original negative at the Boulogne studios was destroyed by Allied bombs. *La Règle du Jeu* was re-released in mutilated form in 1945 and 1948. But it was not reconstituted into its original form until 1956 by Jean Gaborit, Jacques Durand, with the help of Jacques Maréchal, Joseph Kosma, and a consultation with Renoir. Gaborit and Durand had to work from two hundred cans of fragments: mixed scenes, bits of sound track, positive and negative prints. In 1962 an international poll of film critics named it the third greatest film ever made.

Renoir directed only the first scenes of *La Tosca* (1940), and then turned it over to Carl Koch, who had worked with Renoir on *La Marseillaise* and *La Règle du Jeu*. (His wife, Lotte Reiniger, had done the shadow-theater sequence in *La Marseillaise*.) Renoir had already had offers from the United States. But he felt obligations both to France and to the Scalera company who produced *La Tosca*. In late 1939, he entered the French Army as a lieutenant in the Service Cinématographique. In early 1940 he went to Italy; Italy entered the war in June, but in August Renoir wrote to Robert Flaherty that he could not leave until he believed both that Scalera no longer needed his services and that he couldn't work in France; he wanted to stay in France until things settled and then he could leave more naturally to make a film in another country, as he had frequently wanted to.

By mid-August Renoir had decided that since Italy was at war, Scalera probably did not want him to fulfill his contract at the present time. He left for Vichy to ask the film industry head, Tixier Vignancourt, if he were needed in France. Renoir was two years short of the age (forty-eight) necessary to leave the country without question, but thought that because of his severe World War I wounds, he might be excused. Meanwhile, Flaherty arranged with the State Department to expedite the passage of Renoir and his companion Dido Freire, Alberto Cavalcanti's niece and the script girl for La Règle du Jeu.

Flaherty and Albert Lewin undertook to attest that Renoir would be an important addition to the American film industry and was in no danger of becoming a ward of the state. After telegrams and letters, first Renoir and then Dido Freire arrived in Lisbon and then in late December both flew to the United States. Renoir had tried to bring his son Alain over with him, making it part of his Twentieth Century-Fox contract that Alain receive an acting contract. But Alain was too young to get out of France. He joined the Free French Army and later fought with the American Army as an artillery captain in the Pacific, after training at Camp Roberts in Paso Robles, California. After the war he enrolled as a student at the University of California, Santa Barbara, and is now Professor of Medieval Literature at Berkeley, and head of the Department of Comparative Literature.

America was not entirely new to Renoir. He even had family, a line of cousins founded by his mother's father, who left his wife in 1865 and came to North Dakota to build one of the first farms in the territory. (The family story maintains that he left because his wife drove him crazy

with her insistence on highly polished wood floors, an obsession she passed on to the wife in "La Cireuse Électrique"
section of *Le Petit Théâtre de Jean Renoir*.) Renoir also
felt at home because of the many American films he had
seen. "I knew more about American life from the Harry
Langdon comedies than I did from the most serious documentary." But lacking knowledge of English, he was uncertain about scripts and Fox held him back by giving him
scenarios set in Europe, to which he was supposed to give
his foreign "touch." Fired by a desire to engage an American
theme, he found a Dudley Nichols script, and told Darryl
Zanuck he was going to Georgia to film *Swamp Water*
(1941). Renoir was slow in his production schedule and the
studio chiefs wanted to fire him, but he retained Zanuck's
support. After winning one final conflict, Renoir returned
to the set to find actors and technicians all standing at
attention in tribute. The Fox producer had wanted Renoir to
use Linda Darnell because she was authentically from the
countryside. "She's a good actress but her voice had nothing
of the country in it. I took Anne Baxter instead. She was
unknown at that time and had a perfectly bourgeois and
urban background. But she could talk like a farmgirl."
Swamp Water was also the first film of any importance for
Dana Andrews.

Renoir's relationship with Fox does not seem to have
been happy. In two letters of 1942 to Flaherty (in the
Flaherty collection, Butler Library, Columbia University),
he complains about his inability to do the pictures he wants,
as well as the generally poor quality of Hollywood films then
being made. Universal proposed a picture with Deanna Dur-
bin. The project was begun but never got anywhere because
Renoir was uncomfortable working in the style Henry Koster
had established for her films. Another abortive project was

a film of Saint-Exupéry's *Terre des Hommes,* for which Renoir and Saint-Exupéry had worked out a treatment.

By 1943 Renoir had signed with RKO and was feeling easier; he told Flaherty that the experience working there was much more pleasant than any he had had so far in Hollywood. By March he had finished *This Land Is Mine* for RKO. The Premier Plan volume on Renoir reports that its reception in France after the war was generally unfavorable, as was the reception of almost all of Renoir's American films until Eric Rohmer attempted a re-evaluation in 1952. Renoir himself says the reception was neither good nor bad, but thought that it was a mistake to release it in France. During this period he also made several films for the Office of War Information, including *Salute to France,* considering these propaganda pieces to be work that he owed to the United States for taking him in. He disclaims any directorial credit for the films and says he gave mainly technical assistance. On February 6, 1944 he and Dido Freire were officially married, with Dudley Nichols and Charles Laughton among the witnesses.

The Southerner (1945) was Renoir's first independent project in Hollywood. It was produced by Robert Hakim, who had produced *La Bête Humaine,* and David Loew, the partner of Albert Lewin, director of *The Picture of Dorian Gray.* William Faulkner was consulted a few times by Renoir, mainly about dialogue. The film was a great popular success, not least because it was the target of a Ku Klux Klan-supported boycott that had also been aimed at John Ford's *Grapes of Wrath,* even though that film had been made in 1940. *The Southerner* was not released in France until 1950, which prompted one French critic to deduce that United Artists, the distribution company, was trying to soft-pedal the film because of the boycott.

Renoir has said that he was as free in making *Diary of*

a Chambermaid (1946) as he was in making *The Southerner*. But the "naturalistic" *Southerner* was more obviously a "Renoir" film. When it appeared in France in 1948, André Bazin treated it mainly as a "deficient *Règle du Jeu*," but later revised his views to praise it highly. The filming of Mirbeau's novel had been an old project from silent days, conceived in "a romantic fashion, very Nana." Like Zola, Mirbeau had been connected with the Impressionist circle. In his art criticism he was one of the fiercest defenders of Auguste Renoir's paintings. Renoir also had wanted for some time to do a film with Paulette Goddard. Although the use of studio sets give the film a formal tone, much was improvised, including the final "lynching" scene, which was not in the script. As I mentioned above, Luis Buñuel made his own film version of the novel in 1964.

Renoir wrote to Flaherty that he considered the subject of *Woman on the Beach* (1946) insignificant, but enjoyed working with the actors and writers. Joan Bennett had in fact asked RKO to make the film. After a very negative preview audience in Santa Barbara, Renoir cut the film severely and reshot about a third of it—mostly scenes between Robert Ryan and Joan Bennett.

After *Woman on the Beach* Renoir helped form the Film Group to encourage young directors to make classical theater pieces into films, but the project was abandoned for lack of money. Other Hollywood projects foundered and Renoir worked on a book until in 1949 he read Rumer Godden's novel *The River* and wrote for an option. He didn't want to make a film of the novel, but only to use it as an inspiration for another scenario. Then he became more interested in a film based on the Godden novel. The producers he approached thought of the project in terms of elephants and maharajas, but Renoir wanted a film that would be related to his own experience as a stranger in India. Finally

Renoir found a sympathetic backer who also had contacts in India. In April 1949 he went to India with his wife Dido, producer Kenneth McEldowney, and associate producer Forrest Judd to scout locations. Shooting was slated to begin on November 20 but was delayed until December 5, 1949. The lead role of Harriet was played by Patricia Walters, a non-professional whom Renoir found in a Calcutta school. All the sound was recorded on the spot because of Renoir's distaste for postdubbing. *The River* marked the first use in films of Western Electric's magnetic tape-recording equipment—a further example of Renoir's interest in technical innovation.

Renoir returned to France in mid-1951 after the French courts had decided not to press bigamy charges against him for his marriage to Dido, which, although perfectly legal in the United States, had run into trouble under French law. Renoir made plans to film Camus' *L'Étranger* and proposed Gérard Philippe as Meursault. But the chance of working with Anna Magnani on *Le Carrosse d'Or* (1953) brought him to Italy instead. The film was made in English, French, and Italian versions. The original scenario opened in Venice with Ramon, but the final film stayed in the Peruvian locale. In line with his frequent statement that his films of the 1950s were mere *jeux d'esprit,* Renoir wrote an article about *Le Carrosse d'Or* entitled "Je n'ai pas tourné mon film au Perou," his adaptation of the French idiom meaning "it's no big thing."

In 1954 Renoir toyed with a film project about the life of Vincent van Gogh, a film set one hundred years ago in Bourgogne to be called *Les Braconniers,* and an adaptation of Turgenev's *First Love.* In July he directed *Julius Caesar* in the Roman Arena at Arles, with Jean-Pierre Aumont (Marc Antony) and Paul Meurisse (Brutus) in the cast. *French Cancan* (1955) took six months to make because of the elaborate sets. Jean Gabin was somewhat apprehensive about working with Renoir after so many years, but found him the same as he had been in *La Grande Illusion* and *La Bête Humaine*. Pierre Leprohon reports seeing a work photo from the film of Degas, Pissarro, and van Gogh that does not appear in the final version.

Between *French Cancan* and *Elena* Renoir directed his own play *Orvet* at the Théâtre de la Renaissance, opening March 12, 1955. Originally written in 1953 for Leslie Caron (whom Renoir had met in Hollywood) as an adaptation from the scenario for *Les Braconniers, Orvet* was rewritten by Renoir to suit the talents of Paul Meurisse, whom Renoir had been very impressed by in *Julius Caesar*.

Elena et les Hommes (1956) began as a direct romantic adaptation of the life of General Boulanger that was gradually changed because Renoir and the producer did not want to offend Boulanger's family. *Variety* reported that an English version was to be made by Warners, with Cy Howard helping Renoir on the script. But nothing seems finally to have come of the project.

In 1957 Renoir directed again for the stage, this time an adaptation of Clifford Odets' *The Big Knife,* with Daniel Gélin, Claude Génia, and Paul Bernard in the cast.

In 1959 a planned film version of Simenon's *Trois Chambres à Manhattan,* to have starred Leslie Caron, fell through and Renoir moved enthusiastically into television. *Le Testament du Docteur Cordelier* (1959) arose, says Renoir, from a mingling of Faust and Stevenson. In an interview with Jean-Luc Godard in *Arts* (21 avril 1959), Renoir explained why he enjoyed working in television: "The technicians must necessarily become actors, invisible actors of course, but actors who have their own part in the creation of the work." Renoir's own role in directing these "free agent technicians" resembles the position of the eighteenth-century watchmaker-

Woman on the Beach. Lieutenant Scott Burnett (Robert Ryan) meets Peggy Butler (Joan Bennett) collecting driftwood on the beach next to a wrecked ship. Below, Scott Burnett passes a cigarette to Peggy Butler in front of her blind husband Tod (Charles Bickford). Even in this darker film, once again the order of the dinner table.

The River. Above left, "We welcome you to this film." The ceremonial floor painting before the credits. Below left, Melanie (Rahda) in an inlet of the Ganges. Above, the house that lets the world in. From left to right: Ram Singh (Sahjn Singh), Nan (Suprova Mukerjee), and the Mother (Nora Swinburne). Below, a production shot of Jean Renoir and Rumer Godden with all the children in the film including Harriet (Patricia Walters) (at Renoir's left) and Bogey (Richard Foster) (on the ground in front of Harriet).

Le Carrosse d'Or. The traveling *commedia dell'arte* company has set up its stage in the courtyard of an inn in eighteenth-century Peru. On stage holding a lyre is Camilla (Anna Magnani) dressed as Colombine. Above right, over dinner the Viceroy (Duncan Lamont) takes off his formal wig to Camilla to show that he can be out of costume too. Below right, Camilla descending from the coach the Viceroy has given her, just before the Archbishop is to decide who the real owner of the coach is.

Renoir on the set of *French Cancan*. Dido Renoir on the left.

French Cancan. Below, Danglard (Jean Gabin) hears of his upcoming bankruptcy, while Nini (François Arnoul) looks inquisitively at Danglard's valet (Gaston Modot). Near right, in a production shot Renoir gives some idea of the proper cancan technique. Far right, Danglard and Nini dance at a small club where Danglard gets the idea to revive the cancan. Below right, the Grand Opening of the Moulin Rouge and the cancan finale, while Danglard sits backstage and swings his foot in time.

Elena et les Hommes. Miarka (Juliette Greco) enters the house where Rollan (Jean Marais) and Elena (Ingrid Bergman) are meeting. Below, Miarka, the gypsy singer, once again off to the side, this time, while Elena and Rollan embrace.

Le Testament du Dr. Cordelier. Opale (Jean-Louis Barrault) on the psychiatrist's couch. Below, Opale taking care of a cripple.

Le Déjeuner sur l'Herbe. Nino (Fernand Sardou) eating with Ritou (Jean-Pierre Granval) while Ritou's wife Titine (Jacqueline Morane) serves. Below, another lunch. This time the official picnic to announce the upcoming marriage of Etienne Alexis (Paul Meurisse) (at the center table) and Marie-Charlotte (Ingrid Nordine) (sitting with him). At the right hand table are M. and Mme. Poignant (J. Danoville and Marguerite Cassan), the first parents to have a child by Etienne's methods of artificial insemination. Behind Etienne is Nénette (Catherine Rouvel). Surrounding the picnic group is a recently descended group of paparazzi. Above right, Etienne Alexis and Nénette after Pan's wind has taken over.

Le Déjeuner sur l'Herbe. Intoxicated by the strange wind, the Poignants dance in a ruined temple of Diana, while Gaspard (Charles Blavette) and his goat Cabri sit by the proscenium.

Le Caporal Epinglé. Left, the Corporal (Jean-Pierre Cassel) tries figure out an escape route. Right, in a railroad compartment a sold disguised as a woman (Sacha Briquet) explains his plans to t escaping Corporal. Below, Renoir poses with his actors. On Renoi left is Claude Brasseur (Pater). Jean-Pierre Cassel sits on the flo and Claude Rich (Ballochet) is wearing glasse

God. "My work consists solely in placing several forces in relations like a clockmaker would assemble the various wheels of his mechanism. Then everything is let go, and each wheel plays its personal note in the final concert." Some critics have said that the film cost only about $8000, but Renoir has recently asserted that it was $100,000, still cheap but not extraordinarily so. *Cordelier* was the first TV-cinema co-production in France. It required fifteen days of rehearsal and ten and a half of shooting.

Le Déjeuner sur l'Herbe (1959), like *Cordelier,* was made with television methods, using five cameras and constructed by scenes rather than by shots. The search for proper exteriors took about a month, then three weeks of rehearsal for the technicians and the actors, and finally twenty days of actual shooting time. Despite the television methods, the film cost almost as much as a traditional one. Renoir has said that he used television methods, not necessarily for economy, but "to direct a kind of filmed poem."

Le Caporal Épinglé (1962) was first turned down as a project by Renoir, because he wanted to finish the biography of his father. Then he read the Jacques Perret novel and accepted.

In 1962 Renoir also published his biography of his father, and planned a collection of short films to be entitled *C'est la Révolution* and star Paul Meurisse and Simone Signoret. His first novel *Les Cahiers du Capitaine Georges* was published in 1966. At about this time he was to contribute a film version of Poe's "The Strange System of Dr. Tarr and Professor Feather" to a film that would also include sections by Fellini and Roger Vadim. But Claude Chabrol had already done a script, and Renoir withdrew from the project.

For several years Renoir had been trying to interest producers in a script entitled *La Clocharde,* in which Jeanne Moreau would play the leading role. He also put together a group of short pieces in the form now called *Le Petit Théâtre de Jean Renoir* (1969). The French Film Center refused funds, believing that Renoir could not at his advanced age make or finish the film. Finally French and Italian television decided to co-produce it and it was filmed in the summer of 1969 and first shown in the United States, unfortunately without subtitles, at the Los Angeles County Museum on May 15, 1970, and then at the Metropolitan Museum of Art in New York in the fall. Renoir was disappointed that the film had no subtitles and did not want it shown without them, but was prevailed upon to allow the showing. The film received its European television showing in December 1970; by contract it cannot have commercial release until sixteen months later. There are no plans for U.S. release as yet.

Renoir has one other script that he will probably not now film himself. Called *Julienne et Son Amour*, it is the story of a prostitute and the rich man who discovers that he can fall asleep only when he is in bed with her. Meanwhile, Renoir is working on a book of reminiscences that will, he says, deal in part with his life in films.

Filmography

UNE VIE SANS JOIE

DATE: 1924 (re-edited in 1927 and released under the title *Catherine*)
TIME: 80 min.
INTERIORS: Gaumont Studios
EXTERIORS: Saint-Paul de Vence, Cagnes-sur-mer
PRODUCTION SCHEDULE: Spring 1924
FIRST FRENCH SHOWING: Paris, 1924
DIRECTOR: Albert Dieudonné
SCENARIO: Jean Renoir
PHOTOGRAPHY: Jean Bachelet, Gibory
PRODUCER: Jean Renoir
CAST: Catherine Hessling (*Catherine Ferand*)
    Albert Dieudonné (*M. Mallet, the owner*)
    Pierre Philippe (pseudonym of Pierre Lestringuez)
      (*the pimp*)
    Pierre Champagne (*the owner's son*)
    Oléo (*a prostitute*)
    Georges Térof (*Gédéon Grané*)
    Eugénie Naud (*Madame Laisné*)
    Jean Renoir (*le sous préfet*)
    Louis Gauthier (*Georges Mallet*)
    Monfils

LA FILLE DE L'EAU

DATE: 1924

BRITISH TITLE: The Whirlpool of Fate

INTERIORS: "La Nicotière," property of Paul Cézanne *fils*
at Marlotte; "Au Bon Coin" bar

EXTERIORS: Marlotte, borders of the forest of Fontainebleau;
Loing River at Montigny

PRODUCTION SCHEDULE: Summer 1924

FIRST FRENCH SHOWING: Paris, December 12, 1924; public
showing, April 1925

TIME: 80 min.

SCENARIO: Pierre Lestringuez

PHOTOGRAPHY: Jean Bachelet, Gibory

SET DESIGN: Jean Renoir

ASSISTANT DIRECTOR: Pierre Champagne

PRODUCER: Jean Renoir

DISTRIBUTION: G.-M. Films

PRINTS OWNED BY: Cinémathèque Française (multilated),
British Film Institute

CAST: Catherine Hessling (*Virginie*)
Pierre Philippe (*Uncle Jeff*)
Pierre Champagne (*Justin Crépoix*)
Harold Lewingston (*Georges Lanval*)
Maurice Touzé (*Ferret*)
Georges Térof (*M. Raynal*)
Henriette Moret (*La Roussette*)
Charlotte Clasis (*Mme. Maubien*)
Fockenberghe (*Mme. Raynal*)
Pierre Renoir (*a peasant with a pitchfork*)
André Derain (*owner of "Au Bon Coin"*)
Van Doren

NANA

DATE: 1926
INTERIORS: Grunewald Studios in Berlin, Gaumont Studios in Paris
EXTERIORS: Paris: Montigny
PRODUCTION SCHEDULE: October 1925–February 1926
FIRST FRENCH SHOWING: Paris, April 27, 1926
FIRST U.S. SHOWING: New York, Acme Theatre, December 9, 1926
TIME: 98 min.
SCENARIO: Pierre Lestringuez, based on the novel by Emile Zola
SCRIPT: Intertitles written by Jean Renoir and Mme. Denise Leblond-Zola, Zola's daughter
PHOTOGRAPHY: Jean Bachelet, Edmund Corwin, Holski, Asselin, Périe
SET DESIGN: Claude Autant-Lara, constructed by Robert-Jules Garnier
ASSISTANT DIRECTOR: André Cerf
PRODUCER: Jean Renoir
PRODUCTION MANAGER: R. Turgy
DISTRIBUTION: Aubert, Moviegraph (U.S.)
PRINTS OWNED BY: Cinémathèque Française, Eastman House, British Film Institute (incomplete)
CAST: Catherine Hessling (Nana)
 Werner Krauss (Count Muffat)
 Jean Angelo (Count de Vandeuvres)
 Raymond Guérin-Catelain (Georges Hugon)
 Pierre Champagne (La Falàise)
 Pierre Philippe (Bordenave)
 Valeska Gert (Zoé, Nana's maid)

Harbacher (*Francis, Nana's hairdresser*)
André Cerf (*Le Tigre, Nana's groom*)
Jacqueline Forzane (*Countess Muffat*)
Claude Moore (pseudonym of Autant-Lara) (*Fauchery*)
Jacqueline Ford (*Rose Mignon*)
Nita Romani (*Satin*)
Marie Prévost (*Gogo*)
René Koval (*Fontan*)
Pierre Braunberger (*a pretty girl*)
R. Turgy (*a spectator*)

SUR UN AIR DE CHARLESTON

DATE: 1927
INTERIORS: Épinay Studios
PRODUCTION SCHEDULE: 3 days in autumn, 1926
FIRST FRENCH SHOWING: Paris, March 19, 1927
TIME: 22 min.
SCENARIO: Pierre Lestringuez, from an idea by André Cerf
PHOTOGRAPHY: Jean Bachelet
SET DESIGN: Jean Renoir(?) The set is so elaborate, yet no
    designer is listed in the credits.
MUSIC: Clément Doucet
ASSISTANT DIRECTORS: André Cerf, Claude Heymann
PRINTS OWNED BY: British Film Institute
CAST: Catherine Hessling (*the dancer*)
      Johnny Higgins (*the explorer*)
      Pierre Braunberger (*an angel*)
      Pierre Lestringuez (*another angel*)

LA P'TITE LILI
(*Tragédie sur une toile d'emballage*)

DATE: 1929
TIME: 11 min.
INTERIORS: Billancourt Studios
FIRST FRENCH SHOWING: October 1929
DIRECTOR: Alberto Cavalcanti
SCENARIO: Alberto Cavalcanti, from a 1900 song by Louis
    Benech
PHOTOGRAPHY: Rogers
SET DESIGN: Eric Aës
PRODUCER: Pierre Braunberger
PRODUCTION COMPANY: Néo-Film
CAST: Catherine Hessling (*La P'tite Lili*)
    Jean Renoir (*the pimp*)
    Guy Ferrand (*the singer*)
    Roland Caillaux (*la concierge*)
    Eric Aës
    Dido Freire
    Rogers

MARQUITA

DATE: 1927
INTERIORS: Gaumont Studios at Buttes-Chaumont
EXTERIORS: Nice, Moyenne Corniche
PRODUCTION SCHEDULE: late 1926
FIRST FRENCH SHOWING: Paris, July 1927; public, August
    1927
TIME: 87 min.

SCENARIO: Pierre Lestringuez
PHOTOGRAPHY: Jean Bachelet, Raymond Agnel
SET DESIGN: Robert-Jules Garnier
ASSISTANT DIRECTOR: M. Gargour
PRODUCTION COMPANY: Artistes Réunis (Films Renoir)
DISTRIBUTION: Jean de Merly
CAST: Jean Angelo (*Prince Vlasco*)
     Marie-Louise Iribe (*Marquita*)
     Henri Debain (*the Chamberlain*)
     Lucien Mancini (*the step-father*)
     Pierre Philippe (*the casino director*)
     Pierre Champagne (*a taxi driver*)
     Simone Cerdan

LA PETITE MARCHANDE D'ALLUMETTES

DATE: 1928
AMERICAN TITLE: The Little Match Girl
INTERIORS: Attic of the Vieux-Colombier Théâtre, Paris
EXTERIORS: Dunes near Marly; Bourbon Marlotte near Fontainebleau
PRODUCTION SCHEDULE: shooting over by January 1928
FIRST FRENCH SHOWING: Silent version shown at Geneva, March, 1928; Sound, Paris, July 1929
FIRST U.S. SHOWING: New York, Museum of Modern Art, February 1, 1954
TIME: 29 min.
DIRECTOR: Jean Renoir, with the collaboration of Jean Tedesco
SCENARIO: Jean Renoir, based on the story by Hans Christian Andersen, entitled in French, "La Petite Fille aux Allumettes"

PHOTOGRAPHY: Jean Bachelet
SET DESIGN: Eric Aës
MUSIC: For the sound version, not an integral part of the
    film: Strauss, Wagner, Mendelssohn, etc., arranged by
    Manuel Rosenthal, Michael Grant
ASSISTANT DIRECTORS: Claude Heymann, Simone Hamiguet
PRODUCERS: Jean Renoir and Jean Tedesco
DISTRIBUTION: Films SOFAR
PRINTS OWNED BY: Museum of Modern Art, Cinémathèque
    Française, British Film Institute (incomplete)
LAB: Neuilly, developed by Ralleigh
CAST: Catherine Hessling (*The Little Match Girl*)
    Jean Storm (*the Young Man and the Soldier*)
    Manuel Raaby (pseudonym of Rabinovitch) (*the Po-
    liceman and the emissary of Death*)
    Amy Wells (*the dancing doll*)

TIRE-AU-FLANC

DATE: 1928
INTERIORS: Billancourt Studios
EXTERIORS: Cent Gardes barracks in the Bois de Saint-Cloud
PRODUCTION SCHEDULE: Summer 1928
FIRST FRENCH SHOWING: Paris, July 1928; public showing,
    December 1928
TIME: 80 min.
SCENARIO: Jean Renoir and Claude Heymann from the play
    by A. Mouézy-Eon and A. Sylvane
TITLES: André Rigaud and Jean Renoir(?)
PHOTOGRAPHY: Jean Bachelet
SET DESIGN: Eric Aës
ASSISTANT DIRECTOR: André Cerf, Lola Markovitch
PRODUCER: Pierre Braunberger

PRODUCTION COMPANY: Néo-Film
DISTRIBUTION: Films Armor
PRINTS OWNED BY: Cinémathèque Française
CAST: Georges Pomiès (*Jean Dubois d'Ombelles*)
Michel Simon (*Joseph*)
Félix Oudart (*Colonel Brochard*)
Jeanne Helbling (*Solange*)
Jean Storm (*Lieutenant Daumel*)
Paul Velsa (*Corporal Bourrache*)
Manuel Raaby (*the Sergeant*)
Fridette Fatton (*Georgette*)
Maryanne (*Mme. Blandin*)
Zellas (*Muflot*)
Kinny Dorlay (*Lili*)
Esther Kiss (*Madame Fléchais*)
André Cerf (*a soldier*)
Max Dalban (*a soldier*)

LE TOURNOI DANS LA CITÉ

DATE: 1929
INTERIORS: St. Maurice Studios
EXTERIORS: Carcassonne, during the 2000th anniversary cele-
bration
PRODUCTION SCHEDULE: Summer and autumn 1928
FIRST FRENCH SHOWING: Before Belgian royal family toward
the end of 1928; Paris, February 1929
TIME: 73 min.(?)
SCENARIO: Jean Renoir, from the novel by Henri Dupuy-
Mazuel
PHOTOGRAPHY: Marcel Lucien, Maurice Desfassiaux
CAMERAMAN: J.-L. Mundwiller
SET DESIGN: Robert Mallet-Stevens

COSTUMES: Georges Barbier
SPECIAL EFFECTS: Tournament staged by Captain Wemaere
    of the Saumur Cavalry School
ASSISTANT DIRECTOR: André Cerf
EDITOR: André Cerf
PRODUCER: Henri Dupuy-Mazuel
PRODUCTION ASSISTANT: Pierre Delmonde
PRODUCTION COMPANY: Société des Films Historiques (De
    Maroussen and François Harlspuru)
DISTRIBUTION: Jean de Merly, Fernand Weil
PRINTS OWNED BY: Ten minutes owned by Cinémathèque
    Française
CAST: Aldo Nadi (*François de Baynes*)
        Jackie Monnier (*Isabelle Ginori*)
        Enrique Rivero (*Henri de Rogier*)
        Manuel Raaby (*Count Ginori*)
        Blanche Bernis (*Catherine de Médicis*)
        Suzanne Desprès (*Countess de Baynes*)
        Gérard Mock (*Charles IX*)
        Viviane Clarens (*Lucrèce Pazzi*)
        Narval (*Antonio the dwarf*)
        Janvier (*the King's aide*)
        William Aguet (*Master of the Horse*)
        Max Dalban (*Captain of the Watch*)
        Students of the Saumur Cadre Noir

LE BLED

DATE: 1929
INTERIORS: Joinville Réservoirs Studios
EXTERIORS: Algiers, Sidi Ferruch, Biskra, Boufarik, Staouéli
PRODUCTION SCHEDULE: February–March 1929
FIRST FRENCH SHOWING: Paris, May 1929

TIME: 87 min.

SCENARIO: Henri Dupuy-Mazuel, André Jaeger-Schmidt

TITLES: André Rigaud

PHOTOGRAPHY: Marcel Lucien, Morizet, André Bac, Boissey

SET DESIGN: William Aguet

SPECIAL EFFECTS: Technical Director: J.-L. Mundwiller

ASSISTANT DIRECTOR: André Cerf, René Arcy-Hennery

PRODUCER: Henri Dupuy-Mazuel

PRODUCTION COMPANY: Société des films historiques, aided
    by the French Government

DISTRIBUTION: Mappemonde Films

PRINTS OWNED BY: Cinémathèque Française

CAST: Jackie Monnier (*Claudie Duvernet*)
      Enrique Rivero (*Pierre Hoffer*)
      Arquillière (*Christian Hoffer*)
      Diana Hart (*Diane Duvernet*)
      Manuel Raaby (*Manuel Duvernet*)
      Bérardi Aïssa (*Zoubir*)
      Jacques Becker (*one of Christian Hoffer's farm
          hands*)
      Hadj Ben Yasmina (*the chauffeur*)
      M. Martin (*the falconer*)
      Rozier (*Marie-Jeanne*)

LE PETIT CHAPERON ROUGE

DATE: 1929

INTERIORS: Billancourt Studios

EXTERIORS: Marlotte

FIRST FRENCH SHOWING: Paris, July 1929

DIRECTORS: Albert Cavalcanti, Jean Renoir

SCENARIO: Adapted by Alberto Cavalcanti and Jean Renoir
    from the story by Charles Perrault
PHOTOGRAPHY: Marcel Lucien
MUSIC: Maurice Jaubert; song "La Java du Loup" by
    Claude André Puget
CAST: Catherine Hessling (*Little Red Riding Hood*)
    Jean Renoir (*the Wolf*)
    André Cerf (*the notary*)
    Pierre Prévert (*a little girl*)
    Pablo Quevedo (*the young man*)
    La Montagne (*a farmer*)
    William Aguet (*an old Englishwoman*)
    Mme. Nekrassof
    Viviane Clarens
    Pola Illery
    Amy Wells
    Raymond Guérin

ON PURGE BÉBÉ

DATE: 1931
INTERIORS: Billancourt Studios
PRODUCTION SCHEDULE: 6 days in July 1931
FIRST FRENCH SHOWING: Paris, Aubert-Palace, August 1931
TIME: 62 min.
SCENARIO: Jean Renoir, from the play by Georges Feydeau
DIALOGUE: Georges Feydeau
PHOTOGRAPHY: Théodore Sparkuhl, Roger Hubert
STILLS: Roger Forster
SET DESIGN: Gabriel Scognamillo
SOUND: D. F. Scanlon and Bugnon for Western Electric
ASSISTANT DIRECTOR: Claude Heymann, Pierre Schwab
EDITOR: Jean Mamy

PRODUCER: Production Director: Charles David; Administrator: Roger Woog; Production Assistant: Gaillard
PRODUCTION COMPANY: Braunberger-Richebé
PRINTS OWNED BY: Cinémathèque Française
CAST: Louvigny (*Follavoine*)
    Marguerite Pierry (*Julie Follavoine*)
    Michel Simon (*Chouilloux*)
    Olga Valery (*Clémence Chouilloux*)
    Sacha Tarride (*Toto Follavoine*)
    Nicole Fernandez (*Rose*)
    Fernandel (*Truchet*)

LA CHIENNE

DATE: 1931
INTERIORS: Billancourt Studios
EXTERIORS: Paris, Montmartre, Nogent, Avenue Matignon
PRODUCTION SCHEDULE: Summer 1931
FIRST FRENCH SHOWING: Nancy; Biarritz; Paris, Colisée, November 1931
FIRST U.S. SHOWING: New York, Museum of Modern Art, February 2, 1954
TIME: 100 min.
SCENARIO: Jean Renoir and André Girard, after the novel of Georges de la Fouchardière
SCRIPT: Jean Renoir, Pierre Schwab
PHOTOGRAPHY: Théodore Sparkuhl, Roger Hubert
SET DESIGN: Gabriel Scognamillo
SOUND: Courme, Joseph de Bretagne and Courme, with the advice of Hotchkiss and Bell of Western Electric
ASSISTANT DIRECTOR: Claude Heymann, Pierre Prévert
EDITOR: Marguerite Renoir

PRODUCTION COMPANY: Braunberger-Richebé; Production
    Director: Charles David; Administrator: Roger Woog;
    Production Assistant: Gaillard
DISTRIBUTION: Europe-Films (C.S.C.)
PRINTS OWNED BY: Cinémathèque Française
CAST: Michel Simon (*Maurice Legrand*)
    Janie Marèze (*Lulu*)
    Georges Flamant (*Dédé*)
    Madeleine Bérubet (*Adèle Legrand*)
    Gaillard (*Alexis Godard*)
    Jean Gehret (*Dagodet*)
    Lucien Mancini (*the gallery owner*)
    Sylvain Itkine (*the lawyer*)
    Alexandre Rignault (*the art critic*)
    Max Dalban (*Bonnard*)
    Colette Borelli (*Lulu's friend*)
    Romain Bouquet (*the owner of the drygoods store*)
    Pierre Destys (*Gustave*)
    Jane Pierson (*the concierge*)
    Henri Guisol (*Amédée*)

LA NUIT DU CARREFOUR

DATE: 1932
INTERIORS: Billancourt Studios
EXTERIORS: Bouffemont
PRODUCTION SCHEDULE: January–February 1932
FIRST FRENCH SHOWING: Paris, April 1932
TIME: 80 min.
SCENARIO: Jean Renoir, after the novel by Georges Simenon
SCRIPT: Jean Renoir
SCRIPT GIRL: Suzanne de Troyes
PHOTOGRAPHY: Marcel Lucien, Asselin, Fabian

SET DESIGN: William Aguet, assisted by Jean Castanier
SOUND: Bugnon, Joseph de Bretagne
SCRIPT GIRL: Suzanne de Troyes
ASSISTANT DIRECTOR: Jacques Becker, Maurice Blondeau
EDITOR: Marguerite Renoir
PRODUCTION COMPANY: Europa-Films
DISTRIBUTION: Comptoir Francais Cinématographique
PRINTS OWNED BY: Cinémathèque Française
CAST: Pierre Renoir (*Inspector Maigret*)
      Winna Winfried (*Else Andersen*)
      Georges Koudria (*Carl Andersen*)
      Georges Térof (*Lucas*)
      Dignimont (*Oscar*)
      G. A. Martin (*Grandjean*)
      Jean Gehret (*Michonnet*)
      Michel Duran (*Jojo*)
      Jean Mitry (*Arsène*)
      Max Dalban (*the Doctor*)
      Gaillard (*the butcher*)
      Jeanne Pierson (*Mrs. Michonnet*)
      Lucie Vallat (*Oscar's wife*)
      Boulicot (*the policeman*)
      Manuel Raaby (*Guido*)

BOUDU SAUVÉ DES EAUX

DATE: 1932
AMERICAN TITLE: Boudu Saved from Drowning
INTERIORS: Épinay (Éclair Studios)
EXTERIORS: Paris, Seine; Joinville, Marne
PRODUCTION SCHEDULE: Summer 1932
FIRST FRENCH SHOWING: Paris, November 11, 1932
FIRST U.S. SHOWING: New York, New Yorker, February
    23, 1967

TIME: 87 min.

SCENARIO: From the play by René Fauchois

SCRIPT: Jean Renoir, Albert Valentin

PHOTOGRAPHY: Marcel Lucien, Asselin

SET DESIGN: Laurent, Jean Castanier

MUSIC: Raphael, Johann Strauss, Jean Boulze, Edouard Dumoulin

SOUND: Kalinowski

ASSISTANT DIRECTOR: Jacques Becker

EDITOR: Marguerite Renoir, Suzanne de Troyes

PRODUCER: Michel Simon, Jean Gehret; Studio Management: Clément Oliver

DISTRIBUTION: Les Établissements Jacques Haïk; Pathé Contemporary

PRINTS OWNED BY: Cinémathèque Française, Contemporary Films-McGraw Hill

CAST: Michel Simon (*Boudu*)
   Charles Granval (*Lestingois*)
   Marcelle Hainia (*Mme. Lestingois*)
   Séverine Lerczinska (*Anne-Marie*)
   Jean Dasté (*the student*)
   Max Dalban (*Godin*)
   Jean Gehret (*Vigour*)
   Jacques Becker (*the poet on the park bench*)
   Jane Pierson (*Rose*)
   Georges Darnoux (*a marriage guest*)

CHOTARD & COMPAGNIE

DATE: 1933

INTERIORS: Pathé-Natan Studios at Joinville

PRODUCTION SCHEDULE: November–December 1932

FIRST FRENCH SHOWING: Paris, March 1933

TIME: 113 min.

SCENARIO: From the play by Roger Ferdinand
SCRIPT: Jean Renoir, Roger Ferdinand
PHOTOGRAPHY: J.-L. Mundwiller, R. Ribault
SET DESIGN: Jean Castanier
SOUND: Kalinowski
SPECIAL EFFECTS: Ralleigh
ASSISTANT DIRECTOR: Jacques Becker
EDITOR: Marguerite Renoir, Suzanne de Troye
PRODUCER: Roger Ferdinand
PRODUCTION COMPANY: Sté des Films R.F.
DISTRIBUTION: Universal
PRINTS OWNED BY: Cinémathèque Française
CAST: Georges Pomiès (*Julien Collinet*)
　　　Fernand Charpin (*François Chotard*)
　　　Jeanne Boitel (*Reine Collinet*)
　　　Jeanne Lory (*Marie Chotard*)
　　　Malou Treki (*Augustine*)
　　　Louis Tunk (*the subprefect*)
　　　Dignimont (*Parpaillon*)
　　　Louis Seigner (*police captain*)
　　　Max Dalban (*employee in the grocery store*)
　　　Robert Seller (*the Commandant*)
　　　Fabien Loris (*a guest at the Ball*)

MADAME BOVARY

DATE: 1934
INTERIORS: Paris-Studio-Cinema at Billancourt
EXTERIORS: Ry, Rouen, and Lyons-la-Forêt
PRODUCTION SCHEDULE: August–October 1933
FIRST FRENCH SHOWING: Paris, January 13, 1934
FIRST U.S. SHOWING: New York, Acme, November 17,
　　　1934 (102-minute version)

TIME: over three hours, then cut to 120 min.
SCENARIO: From the novel by Gustave Flaubert
SCRIPT: Jean Renoir
PHOTOGRAPHY: Jean Bachelet, Gibory
ASSISTANT CAMERAMAN: Claude Renoir
SET DESIGN: Eugène Lourié, Robert Gys
COSTUMES: Medgyes
MUSIC: Darius Milhaud, Donizetti
SOUND: Courme and Joseph de Bretagne
ASSISTANT DIRECTORS: Jacques Becker, Pierre Lesouches
EDITOR: Marguerite Renoir
PRODUCER: Gaston Gallimard
PRODUCTION COMPANY: Nouvelle Société de Films
DISTRIBUTION: U.S. Distribution: John S. Tapernoux; Télédis
PRINTS OWNED BY: Cinémathèque Française
CAST: Valentine Tessier (*Madame Bovary*)
      Pierre Renoir (*Charles Bovary*)
      Max Dearly (*Homais*)
      Daniel Lecourtois (*Léon*)
      Fernand Fabre (*Rodolphe*)
      Alice Tissot (*Charles Bovary's mother*)
      Héléna Manson (*Charles Bovary's first wife*)
      Pierre Larquey (*Hippolyte*)
      Robert Le Vigan (*Lheureux*)
      Maryanne (*Mme. Homais*)
      Léon Larive (*the prefect*)
      Florencie (*Abbé Bournisien*)
      Romain Bouquet (*the notary*)
      Georges Cahuzac (*Rouault*)
      Alain Dhurtal (*the surgeon*)
      Henry Vilbert (*Canivet*)
      Robert Moor (*the bailiff*)
      Georges Deneubourg (*the Marquis*)

Edmond Beauchamp (*Binet*)
André Fouché (*Justin*)
Jean Gehret (*the prefect*)
Marthe Mellot (*old Nicaise*)
Monette Dinay (*Félicité*)
Christiane d'Or (*Mme. Lefrancois*)
Odette Dynès (*Mlle. Musette*)
Paulette Elambert
Pierre Bost
René Bloch (*the cabman*)
Max Tréjean
Albert Malbert

TONI

DATE: 1935
INTERIORS: Marcel Pagnol Studios at Marseilles
EXTERIORS: Martigues
PRODUCTION SCHEDULE: Summer 1934
FIRST FRENCH SHOWING: Paris, Ciné Opéra, February 22, 1935
FIRST U.S. SHOWING: New York Film Festival, September 18, 1968
TIME: 90 min.
SCENARIO: from documents collected by Jacques Levert (pseudonym of Jacques Mortier)
SCRIPT: Jean Renoir, Carl Einstein; Dialogue: Carl Einstein
PHOTOGRAPHY: Claude Renoir, Roger Ledru
SET DESIGN: Marius Brauquier, Léon Bourelly
MUSIC: Paul Bozzi
SOUND: Barbishanian, assisted by Sarrazin
ASSISTANT DIRECTORS: Georges Darnoux, Antonio Canor
EDITOR: Marguerite Renoir, Suzanne de Troyes, assisted by Guy Darnoux

PRODUCER: Pierre Gaut; Production manager: E. Boyer
PRODUCTION COMPANY: Films d'aujourd'hui
DISTRIBUTION: Films Marcel Pagnol
PRINTS OWNED BY: Cinémathèque Française, Contemporary
    Films-McGraw Hill
CAST: Charles Blavette (*Antonio Canova, called Toni*)
       Celia Montalvan (*Josefa*)
       Jenny Hélia (*Maria*)
       Max Dalban (*Albert*)
       Edouard Delmont (*Fernand*)
       Andrex (*Gaby*)
       André Kovatchevitch (*Sebastien*)
       Paul Bozzi
       Jacques Levert

LE CRIME DE MONSIEUR LANGE

DATE: 1936
AMERICAN TITLE: The Crime of Monsieur Lange
INTERIORS: Billancourt Studios
EXTERIORS: Paris, Tréport
PRODUCTION SCHEDULE: October–November 1935
FIRST FRENCH SHOWING: Paris, January 24, 1936
FIRST U.S. SHOWING: New York, Normandie, April 3, 1964
TIME: 90 min.
SCENARIO: Jean Castanier, Jean Renoir, and Jacques Prévert
DIALOGUE: Jacques Prévert
PHOTOGRAPHY: Jean Bachelet; Photographe: Dora Maar
SET DESIGN: Jean Castanier, Robert Gys, assisted by Roger
    Blin
MUSIC: Jean Wiener, song by Joseph Kosma
SOUND: Moreau, L. Bogé, Robert Teisseire
ASSISTANT DIRECTORS: Pierre Prévert, Georges Darnoux

EDITOR: Marguerite Renoir
PRODUCER: André Halley des Fontaines
PRODUCTION COMPANY: Oberon
DISTRIBUTION: Minerva
PRINTS OWNED BY: Cinémathèque Française, Brandon Films
CAST: René Lefèvre (*Amédée Lange*)
    Jules Berry (*Batala*)
    Florelle (*Valentine*)
    Nadia Sibirskaïa (*Estelle*)
    Sylvia Bataille (*Edith*)
    Henri Guisol (*Meunier*)
    Maurice Baquet (*Charles*)
    Marcel Levesque (*the concierge Bessard*)
    Odette Talazac (*the concierge's wife*)
    Marcel Duhamel (*a printer*)
    Jacques Brunius (*Baigneur*)
    Jean Dasté (*a printer*)
    Sylvain Itkine (*the retired police inspector*)
    Edmond Beauchamp (*the priest on the train*)
    René Génin (*a customer in the café*)
    Guy Decomble (*a printer*)
    Paul Grimault (*a printer*)
    Paul Demange (*a creditor*)
    Claire Gérard (*the prostitute*)
    Henri Saint-Isles
    Charbonnier
    Max Morise
    Fabien Loris
    Yves Deniaud
    Pierre Huchet
    Marcel Lupovici
    Jean Brémaud
    Janine Loris

LA VIE EST À NOUS

DATE: 1936

AMERICAN TITLE: People of France . . .

INTERIORS: Francoeur Studios

AMERICAN TITLES: Muriel Rukeyser

FIRST FRENCH SHOWING: Forbidden by the censors and shown only in private showings until 1969

FIRST U.S. SHOWING: New York, Squire, December 4, 1937 (62 minutes)

TIME: 66 min.

DIRECTOR: Jean Renoir, with the assistance of Jacques Becker, Jean-Paul Le Chanois, Henri Cartier-Bresson, Pierre Unik, Jacques B. Brunius, André Vaillant-Couturier

SCENARIO: André Zwoboda

PHOTOGRAPHY: Alain Douarinou, Claude Renoir, Jean Isnard, Jean Bourgoin

MUSIC: Chorale Populaire de Paris singing "L'Internationale," "Ronde des Saint-Simoniens" and other Popular Front songs

EDITOR: Marguerite Renoir

PRODUCTION COMPANY: Parti Communiste Française

DISTRIBUTION: Cinémas Associés (1969)

PRINTS OWNED BY: L'Avant-Scène

CAST: Jean Dasté (*the schoolteacher*)
   Jacques B. Brunius (*the president of the administrative council*)
   Max Dalban (*Brochard the foreman*)
   Madeleine Sologne (*a worker*)
   Charles Blavette (*Tonin*)
   Jean Renoir (*the bar-owner*)
   Edy Debray (*the bailiff*)

Henri Pons (*M. Lecocq*)
Gaston Modot (*M. Lecocq's nephew Philippe*)
Léon Larive (*the customer at the auction*)
Julien Bertheau (*an unemployed worker*)
Nadia Sibirskaïa (*Ninette*)
Marcel Duhamel (*the National Volunteer*)
O'Brady (*the car washer*)
Guy Favières (*the old unemployed worker*)
Jacques Becker (*an unemployed worker*)
Jean-Paul Le Chanois (*P'tit Louis*)
Emile Drain (*a worker*)
Sylvain Itkine (*the accountant*)
Gabrielle Fontant (*Mme. Lecocq*)
Fabien Loris (*a worker*)
Simone Sylvain
Vladimir Sokoloff

As themselves:

Marcel Cachin
André Marty
Paul Vaillant-Couturier
Jean Renaud
Martha Desrumeaux
Marcel Gitton
Jacques Duclos
Maurice Thorez
and, involuntarily
Colonel de la Rocque
Hitler

[The original credits read "Un film réalisé collectivement
    par une équipe de techniciens, d'artistes at d'ouvriers"
    with no individual credits.]

UNE PARTIE DE CAMPAGNE

DATE: 1936
AMERICAN TITLE: A Day in the Country
BRITISH TITLE: Country Excursion
EXTERIORS: Loing River, near Montigny and Marlotte
PRODUCTION SCHEDULE: July 15–September 5, 1936
FIRST FRENCH SHOWING: Paris, May 8, 1946. (As part of a
   three-part film)
TIME: 37 min.
SCENARIO: From the short story by Guy de Maupassant
SCRIPT: Jean Renoir
PHOTOGRAPHY: Claude Renoir, Jean Bourgoin; Assistant
   Cameramen: Eli Lotar, A. Viguier
MUSIC: Joseph Kosma; song sung by Germaine Montero
SOUND: Joseph de Bretagne
ASSISTANT DIRECTOR: Yves Allégret, Jacques Becker, Jacques
   Brunius, Henri Cartier-Bresson, Luchino Visconti,
   Claude Heymann
EDITOR: Marguerite Renoir, Marinette Cadix
PRODUCER: Pierre Braunberger; Production Manager: Jacques
   Brunius; Production Director: Roger Woog
PRODUCTION COMPANY: Pantheon
DISTRIBUTION: Films de la Pléiades
PRINTS OWNED BY: Cinémathèque Française, British Film
   Institute, Contemporary Films-McGraw Hill
CAST: Sylvia Bataille (*Henriette Dufour*)
   Georges Saint-Saëns (pseudonym of Georges Dar-
   noux) (*Henri*)
   Jacques Borel (pseudonym of Jacques Brunius) (*Ro-
   dolphe*)
   Jeanne Marken (*Mme. Dufour*)

André Gabriello (*M. Dufour*)
Paul Temps (*Anatole*)
Gabrielle Fontan (*Grandmother Dufour*)
Jean Renoir (*Poulain the inkeeper*)
Marguerite Renoir (*the servant*)
Pierre Lestringuez (*the curé*)
Jacques Becker (*seminary student*)
Alain Renoir (*little boy fishing*)

LES BAS-FONDS

DATE: 1936
AMERICAN TITLE: The Lower Depths
INTERIORS: Éclair Studios at Épinay
EXTERIORS: Vicinity of the Seine between Épinay and Saint-Denis, Villeneuve-la Garenne
PRODUCTION SCHEDULE: August–October 1936
FIRST FRENCH SHOWING: Paris, December 1936
FIRST U.S. SHOWING: New York, September 10, 1937
TIME: 91 min.
SCENARIO: Jacques Companeez, Eugene Zamiatin, after the play by Maxim Gorki
SCRIPT: Charles Spaak, Jean Renoir
PHOTOGRAPHY: Jean Bachelet
CAMERAMAN: R. Bourgas, Jacques Mercanton
SET DESIGN: Eugène Lourié, Hughes Laurent
COSTUMES: Art Director: Alexander Kamenka
MUSIC: Jean Wiener in collaboration with Roger Desormières
SOUND: Robert Ivonnet on Tobis Klangfilm
ASSISTANT DIRECTOR: Jacques Becker, Joseph Soiffer
EDITOR: Marguerite Renoir

PRODUCER: Alexander Kamenka; Production Director: Vladimir Zederbaum

PRODUCTION COMPANY: Albatros

DISTRIBUTION: U.S. Distribution: Arthur Mayer, Joseph Burstyn

PRINTS OWNED BY: Eastman House, Contemporary Films-McGraw Hill

CAST: Louis Jouvet (*the Baron*)
    Jean Gabin (*Pepel*)
    Suzy Prim (*Vasilissa*)
    Vladimir Sokoloff (*Kostilev*)
    Junie Astor (*Natacha*)
    Robert Le Vigan (*the actor*)
    André Gabriello (*the inspector*)
    Camille Bert (*the count*)
    Léon Larive (*Félix*)
    René Génin (*the drunkard*)
    Jany Holt (*the prostitute*)
    Maurice Baquet (*the accordionist*)
    Lucien Mancini (*the restaurant owner*)
    Paul Temps
    René Stern
    Sylvain Itkine
    Henri Saint-Isles
    Robert Ozanne
    Alex Allin
    Fernand Bercher
    Annie Cérès
    Nathalie Alexeieff
    Jacques Becker

LA GRANDE ILLUSION

DATE: 1937
TIME: 114 min. (1938 version: 94 min.)
INTERIORS: Billancourt Studios, Éclair Studios, at Épinay
EXTERIORS: Neuf-Brisach, Haut-Koenigsbourg (Alsace); Colmar barracks
PRODUCTION SCHEDULE: Winter 1936–37
FIRST FRENCH SHOWING: Paris, June 4, 1937; reissued May 27, 1955
FIRST U.S. SHOWING: New York, September 12, 1938 (played for 26 weeks)
SCENARIO: Charles Spaak, Jean Renoir
TECHNICAL CONSULTANT: Carl Koch
PHOTOGRAPHY: Christian Matras
CAMERAMEN: Claude Renoir, Bourreaud, Jean Bourgoin
SCRIPT GIRL: Gourdji
SET DESIGN: Eugène Lourié
PHOTOGRAPHIE: Sam Levin
MUSIC: Joseph Kosma, song by Vincent Telly and A. Valsien
SOUND: Joseph de Bretagne
ASSISTANT DIRECTOR: Jacques Becker
EDITOR: Marguerite Renoir; Marthe Huguet; 1958: Renée Lichtig
PRODUCERS: Frank Rollmer, Albert Pinkovitch
PRODUCTION COMPANY: R.A.C (Réalisations d'Art Cinématographique); Production Director: Raymond Blondy
PRINTS OWNED BY: Cinémathèque Française, British Film Institute, Janus, Museum of Modern Art (censored)
CAST: Jean Gabin (*Maréchal*)
      Pierre Fresnay (*Boeldieu*)
      Erich von Stroheim (*Rauffenstein*)

Marcel Dalio (*Rosenthal*)
Dita Parlo (*Elsa*)
Julien Carette (*the actor*)
Gaston Modot (*the engineer*)
Jean Dasté (*the teacher*)
Georges Péclet (*a French soldier*)
Jacques Becker (*an English officer*)
Sylvain Itkine (*Demolder*)
Werner Florian
Claude Sainval
Michel Salina

[The restored version of *La Grande Illusion* frequently includes a prefatory statement by Renoir made in 1958]

LA MARSEILLAISE

DATE: 1938

INTERIORS: Billancourt Studios

EXTERIORS: Provence, Alsace, Fontainebleau, Haute Provence, Antibes

PRODUCTION SCHEDULE: exteriors, nine weeks in autumn 1937

FIRST FRENCH SHOWING: Paris, February 10, 1938

FIRST U.S. SHOWING: New York, November 2, 1939

TIME: 135 min.

SCENARIO: Jean Renoir, with the assistance of Carl Koch, and M. and Mme. N. Martel-Dreyfus for the historical details

PHOTOGRAPHY: Jean Bourgoin, Alain Douarinou, Jean-Marie Maillols, Jean-Paul Alphen

CAMERAMAN: Jean Louis

SET DESIGN: Léon Barsacq, Georges Wakhevitch, Jean Perrier

MUSIC: Joseph Kosma, Sauveplane; Lalande, Grétry, Rameau, Mozart, Bach, Rouget de Lisle

SOUND: Joseph de Bretagne, Jean-Paul Alphen, J. Demede

SHADOW THEATER: Lotte Reiniger

ASSISTANT DIRECTOR: Jacques Becker, Claude Renoir (nephew), Jean-Paul Le Chanois, Claude Renoir (brother)

EDITOR: Marguerite Renoir, Marthe Huguet

PRODUCER: C.G.T. (André Zwoboda) Marc Maurette

PRODUCTION COMPANY: Société de Production and d'Exploitation du film *La Marseillaise*

DISTRIBUTION: R.A.C.; World Pictures

ADMINISTRATION: Louis Joly

PRINTS OWNED BY: British Film Institute, Contemporary Films-McGraw Hill

CAST: *The Court:*
    Pierre Renoir (*Louis XVI*)
    Lise Delamare (*Marie Antoinette*)
    Léon Larive (*Picard, Louis XVI's valet*)
    William Aguet (*La Rochefoucauld*)
    Elisa Ruis (*Mme. de Lamballe*)
    G. Lefébure (*Mme. Elisabeth*)
  The civil and military authorities:
    Louis Jouvet (*Roederer*)
    Jean Aquistapace (*the mayor of the village*)
    Georges Spanelly (*La Chesnaye*)
    Jaque Catelain (*Langlade*)
    Pierre Nay (*Dubouchage*)
    Edmond Castel (*Leroux*)
  The aristocrats:
    Aimé Clariond (*Saint-Laurent*)
    Maurice Escande (*the lord of the village*)
    André Zibrol (*Saint-Méry*)
    Jean Aymé (*Fougerolles*)
    Irène Joachim (*Mme. de Saint-Laurent*)

The inhabitants of Marseille:
   Andrex (*Arnaud*)
   Edmond Ardisson (*Bonnier*)
   Jean-Louis Allibert (*Moissant*)
   Jenny Hélia (*the questioner*)
   Paul Dulac (*Javel*)
   Ferdinand Flament (*Ardisson*)
   Georges Péclet (*a Marseille leader*)
   Géo Dorlys (*a Marseille leader*)
   Géo Lastry (*Captaine Massugue*)
   Adolphe Autran (*the drummer*)
   Alex Truchy (*Cuculière*)
The People:
   Nadia Sibirskaïa (*Louison*)
   Edouard Delmont (*Cabri*)
   Séverine Lerczinska (*peasant woman*)
   Edmond Beauchamp (*the curé*)
   Gaston Modot (*a volunteer*)
   Julien Carette (*a volunteer*)
   Marthe Marty (*Bonnier's mother*)
   Roger Pregor
   Pierre Ferval
   Fernand Bellan
   Jean Boissemond
   Pamela Stirling
   Blanche Destournelles
   Lucy Kieffer

LA BÊTE HUMAINE

DATE: 1938
BRITISH TITLE: Judas Was a Woman
INTERIORS: Billancourt Studios
EXTERIORS: Gare St-Lazare, Le Havre

PRODUCTION SCHEDULE: August 12, 1938–September 1938
FIRST FRENCH SHOWING: Paris, December 23, 1938
FIRST U.S. SHOWING: New York, February 19, 1940
TIME: 105 min.
SCENARIO: Jean Renoir, from the novel by Émile Zola
SCRIPT: Jean Renoir, assisted by Denise Leblond-Zola
SCRIPT GIRL: Suzanne de Troyes
PHOTOGRAPHY: Curt Courant, Claude Renoir, assisted by
     Pecqueux, J. Natteau; Maurice Pecqueux, Guy Ferrier,
     Alain Renoir
SET DESIGN: Eugène Lourié
MUSIC: Joseph Kosma
SOUND: Robert Teisseire
ASSISTANT DIRECTOR: Claude Renoir (brother), Suzanne de
     Troyes
EDITOR: Marguerite Renoir
PRODUCER: Robert Hakim; Director of Production: Roland
     Tual
PRODUCTION COMPANY: Paris-Film-Productions
DISTRIBUTION: Juno
PRINTS OWNED BY: Cinémathèque Française, William K.
     Everson
CAST: Jean Gabin (*Jacques Lantier*)
          Simone Simon (*Séverine Roubaud*)
          Fernand Ledoux (*Roubaud*)
          Julien Carette (*Pecqueux*)
          Blanchette Brunoy (*Flore*)
          Gérard Landry (*Lauvergne*)
          Jacques Berlioz (*Grandmorin*)
          Jean Renoir (*Cabuche*)
          Marcel Perez (*railway workman*)
          Jenny Hélia (*Philomène*)
          Marceau (*a mechanic*)
          Tony Corteggiani (*the section boss*)

André Tavernier (*the examining magistrate*)
Colette Régis (*Mme. Victoire*)
Claire Gérard (*a traveler*)
Charlotte Clasis (*Mme. Misard*)
Georges Spanelly (*Grandmorin's secretary*)
Guy Decomble (*the crossing guard*)
Georges Péclet (*a railroad worker*)
Emile Gènevois (*a farmhand*)
Jacques Brunius (*a farmhand*)
André Tavernier
Jacques Roussel

LA RÈGLE DU JEU

DATE: 1939
AMERICAN TITLE: The Rules of the Game
INTERIORS: Joinville, Billancourt
EXTERIORS: Sologne, château of Le Ferté-Saint-Aubin, La Motte-Beuvron, Aubigny
PRODUCTION SCHEDULE: February 15, 1939–spring 1939
FIRST FRENCH SHOWING: Paris, July 7, 1939
FIRST U.S. SHOWING: New York, April 10, 1950 (short version); January 28, 1961 (100 minutes)
TIME: 113 min.
SCENARIO: Jean Renoir, with the collaboration of Carl Koch
SCRIPT GIRL: Dido Freire
PHOTOGRAPHY: Jean Bachelet
CAMERAMAN: Jacques Lemare, assisted by Jean-Paul Alphen, Alain Renoir
SET DESIGN: Eugène Lourié, Max Douy
COSTUMES: Coco Chanel
MUSIC: Mozart, Monsigny, Saint-Saëns, Johann Strauss, arranged by Robert Desormières and Joseph Kosma

SOUND: Joseph de Bretagne

ASSISTANT DIRECTOR: André Zwoboda, Henri Cartier-Bresson

EDITOR: Marquerite Renoir; Assistant Editor: Marthe Huguet

PRODUCER: Jean Renoir; Production Director: Claude Renoir

PRODUCTION COMPANY: Nouvelle Edition Française; Administrator: Camille François

DISTRIBUTION: Gaumont; Les Grands Films Classiques

PRINTS OWNED BY: Eastman House, Janus Films

CAST: Marcel Dalio (*Robert de la Chesnaye*)
   Nora Grégor (*Christine de la Chesnaye*)
   Roland Toutain (*André Jurieu*)
   Jean Renoir (*Octave*)
   Mila Parély (*Geneviève de Marrast*)
   Paulette Dubost (*Lisette*)
   Gaston Modot (*Schumacher*)
   Julien Carette (*Marceau*)
   Odette Talazac (*Charlotte de la Plante*)
   Pierre Magnier (*the General*)
   Pierre Nay (*Saint-Aubin*)
   Richard Francoeur (*La Bruyère*)
   Eddy Debray (*Corneille*)
   Léon Larive (*the cook*)
   Claire Gérard (*Mme. de la Bruyère*)
   Anne Mayen (*Jackie, Christine's niece*)
   Lise Elina (*the radio reporter*)
   Roger Forster (*the homosexual*)
   Nicolas Amato (*the South American*)
   Tony Corteggiani (*Berthelin*)
   Camille François (*the radio announcer*)
   André Zwobada (*the engineer at Caudron*)
   Henri Cartier-Bresson (*the English servant*)
   Jenny Hélia (*a kitchen servant*)

LA TOSCA

DATE: 1940
INTERIORS: Scalera Studios
EXTERIORS: Rome
FIRST FRENCH SHOWING: Paris, September 30, 1942
FIRST U.S. SHOWING: New York, December 18, 1947
DIRECTOR: Carl Koch
SCENARIO: Adapted by Jean Renoir, Carl Koch, Luchino
    Visconti from the play by Victorien Sardou
PHOTOGRAPHY: Ubaldo Arata
MUSIC: Puccini, arranged by Umberto Mancini; songs sung
    by Mafalda Favero, Ferruccio Tagliavini
EDITOR: Gino Bretone
PRODUCER: Arturo A. Ambrogio
PRODUCTION COMPANY: Scalera-Film
DISTRIBUTION: Superfilm
CAST: Imperio Argentina (*Tosca*)
      Michel Simon (*Scarpia*)
      Rossano Brazzi (*Cavaradossi*)
      Massimo Girotti (*Angeloti*)
      Carla Candiani
      Juan Calvo
      Adriano Rimoldi
      Nicolas Perchicot

SWAMP WATER

DATE: 1941
FRENCH TITLE: L'Étang Tragique
BRITISH TITLE: The Man Who Came Back

EXTERIORS: Okefenokee Swamp, Georgia
FIRST FRENCH SHOWING: Paris, April 23, 1948
FIRST U.S. SHOWING: New York, November 16, 1941
TIME: 86 min.
SCENARIO: Dudley Nichols, from the novel by Vereen Bell
PHOTOGRAPHY: Peverell Marley
SET DESIGN: Thomas Little; Artistic Director: Richard Day
COSTUMES: Gwen Wakeling
MUSIC: David Buttolph
EDITOR: Walter Thompson
PRODUCER: Irving Pichel; Associate Producer: Len Hammond
PRODUCTION COMPANY: Twentieth-Century Fox
CAST: Walter Brennan (*Tom Keefer*)
　　　Walter Huston (*Thursday Ragan*)
　　　Anne Baxter (*Julie Keefer*)
　　　Dana Andrews (*Ben Ragan*)
　　　Mary Howard (*Hannah Ragan*)
　　　John Carradine (*Jesse Wick*)
　　　Virginia Gilmore (*Mabel McKenzie*)
　　　Eugene Pallette (*Sheriff Jeb McKane*)
　　　Ward Bond (*Jim Dorson*)
　　　Guinn Williams (*Bud Dorson*)
　　　Russell Simpson (*Marty McCord*)
　　　Joseph Sawyer (*Hardy Ragan*)
　　　Paul Burns (*Tulle McKenzie*)
　　　Dave Morris (*Barber*)
　　　Frank Austin (*Fred Ulm*)
　　　Matt Willis (*Miles Tonkin*)

THIS LAND IS MINE

DATE: 1943
FRENCH TITLE: Vivre Libre
FIRST FRENCH SHOWING: Paris, July 10, 1946
FIRST U.S. SHOWING: New York, Rivoli, May 27, 1943
TIME: 103 min.
SCENARIO: Dudley Nichols, Jean Renoir
SCRIPT: Dialogue: Dudley Nichols
PHOTOGRAPHY: Frank Redman
SET DESIGN: Albert S. d'Agostino, Walter E. Keller, Eugène
     Lourié
MUSIC: Lothar Perl; Musical Director: C. Bakaleinikoff
EDITOR: Frederick Knudtsen
PRODUCER: Jean Renoir, Dudley Nichols; Deputy Producer:
     Eugène Lourié
PRODUCTION COMPANY: R.K.O.
DISTRIBUTION: R.K.O.
PRINTS OWNED BY: Films Incorporated, British Film Insti-
     tute, Library of Congress
CAST: Charles Laughton (*Albert Mory*)
     George Sanders (*Georges Lambert*)
     Maureen O'Hara (*Louise Martin*)
     Kent Smith (*Paul Martin*)
     Walter Slezak (*Major von Keller*)
     Una O'Connor (*Albert Mory's mother*)
     Philip Merivale (*Professor Sorel*)
     Thurston Hall (*Major Henry Manville*)
     Georges Coulouris (*the Prosecutor*)
     Nancy Gates (*Julie Grant*)
     Ivan Simpson (*the Presiding Judge*)
     John Donat (*Edmond Lorraine*)

Frank Alten (*Lieutenant Schwartz*)
Leo Bulgakov (*the little man*)
Wheaton Chambers (*Lorraine*)
Cecile Weston (*Mrs. Lorraine*)

SALUTE TO FRANCE

DATE: 1944
FRENCH TITLE: Salut à la France
FIRST FRENCH SHOWING: Paris, 1946
TIME: 20 min.
DIRECTOR: Jean Renoir, Garson Kanin
SCENARIO: Philippe Dunne, Jean Renoir, Burgess Meredith, etc.
PHOTOGRAPHY: Army Pictorial Service
MUSIC: Kurt Weill
EDITOR: Helen van Dongen
PRODUCER: Office of War Information, New York
DISTRIBUTION: Associated Artists
PRINTS OWNED BY: Library of Congress
CAST: Claude Dauphin
      Burgess Meredith
      Garson Kanin
      others

THE SOUTHERNER

DATE: 1945
FRENCH TITLE: L'Homme du Sud
BRITISH TITLE: Hold Autumn in Your Hand
FIRST FRENCH SHOWING: Paris, May 30, 1950
FIRST U.S. SHOWING: Beverly Hills, April 30, 1945; New York, August 26, 1945

TIME: 91 min.

SCENARIO: Jean Renoir, from the novel *Hold Autumn in Your Hand* by George Sessions Perry

SCRIPT: Adaptation: Hugo Butler

PHOTOGRAPHY: Lucien Andriot

SET DESIGN: Eugène Lourié

MUSIC: Werner Jannsen

SOUND: Frank Webster

ASSISTANT DIRECTOR: Robert Aldrich

EDITOR: Gregg Tallas

PRODUCER: David L. Loew, Robert Hakim; Associate Producer: Samuel Rheiner

PRODUCTION COMPANY: Producing Artists

DISTRIBUTION: United Artists

PRINTS OWNED BY: David Loew, Eastman House

CAST: Zachary Scott (*Sam Tucker*)
   Betty Field (*Nona Tucker*)
   J. Carroll Naish (*Henry Devers*)
   Beulah Bondi (*Grandma*)
   Percy Kilbride (*Harmie Jenkins*)
   Blanche Yurka (*Mother*)
   Charles Kemper (*Tim*)
   Norman Lloyd (*Finley Hewitt*)
   Estelle Taylor (*Lizzie*)
   Noreen Nash (*Becky*)
   Jack Norworth (*the Doctor*)
   Paul Harvey (*Ruston*)
   Jay Gilpin (*Jot*)
   Nestor Piva (*the bartender*)
   Jean Vanderbilt (*Daisy*)
   Paul Burns (*Uncle Pete*)
   Dorothy Granger (*the young girl at the dance*)
   Earl Hodgkins (*the wedding guest*)
   Almira Sessions (*the client in the store*)
   Rex (*Zoonie*)

THE DIARY OF A CHAMBERMAID

DATE: 1946

FRENCH TITLE: Le Journal d'Une Femme de Chambre

TIME: 86 min. (Variety, N.Y., 1946)

FIRST FRENCH SHOWING: Paris, June 9, 1948

FIRST U.S. SHOWING: New York, June 23, 1946

SCENARIO: Adapted by Jean Renoir and Burgess Meredith from the novel by Octave Mirbeau and the play by André Heuse, André de Lorde, and Thielly Nores

PHOTOGRAPHY: Lucien Andriot

SET DESIGN: Eugène Lourié

COSTUMES: Barbara Karinska; Wardrobe: Greta; Make-up: Otis Malcolm; Hair styles: Scotty Rackin

MUSIC: Michel Michelet

SOUND: William Lynch

SPECIAL EFFECTS: Lee Zavitz

ASSISTANT DIRECTOR: Joseph Depew

EDITOR: James Smith

PRODUCER: Benedict Bogeaus, Burgess Meredith; Assistant to the Producers: Corley Harriman; Production Associate: Arthur M. Landau

DISTRIBUTION: Associated Artists

PRINTS OWNED BY: National Telefilm Associates, Eastman House

CAST: Paulette Goddard (*Celestine*)
      Burgess Meredith (*Mauger*)
      Francis Lederer (*Joseph*)
      Hurd Hatfield (*Georges*)
      Reginald Owen (*Lanlaire*)
      Judith Anderson (*Mrs. Lanlaire*)
      Irene Ryan (*Louise*)

Florence Bates (*Rose*)
Almira Sessions (*Marianne*)

THE WOMAN ON THE BEACH

DATE: 1946
FRENCH TITLE: La Femme Sur La Plage
FIRST FRENCH SHOWING: Paris, June 23, 1948
FIRST U.S. SHOWING: New York, June 8, 1947
TIME: 71 min.
SCENARIO: Jean Renoir, Frank Davis, J. R. Michael Hogan,
    adapted from the novel *None So Blind* by Mitchell
    Wilson
PHOTOGRAPHY: Leo Tover, Harry Wild
SET DESIGN: Darrell Silvera, John Sturtevant
ARTISTIC DIRECTORS: Albert S. d'Agostino, Walter E. Keller
MUSIC: Hans Eisler; Musical Director: C. Bakaleinikoff
SOUND: Jean L. Speak, Clem Portman
SPECIAL EFFECTS: Russell A. Cully
ASSISTANT DIRECTOR: James Casey
EDITOR: Ronald Gross, Lyle Boyer
PRODUCER: Jack Gross; Associate Producer: Will Price
PRODUCTION COMPANY: R.K.O.
PRINTS OWNED BY: Films Incorporated, Library of Congress
CAST: Joan Bennett (*Peggy Butler*)
    Robert Ryan (*Lieutenant Scott Burnett*)
    Charles Bickford (*Tod Butler*)
    Nan Leslie (*Eve Geddes*)
    Walter Sande (*Otto Wernecke*)
    Irene Ryan (*Mrs. Wernecke*)
    Glenn Vernon (*Kirk*)
    Frank Darien (*Lars*)
    Jay Norris (*Jimmy*)

THE RIVER

DATE: 1950
FRENCH TITLE: Le Fleuve
TIME: 98 min.
EXTERIORS: Calcutta, around the Ganges and Houghly rivers
FIRST FRENCH SHOWING: Paris, preview: September 10,
    1951; commercial: December 19, 1951
FIRST U.S. SHOWING: Preview: New York, August 29, 1951
DIRECTOR: Jean Renoir
SCENARIO: Rumer Godden, Jean Renoir, after the novel by
    Rumer Godden
PHOTOGRAPHY: Claude Renoir (Technicolor)
CAMERAMAN: Ramananda Sen Gupta
SET DESIGN: Eugène Lourié, Bansi Chandra Gupta
MUSIC: M. A. Partha Sarathy
SOUND: Charles Poulton, Charles Knott
ASSISTANT DIRECTORS: Forrest Judd, Harishadhan J. Das
    Gupta, Sukhamoy Sen, Bausix Ashe
EDITOR: George Gale
PRODUCER: Kenneth McEldowney; Production Manager:
    Kalyan Gupta
PRODUCTION COMPANY: Oriental-International
DISTRIBUTION: Associated Artists; United Artists
PRINTS OWNED BY: Kenneth McEldowney, Library of Con-
    gress
CAST: Patricia Walters (*Harriet*)
    Radha (*Melanie*)
    Adrienne Corri (*Valerie*)
    Nora Swinburne (*Mother*)
    Esmond Knight (*Father*)
    Thomas E. Breen (*Captain John*)

Arthur Shields (*Mr. John*)
Richard Foster (*Bogey*)
Suprova Mukerjee (*Nan*)
Penelope Wilkinson (*Elizabeth*)
Jane Harris (*Muffie*)
Sahjan Singh (*Ram Prasad Singh*)
Nimai Barik (*Kanu*)
Thilak Jetley (*Anil*)
June Hillman (*narrator*)

LE CARROSSE D'OR

DATE: 1953
AMERICAN TITLE: The Golden Coach
INTERIORS: Cinecittà, Rome
PRODUCTION SCHEDULE: Began February 4, 1952
FIRST FRENCH SHOWING: Paris, February 11, 1953
FIRST U.S. SHOWING: New York, January 21, 1954
TIME: 100 min.
SCENARIO: Jean Renoir, Jack Kirkland, Renzo Avanzo, Giulio
    Macchi, and Ginette Doynel, from the play *Le Carrosse
    du Saint-Sacrement* by Prosper Merimée
PHOTOGRAPHY: Claude Renoir (Technicolor)
CAMERAMEN: H. Ronald, Rodolfo Lombardi
SET DESIGN: Mario Chiari, assisted by Gianni Polidori
COSTUMES: Gino Brosio
MUSIC: Vivaldi, adapted by Gino Marinozzi, played by the
    Rome Symphony
SOUND: Joseph de Bretagne
ASSISTANT DIRECTOR: Marc Maurette, Giulio Macchi
EDITOR: Mario Serandrei, David Hawkins
PRODUCER: Valentine Brosio, Giuseppe Bordognoi; Associate
    Producer: Renzo Avanzo

PRODUCTION COMPANY: Panaria Film-Hoche Production
PRODUCTION MANAGER: Francesco Alliata
DISTRIBUTION: Corona; I.F.E.
PRINTS OWNED BY: British Film Institute
CAST: Anna Magnani (*Camilla*)
   Duncan Lamont (*the Viceroy*)
   Odoardo Spararo (*Don Antonio*)
   Riccardo Rioli (*Ramon*)
   Paul Campbell (*Felipe*)
   Nada Fiorelli (*Isabelle*)
   George Higgins (*Martinez*)
   Jean Debucourt (*the Bishop*)
   Dante Rino (*the Doctor*)
   Gisella Matthews (*the Marquesa Altamirano*)
   Ralph Truman (*Duc de Castro*)
   Elena Altieri (*Duchesse de Castro*)
   Renato Chiantoni (*Captain Fracasse*)
   Giulio Tedeschi (*Baldassare*)
   Alfredo Kolner (*Florindo*)
   Alfredo Medini (*Ploichinelle*)
   Medini Brothers (*the four child acrobats*)
   John Pasetti (*the Captain of the Guards*)
   William Tubbs (*the innkeeper*)
   Cecil Matthews (*the Baron*)
   Fedo Keeling (*the Viscount*)
   Lina Marengo (*the old comedienne*)
   Raf de la Terre (*the Chief Justice*)

FRENCH CANCAN

DATE: 1955
AMERICAN TITLE: Only the French Can
TIME: 102 min.

INTERIORS: Saint-Maurice Studios, Francoeur

PRODUCTION SCHEDULE: October 4, 1954–December 20, 1954

FIRST FRENCH SHOWING: Paris, April 29, 1955

FIRST U.S. SHOWING: New York, April 16, 1956

SCENARIO: Jean Renoir, from an idea by André-Paul Antoine

SCRIPT GIRL: Ginette Doynel

PHOTOGRAPHY: Michel Kelber (Technicolor); Photographe: Serge Beauvarlet

CAMERAMEN: Henri Tiquet; Vladimir Lang, George Barsky

SET DESIGN: Max Douy, assisted by Jean André, Jacques Douy

COSTUMES: Rosine Delamare.

MUSIC: Georges Van Parys; song lyrics by Jean Renoir; voices of Cora Vaucaire, Mario Juillard

SOUND: Antoine Petit-Jean

ASSISTANT DIRECTORS: Serge Vallin, Pierre Kast

EDITOR: Boris Lewin

PRODUCER: Louis Wipf; Production Manager: Lucien Lippens

PRODUCTION COMPANY: Franco-London Film-Joly Film

PRINTS OWNED BY: Contemporary Films-McGraw Hill

CAST: Jean Gabin (*Danglard*)
    Francoise Arnoul (*Nini*)
    Maria Felix (*the Abbesse*)
    Jean-Roger Caussimon (*Baron Walter*)
    Max Dalban (*the owner of the Reine Blanche*)
    Dora Doll (*La Génisse*)
    Gaston Modot (*Danglard's servant*)
    Jean Parédès (*Coudrier*)
    Franco Pastorino (*Paulo*)
    Gianni Esposito (*the Prince*)
    Valentine Tessier (*Madame Olympe, Nini's mother*)
    Michèle Philippe (*Eléonore*)

Lydia Johnson (*Guibole*)
Anna Amendola (*Esther Georges*)
Philippe Clay (*Casimir*)
France Roche (*Béatrix*)
Annik Morice (*Thérèse*)
Jacques Jouanneau (*Bidon*)
Michèle Nadal (*Bigoudi*)
Sylvinne Delannoy (*Titine*)
Anne-Marie Mersen (*Paquita*)
Albert Rémy (*Barjolin*)
Michel Piccoli (*Valorgueil*)
Patachou (*Yvette Guilbert*)
André Claveau (*Paul Delmet*)
Edith Piaf (*Eugénie Buffet*)
Jean Raymond (*Paulus*)
Jean-Marc Tennberg (*Savatte*)
Pierre Olaf (*the whistler*)
Léo Campion (*the Commandant*)
Numès fils (*the neighbor*)
Jaque Catelain (*the Minister*)
Hubert Deschamps (*Isidore*)
Paquerette (*Mimi Prunelle*)
Gaston Gabaroche (*Oscar*)
Pierre Moncorbier (*the process-server*)
Jean Mortier (*the hotel manager*)
Robert Auboyneau (*the elevator operator*)
Laurence Bataille (*the Pygmy*)
Jacques Ciron (*a dandy*)
Claude Arnay (*a dandy*)
Michèle Philippe (*Eléonore*)
R. J. Chauffard (*the police inspector*)
Jacques Hilling (*the surgeon*)
Jedlinska (*la Gigolette*)
Jean Sylvère (*the bellhop*)

Palmyre Levasseur (*a laundress*)
André Phlip
Bruno Balp
Jacques Marin
H. R. Herce
René Pascal
Martine Alexis
Corinne Jansen
Maya Jusanova
Mario Julliard

ELENA ET LES HOMMES

DATE: 1956
AMERICAN TITLE: Paris Does Strange Things
PRODUCTION SCHEDULE: December 1, 1955–March 17, 1956
FIRST FRENCH SHOWING: Paris, September 12, 1956
FIRST U.S. SHOWING: New York, November 9, 1970
TIME: 98 min.
SCENARIO: Jean Renoir
SCRIPT: Jean Renoir, Jean Serge, Cy Howard (English
    version); Dialogue: Jean Renoir
SCRIPT GIRL: Ginette Doynel
PHOTOGRAPHY: Claude Renoir (Eastmancolor)
CAMERAMAN: Gilbert Chain
SET DESIGN: Jean André
COSTUMES: Rosine Delamare, Monique Plotin
MUSIC: Joseph Kosma; Lyrics: Jean Renoir; *Onuit* by
    Juliette Greco
SOUND: William Sivel
ASSISTANT DIRECTOR: Serge Vallin; Production Director:
    Louis Wipf; Production Manager: Lucien Lippens
EDITOR: Boris Lewin

PRODUCTION COMPANY: Franco-London Film, Films Gibé
    (Paris), Electra Compania Cinematografica (Rome)
DISTRIBUTION: Cinedis; Warners (U.S.)
PRINTS OWNED BY: Contemporary Films-McGraw Hill
CAST: Ingrid Bergman (*Eléna*)
        Jean Marais (*General Rollan*)
        Mel Ferrer (*Henri*)
        Jean Richard (*Hector*)
        Magali Noël (*Lolotte*)
        Juliette Greco (*Miarka*)
        Pierre Bertin (*Martin-Michaud*)
        Jacques Jouanneau (*Eugène*)
        Jacques Morel (*Duchêne*)
        Jean Claudio (*Lionel*)
        Renaud Mary (*Fleury*)
        Jacques Hilling (*Lisbonne*)
        Albert Rémy (*Buchez*)
        Elina Labourdette (*Paulette*)
        Jean Castanier (*Isnard*)
        Mirko Ellis (*Marbeau*)
        Gaston Modot (*Romani*)
        Gregori Chmara (*Elena's servant*)
        Paul Demange (*a spectator*)
        Jim Gerald (*the café owner*)
        Dora Doll (*Rosa la Rose*)
        Léo Marjane (*street singer*)
        Michèle Nadal (*Denise Gaudin*)
        Olga Valéry (*Olga*)
        Claire Gérard (*woman walking in the street*)
        Simone Sylvestre
        Robert LeBéal (*the doctor*)
        Léon Larive (*Henri's valet*)
        Gérard Buhr

Frédéric Duvallès
the Zavattas
Jean Ozenne
René Berthier
֍ Hubert de Lapparent
Pierre Duverger
Jaque Catelain
Corinne Jansen
Liliane Ernout
Louisette Rousseau
Palmyre Levasseur
Lyne Carrel

LE TESTAMENT DU DOCTEUR CORDELIER

DATE: 1959
AMERICAN TITLE: The Testament of Dr. Cordelier
BRITISH TITLE: Experiment in Evil
INTERIORS: TV studios, Rue Carducci, Paris
EXTERIORS: Marnes-la-Coquette, Pigalle
PRODUCTION SCHEDULE: Early spring, 1959; 15 days rehearsal; 10½ days shooting
FIRST FRENCH SHOWING: Paris, November 16, 1961
TIME: 90 min.
SCENARIO: Jean Renoir; Artistic Collaborator: Jean Serge
SCRIPT: Dialogue: Jean Renoir; Technical Collaboration: Yves-André Hubert
PHOTOGRAPHY: Georges Leclerc
CAMERAMEN: Bernard Giraux, Jean Graglia, Pierre Guégen, Pierre Lebon, Gilbert Perrot-Minot, Arthur Raymond, Gilbert Sandoz

SET DESIGN: Marcel-Louis Dieulot

MUSIC: Joseph Kosma

SOUND: Joseph Richard

ASSISTANT DIRECTOR: Jean-Pierre Spièro

EDITOR: Renée Lichtig

PRODUCTION COMPANY: Cie Jean Renoir; Radio-Television-Française, Sofirad; Production Director: Albert Hollebecke

DISTRIBUTION: Pathé

PRINTS OWNED BY: Contemporary Films-McGraw Hill

CAST: Jean-Louis Barrault (*Dr. Cordelier, Opale*)
    Michel Vitold (*Dr. Séverin*)
    Teddy Bilis (*Joly*)
    Micheline Gary (*Marguerite*)
    Jean Topart (*Désiré*)
    Gaston Modot (*gardener*)
    Jaque Catelain (*ambassador*)
    Jacqueline Morane (*Alberte*)
    André Certes (*the Inspector*)
    Jacques Dannoville (*the Detective*)
    Jean Renoir (*the narrator*)
    Jean-Pierre Granval (*the hotel-owner*)
    Jean Bertho (*a passerby*)
    Jacques Siron (*a passerby*)
    Didier d'Yd (*Georges*)
    Raymond Jourdan (*the sick man*)
    Régine Blaess (*the ambassador's wife*)
    Raymonde (*Mme. des Essarts*)
    Annick Allieres (*the neighbor*)
    Madeleine Marion (*Juliette*)
    Primerose Perret (*Mary*)
    Sylviane Margolle (*the little girl*)
    Dominique Dangon (*the mother*)

Céline Soles (*a girl*)
Ghislaine Dumont (*Suzy*)
Claudie Bourlon (*Lise*)
Jacqueline Frot (*Isabelle*)
Françoise Boyer (*Françoise*)
Monique Theffa (*Annie*)

LE DÉJEUNER SUR L'HERBE

DATE: 1959
AMERICAN TITLE: Picnic on the Grass
BRITISH TITLE: Lunch on the Grass
TIME: 92 min. (French release); 91 min. (American release)
INTERIORS: Studios Francoeur
EXTERIORS: "Les Collettes," Cagnes, and surrounding areas
PRODUCTION SCHEDULE: Summer 1959: 24 days
FIRST FRENCH SHOWING: Paris, November 11, 1959
FIRST U.S. SHOWING: New York, December 12, 1960
SCENARIO: Jean Renoir; Artistic Collaborator: Jean Serge
SCRIPT: Dialogue: Jean Renoir; Technical Collaborator:
    Yves-André Hubert
PHOTOGRAPHY: Georges Leclerc (Eastmancolor); Laborato-
    ries: FRANAY, L.T.C. Saint-Cloud
SCRIPT GIRLS: Andrée Gauthey, Marinette Pasquet
SET DESIGN: Marcel-Louis Dieulot; Make-up: Yvonne For-
    tuna
COSTUMES: Monique Dunand
MUSIC: Joseph Kosma
SOUND: Joseph de Bretagne
SPECIAL EFFECTS: LAX
EDITOR: Renée Lichtig; General Direction: Maurice Beuchey
PRODUCTION DIRECTOR: Ginette Courtois-Doynel

PRODUCTION COMPANY: Cie Jean Renoir
PRINTS OWNED BY: Contemporary Films-McGraw-Hill, British Film Institute
CAST: Paul Meurisse (*Etienne Alexis*)
      Catherine Rouvel (*Nénette*)
      Jacqueline Morane (*Titine*)
      Fernand Sardou (*Nino*)
      Jean-Pierre Granval (*Ritou*)
      Robert Chandeau (*Laurent*)
      Micheline Gary (*Madeleine*)
      Frédéric O'Brady (*Rudolf*)
      Ingrid Nordine (*Marie-Charlotte*)
      Charles Blavette (*Gaspard*)
      Jean Claudio (*Rousseau*)
      Ghislaine Dumont (*Magda*)
      Hélène Duc (*Isabelle*)
      Jacques Dannoville (*Mr. Poignant*)
      Marguerite Cassan (*Mrs. Poignant*)
      Raymond Jourdan (*Eustache*)
      François Miège (*Barthélmy*)
      Régine Blaess (*Claire*)
      Pierre Leproux (*Bailly*)
      Michel Herbault (*Montet*)
      Jacqueline Fontel (*Miss Michelet*)
      Paulette Dubost (*Miss Forestier*)
      André Brunot (*the curé*)
      M. You (*the foreman*)
      Dupraz
      Lucas
      Roland Thierry
      Michel Péricart

LE CAPORAL ÉPINGLÉ

DATE: 1962
AMERICAN TITLE: The Elusive Corporal
BRITISH TITLE: The Vanishing Corporal
INTERIORS: Vienna
FIRST FRENCH SHOWING: Paris, May 23, 1962
FIRST U.S. SHOWING: New York, February 18, 1963
TIME: 105 min.
SCENARIO: Adapted by Jean Renoir and Guy Lefranc from the novel by Jacques Perret
SCRIPT: Dialogue: Jean Renoir
PHOTOGRAPHY: Georges Leclerc
CAMERAMEN: Jean-Louis Picavet, Gilbert Chain, Antoine Georgakis, Robert Fraisse
COSTUMES: Wolf Witzemann
MUSIC: Joseph Kosma; Orchestra: Serge Baudo
SOUND: Antoine Petitjean, assisted by Jacques Bissière, Gaston Deméde, Jacques Gérardot
SCRIPT GIRL: Charlotte LeFèvre Vuattuox
ASSISTANT DIRECTORS: Guy Lefranc, Marc Maurette, J. E. Kieffer
EDITOR: Renée Lichtig, assisted by Madeleine Lacompère
PRODUCER: General Direction: J. W. Beyer; Production Director: René G. Vuattuox
PRODUCTION COMPANY: Films du Cyclope; Associate Director in Austria: Georges Glass
DISTRIBUTION: Pathé, Omnia
PRINTS OWNED BY: Contemporary Films-McGraw Hill, British Film Institute

CAST: Jean-Pierre Cassel (*the Corporal*)
  Claude Brasseur (*Pater*)
  O. E. Hasse (*the drunk on the train*)
  Claude Rich (*Ballochet*)
  Jean Carmet (*Emile*)
  Jacques Jouanneau (*Penchagauche*)
  Mario David (*Caruso*)
  Conny Froboess (*Erika*)
  Philippe Castelli (*the Electrician*)
  Guy Bédos (*the Stutterer*)
  Raymond Jourdan (*Dupieu*)
  Gerard Darrieu (*the Squinter*)
  Sacha Briquet (*the prisoner escaping dressed as a woman*)
  Lucien Raimbourg (*the guard in the train station*)
  François Darbon (*the French soldier married to a German peasant*)
  Elisabeth Marcus
  Elisabeth Stiepel
  Helmut Janatsch

LE PETIT THÉÂTRE DE JEAN RENOIR

DATE: 1969

INTERIORS: "Le Dernier Réveillon": Studio Saint Maurice; "La Cireuse Électrique": Versailles Grand Siècle Apartment Buildings; "Quand l'Amour meurt": Paris Studio Cinéma

EXTERIORS: "Le Roi d'Yvetôt": Aix-en-Provence, Saint Rémy-en-provence

PRODUCTION SCHEDULE: June–mid-September 1969

FIRST FRENCH SHOWING: TV, December 14, 1970

First U.S. Showing: May 15, 1970, Los Angeles County Museum
Scenario: Jean Renoir
Photography: Georges Leclerc
Set Design: Gilbert Margerie
Music: Joseph Kosma, Jean Weiner; song by Octave Crémieux and G. Millandy
Director of Production: Robert Paillardon; Associate Producer: Pierre Long
Cast: *Le Dernier Réveillon*
  Milly (*La Clocharde*)
  Nino Formicola (*Le Clochard*)
  Roland Betin (*Gontran*)
  André Dumas (*the Manager*)
  Robert Lombard (*the maître d'hôtel*)
 La Cireuse Électrique
  Pierre Olaf (*Gustave*)
  Marguerite Cassan (*Emilie*)
  Jacques Dynam (*Jules*)
  Jean-Louis Tristan (*the salesman*)
  Claude Guillaume
  Denis de Gunzburg
 La Belle Époque
  Jeanne Moreau
 Le Roi d'Yvetot
  Fernand Sardou (*Duvallier, Roi d'Yvetôt*)
  Françoise Arnoul (*Isabelle*)
  Jean Carmet (*Ferand*)
  Andrex (*Blanc*)
  Edmond Ardisson (*César*)
  Roger Prégor (*Joly*)
  Dominique Labourier (*Paulette*)
  Pierre Blanc

Bibliography*

PUBLISHED SCRIPTS
(in chronological order)

This Land Is Mine (with Dudley Nichols) in John Gassner, ed., *Twenty Best Film Plays* (New York: Crown Publishers, 1943).

The Southerner in *Best Film Plays of 1945,* John Gassner, ed. (New York: Crown Publishers, 1946).

Paris-Provence ("Inspiration pour un film"), *Cahiers du Cinéma,* No. 35 (mai 1954), pp. 2–13 (a treatment of an unproduced film).

Le Testament du Docteur Cordelier, L'Avant-Scène, No. 6 (15 juillet 1961).

Une Partie de Campagne, L'Avant-Scène, No. 21 (15 decembre 1962).

La Vie Est à Nous, Premier Plan, Nos. 22–23–24 (mai 1962) (several scenes).

La Grande Illusion (Paris; L'Avant-Scène du Cinéma, 1964). English translation by Marianne Alexandre and Andrew

---

* Pierre Leprohon's book, *Jean Renoir,* contains the most complete bibliography of items published in French, down to newspaper notices of individual films. I have not tried here to be exhaustive, but merely to indicate among the secondary sources works that are interesting or helpful.

Sinclair (New York: Simon and Schuster, 1968) (contains many stills, a note by Renoir, and Erich von Stroheim's reminiscences of his first meeting with Renoir).

La Règle du Jeu (Paris, L'Avant-Scène du Cinéma, 1965). English translation by John McGrath and Maureen Teitelbaum (New York: Simon and Schuster, 1970) (contains many stills and supplementary material; the English language edition is more extensive).

C'est la révolution! (*Crème de beauté*), *Cahiers du Cinéma*, Nos. 200/201 (avril/mai 1968), pp. 33–42 (a short vignette designed for an "anthology" film).

OTHER WORKS BY JEAN RENOIR

Orvet, a play in three acts (Paris, 1955).

Carola ou les Cabotins (section of the play), *Cahiers du Cinéma*, No. 78 (decembre 1957).

Renoir (Paris, 1962); *Renoir, My Father*, translated by Randolph and Dorothy Weaver (Boston: Little, Brown, 1962).

Les Cahiers du Capitaine Georges (Paris, 1966); *The Notebooks of Captain Georges*, translated by Norman Denny (Boston: Little, Brown, 1966.)

BOOKS ABOUT JEAN RENOIR

BAZIN, ANDRÉ. *Jean Renoir* (Paris: Editions Champ Libre, 1971). (Bazin's published essays on Renoir and many of his notes for a never-completed book, together with a long 1938 interview with Renoir, portions of scripts, and an annotated filmography—all collected by François Truffaut.)

CAULIEZ, ARMAND-JEAN. *Jean Renoir* (Paris: Editions Universitaires, 1962).

CHARDÈRE, BERNARD, ed. *Jean Renoir* (*Premier Plan,* Nos. 22–23–24). Lyon, mai 1962. (More than 400 pages of details and opinions about Renoir's career, including extracts from interviews; arranged by film.)

DAVAY, PAUL. *Jean Renoir* (Bruxelles, 1957). (A pamphlet published by the Club du Livre de Cinéma.)

INSTITUT DES HAUTES ÉTUDES CINÉMATOGRAPHIQUES. *Analyse des Films de Jean Renoir* (Paris, 1966). (Student analyses of eleven films, frequently including discussions of technical details.)

IOAN, ANGELA. *Jean Renoir* (Bucuresti, 1966).

LEPROHON, PIERRE. *Jean Renoir* (Paris: Editions Seghers, 1967).

POULLE, FRANÇOIS. *Renoir 1938, ou Jean Renoir Pour Rien, Enquête sur un Cinéaste* (Paris, 1969). (A fascinatingly idiosyncratic effort to discover what, if any, message Renoir's career has for young film-makers.)

INTERVIEWS AND FILMOGRAPHIES

Cahiers du Cinéma, No. 8 (janvier 1952), interviewed by Jacques Doniol-Valcroze. (A special issue devoted in great part to Renoir, including André Bazin's article "Renoir français" and Maurice Scherer's (Eric Rohmer's) "Renoir américain," which revaluated the American films.)

Cahiers du Cinéma, Nos. 34/35 (avril-mai 1954), interviewed by Jacques Rivette and François Truffaut.

Cahiers du Cinéma, No. 78 (Noël 1957), (a special issue devoted to Renoir with the first elaborate filmog-

raphy, including notes by André Bazin, François Truffaut, and Jean-Luc Godard. It appears in expanded form
in the Bazin book.).

Cahiers du Cinéma, No. 180 (juillet 1966), interviewed by
Michel Delahaye and Jean-André Fieschi.

Cahiers du Cinéma, No. 186 (janvier 1967), "Renoir le
patron," interviewed by A. S. Labarthe and Jacques
Rivette.

Positif, No. 93 (mars 1968), "À propos de *La Marseillaise*,"
interviewed by Michel Ciment and Bernard Cohn.

Cinema, vol. 6, No. 1, "Renoir: A Progress Report," interviewed by Alexander Sesonske.

ARTICLES ABOUT JEAN RENOIR*

BERANGER, JEAN. "The illustrious career of Jean Renoir," *Yale
French Studies*, No. 17 (Summer 1956), pp. 27–37.

BONITZER, PASCAL, et al. "*La Vie Est à Nous*: film militant,"
Cahiers du Cinéma, No. 218 (mars 1970), pp. 44–51.

CALLENBACH, ERNEST and SCHULDENFREI, ROBERTA. "The
Presence of Jean Renoir" *Film Quarterly*, vol. 14, No. 2
(Winter 1960), pp. 8–10.

CAREY, GARY. "The Renoir Experience," *Seventh Art*, vol.
1, No. 3 (Summer 1963), pp. 16–17, 27–28.

DYER, PETER JOHN. "Renoir and realism," *Sight and Sound*,
vol. 29, No. 3 (Summer 1960), pp. 130–35.

GILLIATT, PENELOPE. "Le Meneur de Jeu," *The New Yorker*,
August 23, 1969, pp. 34–61.

GREENSPUN, ROGER. "To Love a Renoir Movie Properly,"
New York *Times*, September 6, 1970, pp. D1, D4.

* Many of the special issues cited above have articles about Renoir's
work, among which should be mentioned André Bazin's articles for
Cahiers du Cinéma, *Arts*, and other magazines, collected by Truffaut
in the book cited above.

JOLY, J. "Between Theater and Life: Jean Renoir and *The Rules of the Game*," *Film Quarterly*, vol. 21, No. 2 (Winter 1967–68), pp. 2–9.

KERANS, JAMES. "Classics Revisited: *La Grande Illusion*," *Film Quarterly*, vol. 14, No. 2 (Winter 1960), pp. 10–17.

MILLER, DANIEL. "The Autumn of Jean Renoir," *Sight and Sound*, vol. 37, No. 3 (Summer 1968), pp. 136–41, 161.

RAY, SATYAJIT. "Renoir in Calcutta," *Sequence*, No. 10 (January 1950), pp. 146–150.

ROHMER, ERIC. "La Jeunesse de Jean Renoir," *Cahiers du Cinéma*, No. 102 (decembre 1959), pp. 1–7. (See also the article by Rohmer under the pseudonym of Maurice Scherer in *Cahiers du Cinéma* for avril 1952.)

L'Avant-Scène has produced an album of 120 slides that includes stills and production shots from all of Renoir's films up to *La Règle du Jeu*. Several of these stills are included in this book. The album itself is being published by Grove Press.

INDEX